# Digital Permaculture

design for personal digital sustainability

# Digital Permaculture
design for personal digital sustainability

by Dominik Jais

Bibliografische Information der Deutschen Nationalbibliothek: Die Deutsche Nationalbibliothek verzeichnet diese Publikation in der Deutschen Nationalbibliografie; detaillierte bibliografische Daten sind im Internet über dnb.dnb.de abrufbar.

Die automatisierte Analyse des Werkes, um daraus Informationen insbesondere über Muster, Trends und Korrelationen gemäß §44b UrhG („Text und Data Mining") zu gewinnen, ist untersagt.



1. Edition

Herstellung und Verlag: BoD – Books on Demand, Norderstedt

ISBN: 9783759733283

# Appreciation

I'd like to thank my wife Lumia.

I introduced the concept to digital permaculture back in 2019 to her ,and her first response was: "you are up to something". Without her constant kind words, proofreading, extensive listening, and general support, this book would not have been possible.

**Kiitos Lumia, Minä rakastan sinua!**

I also like to thank my brother Moritz with whom I often speak about permaculture and digital permaculture in particular. As he is not involved in the permaculture bubble he has a different perspective, which I highly appreciate. It is something I generally suggest: have friends who don't share your bubble.

**Thanks Brother. May the 4th be with you.**

I'd like to thank my aunt and my mother for their constant support, especially during difficult times – not just difficult for me but for them too.

I also want to thank Anna-Maria Spehar for initial proofreading and feedback. Special thanks goes to Douglas Locklin, who constantly challenged me on my approach, the topic, and many details. Without him, the book wouldn't be what it is now.

# Summary

The increasing integration of technology into our daily lives presents a unique challenge to those concerned with creating a sustainable and equitable future. While technology has undeniably brought about numerous advancements and conveniences, it is imperative that we critically examine the impact of our digital lives on both the virtual and physical environments. In this context, the concept of "Digital Permaculture" becomes particularly relevant.

Permaculture, with its focus on designing sustainable human habitats, has long been an important approach for those seeking to live in harmony with nature. With the rise of technology, it is necessary to adapt and apply these principles to the digital realm. In "Digital Permaculture," Dominik Jais presents a thought-provoking perspective on the intersection of technology and nature, exploring ways to cultivate sustainable digital systems and communities that promote connection, creativity, and a deep sense of purpose.

The interconnection between our digital and physical lives cannot be overstated. The decisions we make in the virtual world have real-world consequences, and it is our responsibility to ensure that these consequences are positive and sustainable. "Digital Permaculture" invites us to step back and critically assess the impact of our digital lives, encouraging us to make informed choices that contribute to a better future for all.

In this book, Dominik Jais provides a compelling argument for using technology as a tool to create a more equitable and sustainable future. He examines the role of technology in reducing our carbon footprint and protecting the environment, as well as its potential to foster connection, creativity, and community. His focus on a holistic and interconnected approach to our digital and physical lives highlights the importance of considering the impact of our choices on both realms.

The world is rapidly changing, and the line between the virtual and physical is becoming increasingly blurred. In such a context, "Digital Permaculture" serves as a crucial guide for those seeking to build a better world. Whether you are a technologist, an environmentalist, or simply concerned about the impact of technology, this book is a must-read. It is a powerful reminder of the need to take responsibility for our digital lives and to actively work towards creating a more sustainable and equitable future.

In the tradition of critical thinkers, "Digital Permaculture" invites us to question the status quo and to imagine a better world. It is a call to action for those seeking to create a more harmonious and sustainable existence in both the virtual and physical realms.

# About this book

When I started with the concept of Digital Permaculture in 2019, it was intended as a design for my Diploma in Applied Permaculture Design. Some 4.000 words into the design, I realized that a diploma design wouldn't suffice. There were too many things to explain and too many stories to tell. The sheer size of it, now about 60.000 words, is far beyond the suggested size of a diploma design (~2.000 words). The idea to put everything into a book was born.

After writing some chapters, I got side-tracked with other topics, and a year passed without any progress in writing. When I stepped down as chair of the Finnish Permaculture Association, I suddenly had time on my hands and resumed writing. The difficult part was adapting permaculture concepts to Digital Permaculture. What are Zones, Sectors, and Patterns? What do they mean in the digital realm? Do we need other concepts? Not everything was obvious from the beginning.

I opted for a permaculture design approach. The whole book is essentially a design, allowing you to tag along and look over my shoulder. I hope you find great joy in it and that it inspires your own permaculture design journey.

Digital permaculture is the amalgamation of the digital world with permaculture and it is a necessity. In my years of observing the Finnish and parts of the European permaculture community and their behavior I recognized that permaculture design always stopped at every observed person's garden gate. It was neither applied in the social space nor in the digital. The idea that permaculture design can be used for something else than gardens wasn't in people's minds.

In my observations within the permaculture community, I've noticed that there is often a reluctance to embrace or learn about digital tools. However, when we are required to use digital tools, I've observed that we sometimes make uninformed choices that lead to less than optimal outcomes. It is clear to me that there is need for greater awareness, education, and informed decision-making when integrating digital tools into our framework or when developers develop digital tools. By addressing this knowledge gap and understanding the potential benefits and drawbacks of digital technologies and their implications regarding sustainability, we can make more informed choices aligned with our values and contribute to sustainable practices.

**In short:** This book will give you an introduction to permaculture, in particular permaculture ethics and principles as well as permaculture design. Together, we'll embark on a journey through a complete permaculture design process, equipped with a diverse array of tools. By the end of this exploration, you'll have discovered how the principles of permaculture can guide us to make more conscious and ethical decisions – especially in our digital realm.

# Who should read this book?

Before we start into who will benefit most from this book, let's clarify who it might not suit. If you're purely a theorist uninterested in the practical application of digital permaculture, this may not be the read for you. This book isn't for those who prefer to prescribe solutions to others without taking action themselves. Instead, it's crafted for individuals ready to embark on a journey of personal transformation. With "pathways into personal digital sustainability" as our guiding subtitle, the content is action-oriented, designed to empower every reader to make meaningful changes towards a sustainable digital lifestyle.

The primary audience for this book is permaculture designers and people working in IT who find themselves at the intersection of sustainability and IT. It is written for practitioners who want to learn from practical examples of how Digital Permaculture could work. I hope the reader brings an open mind and seeks fruitful connections between disciplines while avoiding territorial definitions. The examples in this book may primarily originate from my own experiences, but the reader should be prepared to view them through a broad lens and try to adapt them for their own use.

In addition to permaculture designers and IT professionals, this book is also intended for sustainability advocates who are passionate about fostering a more sustainable world through the strategic integration of technology. Sustainability advocates, whether they work in environmental organizations, policy development, or community engagement, will find valuable insights in Digital Permaculture.

Moreover, this book is a resource for anyone with a general interest in sustainability, whether you're a concerned citizen, a student exploring environmental topics, or someone who simply wants to lead a more eco-conscious lifestyle. Digital Permaculture offers practical insights into how individuals make more sustainable choices in their daily lives. It provides a window into the world of permaculture and its application in digital contexts, inspiring a deeper appreciation for the interconnectedness of sustainability and the digital realm.

# The content & usage

The structure of the book walks us through the process of a permaculture design, taking readers on a journey through its various stages. Our first stage is *survey*, then we will analyze our findings using different tools.

Continuing the design process we identify patterns and connections, recognizing the interplay between different elements. Armed with these insights, we propose ideas and concepts that will lead to Digital Permaculture. From our design we propose an action plan to navigate the digital realm in a way that aligns with permaculture ethics and principles.

Throughout this journey, there is also a focus on appreciation – acknowledging the valuable contributions and existing initiatives within the digital permaculture space.

There are lots of footnotes, which are more or less links, either as references and/or for further reading to deepen your knowledge. I also put in some QR-codes, which you might find useful.

# Table of Contents

# 1. A brief summary of permaculture

Permaculture, a portmanteau of 'permanent' and 'culture', was originally developed as a method for sustainable land management and settlement design, inspired by the thriving patterns observed in natural ecosystems. The concept was co-originated in the 1970s by Bill Mollison, his partner Reny Mia Slay, and Mollison's student David Holmgren. A key aspect often overlooked is the profound influence of the land management practices of Aboriginal Australians on the development of permaculture principles. Their deep understanding of and harmonious relationship with the land significantly shaped the foundations of permaculture.

Since its inception, permaculture has evolved from its initial focus on agriculture to become a broader approach to sustainable living. In the 2020s, as climate change became a pressing issue worldwide, permaculture was recognized on a larger stage as a solution to contemporary agricultural and environmental challenges. Practices like agroforestry, syntropic farming, and the development of food forests are examples of permaculture techniques that practitioners around the world have refined for decades.

Today, permaculture is acknowledged as a solution to a multitude of problems, ranging from the loss of biodiversity and food insecurity to the erosion of local communities. It is a testament to the enduring wisdom of indigenous peoples, particularly the Aboriginal Australians, whose sustainable living practices have provided valuable insights into creating harmonious, resilient communities in balance with nature.

# Ethics

When I came to permaculture I found it hardest that no one ever wanted to discuss ethics on a meta-level with me. What are ethics, what are their limits? What are current ethics? How did they get defined? Back in the days I needed clarity for myself. Not about the permaculture ethics, but about what ethics in general entail.

Ethics refers to a set of moral principles or values that guide an individual's behavior and decisions. It involves the understanding and analysis of what is right and wrong, good and bad, and just and unjust. Ethics can be personal, societal, or professional, and they often vary based on cultural, philosophical, and religious beliefs.

In a broader context, ethics is the discipline of philosophy that deals with moral conduct, duty, and judgment. It concerns itself with questions like:

- What is the right thing to do in a given situation?
- How should people live their lives in relation to others?

- What are the principles that define good conduct?

Ethics can manifest in various ways, such as:

**Personal ethics:** The individual principles and values that one holds. These are often influenced by upbringing, culture, religion, and personal experiences.

**Professional ethics:** These are standards and practices that govern the behavior of individuals within a profession. For example, medical ethics guide the conduct of healthcare professionals.

**Social ethics:** This pertains to values and principles that govern the behavior of people within a society. They are often codified into laws and social norms. For example in Finland, significant importance is placed on the spoken word; words are chosen deliberately to convey a message effectively. This cultural norm emphasizes the value of meaningful communication, with a preference for saying less and avoiding superfluous small talk. Or as Pythagoras put it: "Be silent or let thy words be worth more than."

**Environmental ethics:** This area of ethics focuses on the relationship between humans and the environment, concerning issues such as conservation, sustainability, and the rights of non-human entities.

Ethics plays a crucial role in decision-making, guiding individuals and groups to make choices that are not only beneficial to themselves but also considerate of others and the broader environment.

Compared to moral, ethics are external. The 3 permaculture ethics were defined by Mollison and then the 3$^{rd}$ ethic has been redefined over the years by the community.

In its heart permaculture is based on its prime directive: "The only ethical decision is to take responsibility for our own existence and that of our children". It is surrounded by the 3 ethics "Earth Care", "People Care", and "Fair Share". All 3 together are required in order to create a permanent culture.

Let's have a look at the **3 permaculture ethics**:

**Earth Care:** Emphasis on preserving and enhancing the health and vitality of natural ecosystems. It recognizes that humans are a part of the natural world and that our actions can have profound impacts on the environment. Earth Care encourages us to work with nature rather than against it, adopting practices that regenerate ecosystems, promote biodiversity, and improve soil health. We have to remember: The infinite cyberspace is bound to finite resources.

**People Care:** fostering social well-being and ensuring that human needs are met in equitable and sustainable ways. People Care encourages the creation of supportive, resilient, and self-reliant communities where individuals can thrive. It promotes practices like sharing resources, building social connections, and encouraging local and participatory decision-making processes. It is also about self care.

**Fair Share (or the limit of resources and consumption, or Return of Surplus or Future Care):** This ethic is centered around the concept of limiting consumption and redistributing surplus resources to promote equity and sustainability. It acknowledges that the earth's resources are finite and that over-consumption contributes to environmental degradation and social inequality. Fair Share encourages us to use resources mindfully, reduce waste, and share what we don't need with others, whether it be knowledge, time, money or material goods.

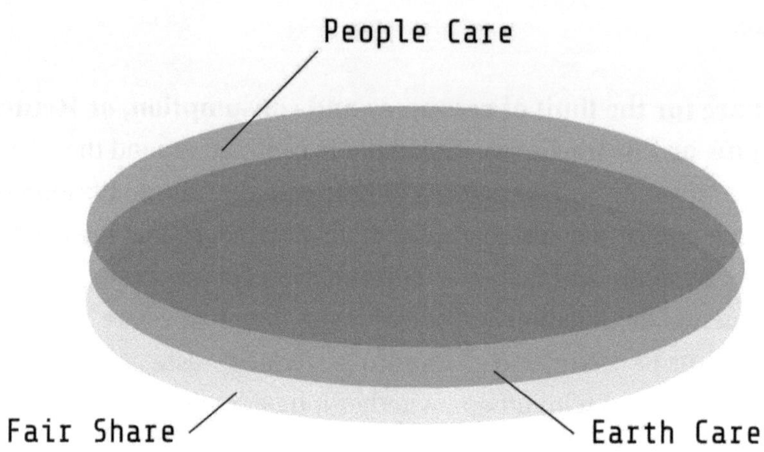


Illustration "Permaculture Cake"

When "People Care", "Earth Care" and "Fair Share" come together as we apply permaculture design we get permaculture.

Just as there are numerous cake recipes to choose from, permaculture offers a diverse range of strategies, techniques, and applications that can be tailored to specific contexts and individual preferences. The beauty of permaculture lies in its adaptability and the creative freedom it provides. It invites us to explore and experiment, celebrating the multiplicity of solutions and approaches that can be integrated into our design practices.

By embracing the metaphor of the cake, we recognize that permaculture is not about rigid adherence to a singular definition of "good permaculture," but rather about the process of continuous learning, adaptation, and innovation. It is through this dynamic and ever-evolving approach that we can create regenerative systems that align with our values and contribute to a more sustainable future.

The 3 ethics don't stop at our garden gate, not when we are using our phone and not when we interact in social media.

To use a slightly modified quote from a small green alien:

*My ally permaculture is, and a powerful ally it is.*

## Permaculture design

Let's first define permaculture design. Permaculture design is a subset of design. Design in general is the process of planning and creating something with a specific function and/or aesthetic in mind. To quote Wikipedia[1]: "Design is the concept of or proposal for an object, process, or system".

Permaculture design focuses on creating sustainable, self-sufficient ecosystems that mimic natural systems. It integrates principles of ecology, sustainable practices, and holistic planning to enhance

---

1    https://en.wikipedia.org/wiki/Design

biodiversity, soil health, water management, and overall ecological balance.

The term *design* is fundamental to permaculture. In fact, to be considered permaculture, a project must involve design. The sum of all permaculture designs results in permaculture.

Bill Mollison's seminal book is titled "Permaculture: A Designer's Manual[2]," emphasizing the central role of design in permaculture practice. Permaculture design requires specific skills and a deep understanding of the subject matter, whether it's a website, a piggy-bank, a product, a house, or a garden.

Design is inherently context-sensitive, meaning that the designer must tailor their approach to the unique characteristics of the project. Designers must possess or acquire the knowledge necessary to initiate the design effectively.

We all have to become permaculture designers and I hope this book helps you to become one!

> I acquired my design skills over decades of designing, starting with advertisement leaflets and party flyers when I was 16, continuing with websites, t-shirt prints, and all kind of different products – and now even entire homesteads.

---

2    https://www.tagaripublications.com

# Design process

A design process is a systematic and iterative method used to create
a plan, solution, or product that meets specific requirements and
objectives. It involves several stages that designers, architects,
engineers, and other professionals follow to bring an idea to fruition.

Most permaculture design processes resemble more or less an action
learning[3] path.

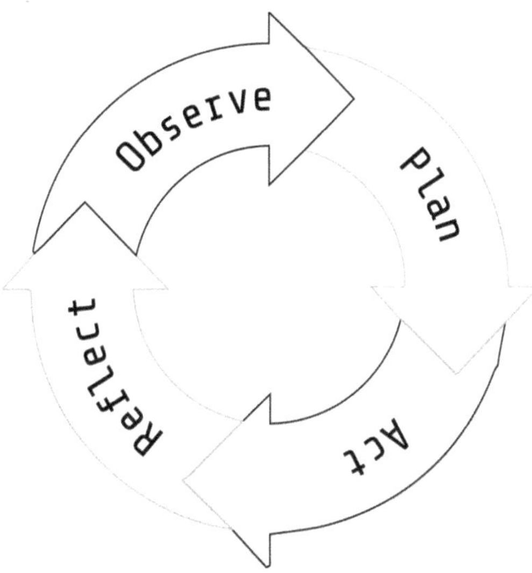


Action learning cycle

To initiate the design process, I select a suitable design framework or
process. There are several recognized processes in permaculture and

_______________

3   https://asb.edu.my/action-learning

design in general. While some have been established for many years, some are more recent.

From the established processes most notable there are SADIMET[4], OBREDIMET[5], CEAP[6], and Looby's Design Web[7]. All of them are used for land- or social permaculture design. CEAP is the original design process developed by Bill Mollison. It is linear. SADIMET and OBREDIMET are circular, hence iterative, using an evaluation and tweaking stage. Looby's Design Web is something entirely different. It is a non-linear non-circular process that allows the designer to use given anchor points in whatever order the designer deems necessary.

For me permaculture design processes come with a lot of benefits:

**Clarity and direction:** A structured design process provides clear steps and stages, which can guide a project from conception to completion, ensuring that all critical aspects are addressed.

**Efficient resource use:** By planning thoroughly and anticipating potential issues, resources such as time, money, and materials can be used more efficiently, reducing waste.

---

4    https://permateachers.eu/wordpress/wp-content/uploads/2014/06/sadimet.pdf
5    https://www.permaculturewomen.com/a-design-cycle-application-gobradimet/
6    https://beyondbuckthorns.com/content/diploma-applied-permaculture-design/welcome-permacafe
7    https://loobymacnamara.com/

**Quality and cohesiveness:** A systematic approach can improve the quality of the final project by ensuring that all components work together cohesively.

**Continuous improvement:** The iterative nature of evaluating and tweaking allows for continuous refinement, leading to progressive improvement in design and outcomes.

**Risk mitigation:** Analysis and regular evaluation can identify risks and issues before they become significant problems, allowing for proactive management.

**Stakeholder satisfaction:** Involving stakeholders throughout the process helps to align the design with their needs and expectations, increasing satisfaction.

**Adaptability to change:** Flexibility is built into the process, allowing for adjustments in response to new information or changing circumstances.

**Enhanced communication:** Documenting each phase of the process improves communication among team members and stakeholders, ensuring that everyone understands the project's progress and direction.

**Knowledge transfer and learning:** Systematic documentation and reflection at each stage of the process create a knowledge base that can be used for training and applied to future projects.

**Sustainability and longevity:** Emphasizing maintenance ensures that the project remains viable and sustainable over the long term, not just upon completion.

The design process SADIMET (or SADIM) is widely used for land-based (you design a piece of land – your garden / homestead / farm) and even social design (you design for yourself / groups / communities) within the permaculture community. It is a suitable process for this book. SADIM is rigid (you will see below). If you are seeking a less rigid and more flexible approach, I recommend Looby Macnamara's "Design Web".

# SADIMET design process

**1. Survey:** This initial stage is about gathering a deep understanding of the current state of the project, whether it's a physical site or a conceptual plan. This includes collecting relevant data and observing existing conditions, resources, limitations, and potential. The aim is to acquire a comprehensive overview to guide the next steps.

**2. Analysis:** In this phase, the information collected during the survey is critically examined to identify patterns, connections, and potential obstacles. This analytical process helps in understanding the project's requirements and opportunities, setting a solid foundation for informed decision-making.

**3. Design / Decision:** The design phase involves creating a plan that integrates the gathered information and analysis. Designers use permaculture principles, strategies and techniques to develop holistic and regenerative solutions.

**4. Implement:** This phase is about bringing the design to life, translating ideas into action. Depending on the project, this could involve executing physical changes, initiating new processes, or applying innovative approaches to achieve the desired outcomes.

**5. Maintain:** Maintaining involves ongoing care and attention to ensure the project continues to function effectively. This could encompass regular monitoring, adjustments, and interventions to address emerging needs or challenges.

**6. Evaluate:** Evaluation involves regularly assessing the performance and outcomes of the design. This phase helps designers identify successes, challenges, and areas for improvement.

**7. Tweak:** We tweak our design according to our findings in Evaluation, basically start the design process again.

The shorter version SADIM, skips the *evaluation* and *tweak* stage.

Like permaculture design processes and software development this book tends to be iterative. The 10th edition might look different than as its first release.

Survey / Observation is both: the beginning and the end; it's from this vantage point that continuous improvement can be made.

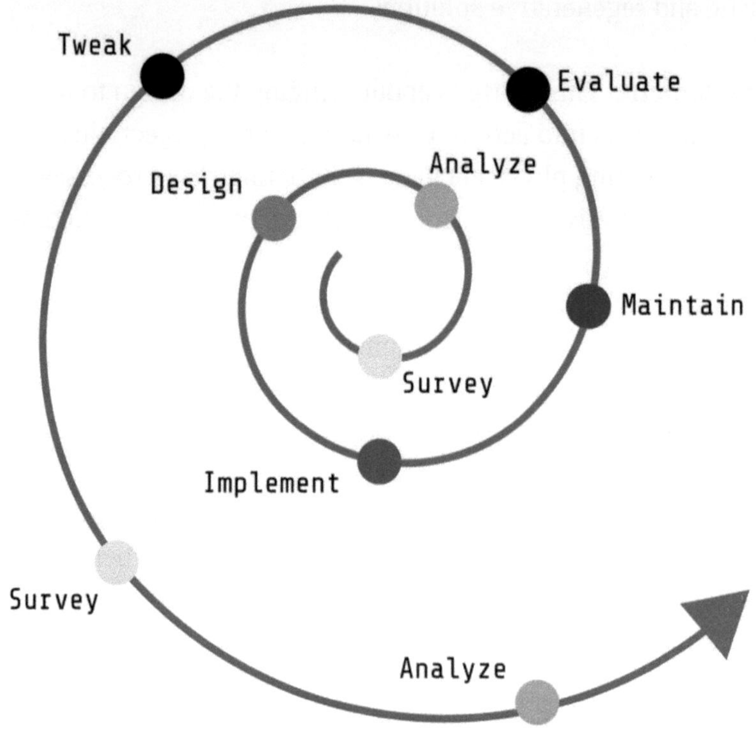


The SADIMET design process as a spiral (linear permaculture design processes are usual circular with no end – hence a spiral.

# 2. IT terminology and concepts

Let's get some clarity about some of the terms and concepts used in IT.

## Open-source software

**Open-source software (OSS)**[8] is software in which the source code is made available to the public, allowing users to view, modify, and distribute the code. This model encourages collaboration, transparency, and community-driven development. Users can customize the software to meet their needs or contribute to its improvement by fixing bugs, adding new features, or optimizing performance.

**Free and Open-Source Software (FOSS)**[9] is a specific category of Open-source software that not only provides access to the source code but also guarantees users the freedom to use, modify, and distribute the software without any restrictions or fees. The term 'free' in FOSS refers to freedom rather than price. This means that while the software is available at no cost, the focus is on the liberties granted to users.

---

8    https://en.wikipedia.org/wiki/Open-source_software
9    https://en.wikipedia.org/wiki/Free_and_open-source_software

Open-source software is a broader term that encompasses all software with publicly accessible source code, while FOSS is a subset of Open-source software that emphasizes user freedom and ensures that the software can be used, modified, and shared without any restrictions or fees.

**One important point:** FOSS or OSS doesn't mean no one gets paid. That is not the case. There are plenty of companies, individuals and organizations who pay developers to create FOSS / OSS. Often developers of (F)OSS can be contacted and paid directly.

# FOSS vs. freeware

Free and Open-source software is distributed under a license that grants users the freedom to use, modify, and distribute the software without restrictions. The source code is also available for anyone to view, modify, and redistribute. This means users have the liberty to control and modify the software as they please. Focus is on the ethical implications of software.

Freeware[10], conversely, pertains to software distributed for free (price), but the source code may not necessarily be accessible. Users can freely use and distribute the software, but they might not have the ability to modify it or distribute modified versions. Freeware is often employed as a marketing tactic to promote paid versions of the software or generate revenue through advertising or donations.

---

10  https://en.wikipedia.org/wiki/Freeware

Unfortunately freeware is often mistaken for (F)OSS and inexperienced users can't distinguish between them. That's why (F)OSS comes with a license.

# The licenses for Open-source software

Open-source software licenses come in various forms. Three of the best-known licenses include:

The **GNU General Public License (GPL)**[11] is perhaps the most well-known. It mandates that any derivative works (changes or additions to the original code) must also be released under the GPL.

The **MIT License**[12] is permissive, imposing very few restrictions on how the software can be used, modified, and distributed.

The **Apache License**[13] resembles the MIT License but also encompasses a patent protection clause, providing an explicit patent license for any patents covered by the software.

Feel free to use a search engine of your choice to explore more Open-source licenses.

---

11  https://www.gnu.org/licenses/gpl-3.0.en.html
12  https://fedoraproject.org/wiki/Licensing:MIT?rd=Licensing/MIT
13  https://www.apache.org/licenses/LICENSE-2.0

A prime example of Open-source software is Thunderbird[14], a mail
client from Mozilla[15]. This software is available free of charge for
users, and its source code is also freely accessible[16]. Besides the
original Thunderbird there are multiple forks available, like for
example Betterbird[17].

# Fork

A fork of software is like taking a copy of a recipe and then deciding
to change it up a bit to suit your taste or add your own flair. Imagine
someone shares a recipe for a cake, and you take that recipe but
decide to add some chocolate chips and a hint of cinnamon to make
it your own. In the world of software, "forking" means taking the
source code (the recipe) of an existing program and developing a
new program from it that might have different features or a different
direction than the original. It's a way for developers to build on
existing work while adding their own ideas and improvements.

# Repository

A repository is like a digital storage space where all the files related
to a project are kept. It's similar to a folder on your computer, but it's
used for storing and organizing things like code, documents or
images. The special thing about a repository is that it keeps track of

---

14   https://www.thunderbird.net/
15   https://www.mozilla.org/
16   https://github.com/mozilla/releases-comm-central
17   https://www.betterbird.eu

all the changes made to the files, kind of like a detailed history or a time machine. This means you can see how the project has evolved over time and go back to older versions if needed. Repositories are often used by people working together on a project, making it easier for them to share updates and work on different parts without getting in each other's way.

## Open-source hardware

Open-source hardware[18] refers to the design and documentation of physical products, such as electronics, scientific equipment and other machinery, that are made publicly available so that anyone can use, modify, and distribute them. Like Open-source software, Open-source hardware is often developed and maintained by a community of volunteers, tightly knit with the Open-design movement[19], and is often distributed for free or at a low cost.

The idea behind Open-source hardware is to allow for the free exchange of knowledge and technology, and to encourage innovation by allowing others to build upon existing designs. Open-source hardware also allows for greater collaboration and customization of products, as well as reducing the cost of production, research and development. Examples of open-hardware include the micro-controller board Arduino[20], and the RepRap[21] 3D printer.

---

18  https://en.wikipedia.org/wiki/Open-source_hardware
19  https://en.wikipedia.org/wiki/Open-design_movement
20  https://www.arduino.cc
21  https://reprap.org/

In contrast, proprietary hardware refers to products with design and documentation that remain secret and unavailable for others to use or modify. The difference between Open source and proprietary hardware parallels the distinction between Open source and proprietary software.

It's crucial to note that Open-source hardware, like Open-source software, also features different licenses. Some may be permissive, while others may be more restrictive. Therefore, it's vital to review the terms and conditions of a specific license before using or distributing open-hardware products.

ChatGPT prompt: use the general concept of Caspar David Friedrich's "Wanderer above the Sea of Fog" to show a landscape full of e-waste.

# 3. Concepts in permaculture design

Let's get some clarity about some of the concepts and terms used in permaculture design. Sectors

## Sectors

One of the key concepts in permaculture is *Sectors*. In permaculture design, *Sectors* refer to influences or forces that affect a particular site or system. These influences can come from various directions, and permaculturists use *Sector* analysis to understand and work with these factors when designing sustainable systems. What are the *Sectors* in the natural world?

**They include Solar, Wind, Water, Access, View, Noise, Social, and Wildlife.**

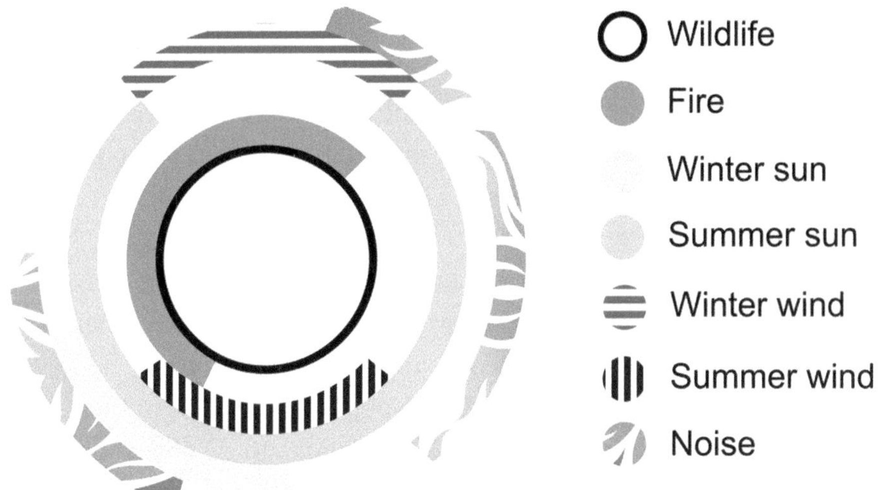


Sectors drawn for the Beyond Buckthorns homestead.

When we draw a circular diagram, a *Sector* is the area between two radii. In land-based design, we draw the sectors in our circular diagram in accordance with the landscape, often as an overlay over our base map (map with boundaries, pathways, roads, buildings, etc). In a map, north is usually at the top. This then gives us a quick overview of where influences are coming from and allows us to design accordingly.

In order to bring sectors into Digital Permaculture we have to repeat the concept: "*Sectors* are influences or forces which affect a system".

Let's ask ourselves: What are those influences or forces in the digital world?

**The manufacturer:** Manufacturers of digital tools and platforms can significantly influence user behavior and choices. Their design decisions, privacy policies, and business models can impact how sustainable and user-friendly their products are. I for example wouldn't buy a Samsung phone. I don't like their design.

**Other users:** The behavior and preferences of other users can affect your experience and choices. In a networked environment, the actions of one user can have a ripple effect on others, influencing trends and norms. For example when a plugin I was working with got a new very unfriendly maintainer I changed that particular plugin for custom code to avoid endless discussions in the plugin's issue queue.

**Peers:** Peer groups can exert a strong influence over individuals, often shaping their attitudes towards technology and sustainability. Peer pressure can lead to the adoption of certain technologies or practices, either positively or negatively impacting sustainable practices. For example when self made drones became a thing I was heavily influenced by peers to build one too.

**Decision Makers:** These could include corporate leaders, heads of institutions, or family members who make decisions about which technologies to adopt or how to implement them. Their choices can have a substantial impact on the digital and environmental footprint of the organization or household they represent.

**Culture:** Cultural norms and values can greatly influence an individual's approach to technology and sustainability. Some cultures might prioritize technological advancement, while others may place a greater emphasis on environmental conservation. For example the preference for different search engines in different regions can be seen as a reflection of cultural differences. These preferences might be influenced by language, local customs, and the specific needs and habits of the people in those regions. For example, Baidu[22] is tailored to the Chinese language and caters to the cultural preferences and internet habits of Chinese users. In Europe we wouldn't use Baidu – we would use one of the many to us available search engines.

**Legislation/Policies:** Government policies and regulations can either encourage or hinder sustainable practices in the digital realm. Laws related to data privacy, energy use, recycling, and production standards can all affect how technology is developed, used, and disposed of. For example in 2023 the EU forced Apple to implement USB-C instead of Apple's proprietary Lightning port[23].

**Economic conditions:** This goes beyond legislation and policy and deals with the broader economic environment which affects technology funding, pricing, and market viability. It is also about ones personal economical situation. Will it be a Xiaomi Redmi smartphone for 160,- €, a Fairphone for 699,- €, or the latest iPhone for 1290,- €?

---

22  https://www.baidu.com/

23  https://www.politico.eu/article/apple-iphone-15-european-union-regulations-charger-usbc-lightning/

**Technological innovations and advancements:** While this may intersect with manufacturer influences, it specifically refers to the broader scope of technology development and breakthroughs that can shape hardware and software options beyond what any single manufacturer produces. In 2014 USB-C[24] got introduced into the market by the USB Implementers Forum[25] (USB-IF) and over time it became a standard in multiple hardware.

When considering *Sectors*, it's crucial to be aware of their presence and to understand the origins of the forces they represent.

In our design, we should ask ourselves the following questions:

- Am I making this decision under the influence of a *Sector*?
- If there is an influence, what is its nature and how does it affect my decision?

## Zones

In permaculture we use *Zones*. In a land based design *Zones* are a function of time[26]. It is about the frequency of visit and the duration of stay. *Zones* are labeled from 0 to 5, where 0 is the center, usually

---


24  https://en.wikipedia.org/wiki/USB-C
25  https://www.usb.org
26  https://www.permaculturenews.org/2015/12/11/permaculture-zones-of-use-a-primer/

the house, and 5 is farthest away, the wilderness. Over the years the concept of *Zones* got extended. We have to deal with *Zone 00* – the mental, physical and spiritual health of the designer – the internal being.

Zones can be used in the survey to see how the natural *Zones* are – how the present is. It can also be used as a design tool – to design what should be. We'll come to that later.

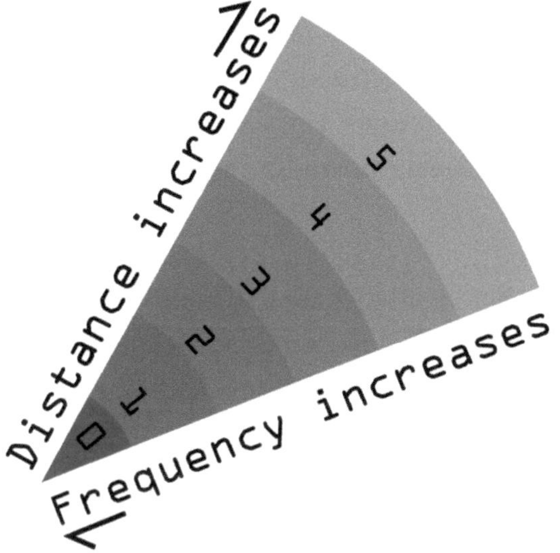


Zones – from 0 to 5 – distance increases while the frequency of visit decreases.

Adapting the *Zones* to Digital Permaculture comes in various forms. One simple adaption is to use the frequency of usage of a soft- / hardware as our main point of reference.

The duration of use will vary based on your personal situation and how much soft- and hardware you use in your life generally. Take my examples below as what they are – just examples of one particular user.

**Zone 0: Core.** Soft- / hardware that are used **several times daily**. For example applications which run continuously or are checked multiple times throughout the day. Examples might include your phone / PC with email clients, instant messaging apps, or essential work tools for certain professions.

**Zone 1:** Soft- / hardware used **at least once daily** but not necessarily multiple times throughout the day. This might include daily task management tools, certain news apps, or professional tools like a professional camera for individuals who need them for work.

**Zone 2:** Soft- / hardware that are used **multiple times a week** but not daily. Examples could be certain video conferencing tools and hardware required for it, photo editing software for hobbyists, or specific educational apps.

**Zone 3:** Soft- / hardware that's used **at least once a week** but not more than a couple of times. This might include certain games, weekly planning or review apps, or specialized software that's only needed for periodic tasks. Occasionally used hardware might be an NVR (network video recorder[27]) on which the video recordings get checked.

---

27  https://en.wikipedia.org/wiki/Network_video_recorder

**Zone 4:** Soft- / hardware or applications that are used less than once a week, perhaps even **monthly or sporadically**. Examples could include tax software, certain utility apps, or niche software for very specific needs. A drone might be a sporadically used hardware. The duration varies but when I fly my drone I will use up a battery pack. It simply takes too much time to get the gear ready for some few minutes of flight.

**Zone 5: Wilderness.** Software that we might use on rare occasion but then use them for hours. One of my personal examples might be the usage of Processing[28] to code art. I only start it for the purpose of art and it takes days until I have finished my work. Another example is browsing through the internet. Staying at websites for hours for inspiration, new ideas – input in general. The websites I then surf to are often not known prior to me.

# Layers

Let's extend on the concept of *Zones* and add *Layers.* In Digital Permaculture we have *3 Layers:*

- The physical layer – the standard permaculture *Zones.* Where are we? At the house? In the field? In the orchard? We still call this Zones.
- The hardware layer – the device used, for example a computer.
- The software layer – the software on a specific device

---

28  https://processing.org

Let's see on the example of a messenger app how this works:

- **Software layer** – WhatsApp on our phone. Shortcut on the home screen – SL 0
- **Hardware layer** – Main phone – *HL 0*
- **Physical layer** – *Zone 0* – the phone is usually always with us.
- Shortcut writing Z 0 | HL 0 | SL 0

From time to time I use the Unreal Engine to create 3D models:

- **Software layer** – No shortcut on my computer's home screen. I have to navigate to it via the Windows menu. The Unreal Engine is actually only accessible within another application – I have to start the Epic Games Store to get to it – SL *3*
- **Hardware layer** – Main computer – *HL 0*
- **Physical layer** – Office – *Zone 0*
- *Shortcut writing Z 0 | HL 0 | SL 3*

Each of the layers are numbered from 0 to 5 like Zones are numbered. *Zone 00* doesn't make any sense in terms of hard- and software layer since *Zone 00* is exclusively internal. We have to wait for humans with brain implants to become a standard before we have *Zone 00* hard- and software.

The software layer is about how you organize your digital device. How you get to apps. It stems from your home screen (Software Layer 0) or the main desktop window, basically what you see first when you access the hardware, to the place from where you would get new software / applications – *software layer 0*. *Software layer 5* (the wilderness) could be an AppStore or a website on the internet. Everything in between is then the amount of clicks or swipes to get there. Do you need to swipe left to see the extension of your home screen? Do you have to open a menu to get to it? The more actions are between your home screen and the application the further outwards the software is in terms of zoning.

A layered approach to organizing your digital space encourages efficiency and mindfulness. You can consider which tools are vital to your daily digital ecosystem and which are better suited for occasional use. By consciously arranging our software applications according to their importance and usage frequency, we create a digital environment that mirrors the efficiency and sustainability of a well-designed permaculture garden.

Furthermore we are able to use the Zone Layer concept to design for a desired outcome. Let's say we want to detox from social media. We could first remove it from your home screen or our virtual screens completely. So that it is buried within the system and it takes us time to get there – we create hurdles.

We could also deinstall it from our smartphone device (*Hardware layer 0)* and only access it from a device within the physical *Zone 2.*

Whatever works best for you according to your needs! In permaculture the placement of this elements, hardware, software within *Zones* is combined under the term *relative locations.*

# Relative locations

In permaculture we designers use *relative locations* to combine different elements. It refers to the placement of elements within a system in relation to each other in a way that maximizes their efficiency and productivity. The idea is to position elements so that they create beneficial relationships and minimize energy need and waste. Every input into the system is work. Every output not utilized by the system is waste. Our goal as designer is to reduce work and waste.

Transferring the concept of *relative location* into the digital realm involves arranging digital tools, platforms, and workflows in a way that maximizes efficiency, reduces redundancy, and enhances productivity.

It comes back to *Zones.* Do I access social media on my desktop in *Zone 0,* or on the tablet in *Zone 2*? Is my social media app on the home screen of my phone (*Zone 0, Hardware Layer 0, Software Layer 0*) or do I have to swipe left or right to get to it? How often do I have to swipe? How are my files stored on my computer – is everything in one place, or is there a strategy used – like for example subject orientated storage? Are often used files combined in a way so I don't have to search? How are my workflows organized? Do I have the necessary tools on one machine or do I have multiple computers with different tools and I have to remember where is what?

Relative location in Digital Permaculture is about how we handle our virtual locations – where our data is stored. We want to maximize efficiency and enhance productivity.

We use *Zones* and *Layers* analysis to see where we are and then design for the outcome we need!

# Principles

Permaculture presents three distinct sets of principles. The first of these, the *attitudinal principles,* can be found in Bill Mollison's influential book A Designers' Manual[29] - a foundational work that has shaped countless lives. The second set, the *ecological principles,* has its roots in the collaborative efforts of Bill Mollison and Reny Mia Slay, a testament to the power of cooperation and shared wisdom. Lastly, there are the *design principles* authored by David Holmgren[30], whose vision has resonated with many and helped to propel the permaculture movement forward.

- **Mollison's attitudinal principles**
  - Work with nature rather than against

---

29  https://www.tagaripublications.com/permaculture-designers-manual/
30  https://permacultureprinciples.com

- The problem is the solution
- Make the least change for the greatest possible effect
- The yield of a system is theoretically unlimited (or only by the imagination & information of the designer)
- Everything gardens (or modifies its environment)
- Everything works both ways, & permaculture is information and imagination-intensive

- **Mollison & Slay's ecological principles**
  - Relative Location
  - Each element performs many functions
  - Each important function is supported by many elements
  - Efficient energy planning: zone, sector & slope
  - Using biological resources
  - Cycling of energy, nutrients, resources
  - Small-scale intensive systems; inc. plant & time stacking
  - Accelerating succession & evolution
  - Diversity, including guilds
  - Edge effect

- **Holmgren's design pinciples**
  1. Observe & Interact
  2. Catch & Store Energy
  3. Obtain a yield
  4. Apply Self regulation & accept feedback
  5. Use & Value Renewable Resources & Services
  6. Produce no waste
  7. Design from patterns to details
  8. Integrate rather than segregate

9.  Use slow & small solutions
10. Use & Value Diversity
11. Use edges & value the marginal
12. Creatively Use & respond to change

There have been a lot of books been published about permaculture and permaculture design. From my perspective the attitudinal principles are the most universal ones while Holmgren's are very versatile.

Let's step through Holmgren's principles in more detail and see how we can use them for Digital Permaculture.

# The design principles

## 1. Observe and interact

In the realm of permaculture, observation serves as the cornerstone for comprehending the intricate natural systems and patterns within a specific environment. In land based design I **adhered to the 24-month rule**, ensuring that I have experienced a place multiple times throughout the year. When the 24-month rule isn't feasible, a 12-month period has to suffice. Grasping a homestead's conditions across various seasons, particularly in winter, is crucial. In Nordic countries like Finland, designs must withstand winter's harshness.

Inspired by designer and book author Philipp Weiss[31] and his dual-zone designs for summer and winter in his applied permaculture design diploma, I adopted a similar approach for Lumia's and my homestead, Beyond Buckthorns[32].

Observation proves to be just as vital in land-based and social designs as it is in the digital world, where it marks the starting point (and end point in a circular design process). (Page 75)

No matter for what we design and what the context is, our observations need to be thorough. The digital world has no seasons and can be very fast-paced but that doesn't mean we can't take the time to observe.

> Out of personal interest I started to map the Finnish permaculture community. I simply wanted to know who is who – who are the key players? While I was working on it I also noticed the digital tools the community used. I found a publicly available Facebook group, a Google mailing-list, and a partly 'official' website. All this information later helped me to create designs.

Understanding the context is paramount, whether in permaculture design, graphic design, or web design. Otherwise, the result may not align with the desired outcome. Observing how people interact with

31  http://skogsträdgården.stjärnsund.nu/wp-content/uploads/Diplomans %C3%B6kan_PhilippWeiss_nov2015.pdf
32  https://www.beyondbuckthorns.com

a specific website – clicking links, reacting to images, assessing spacing, and ensuring mobile compatibility – offers invaluable insights.

Observation is key before starting development. Is there actually a need for the digital product? Or are there other products around that already serve that need to a good extend? Could I contribute to an already existing Open-source project instead of starting a new one?

## 2. Catch and store energy

The principle of catch and store energy revolves around capturing and preserving resources such as water, nutrients, and energy in general for future use. The objective is to harness these resources during times of abundance and conserve them for use during periods of scarcity.

At Beyond Buckthorns, we have implemented rainwater harvesting systems[33] with the help of IBCs[34] and a well, collecting and storing rainwater for various purposes. By capturing and storing water during heavy rainfall we can conserve water, reducing the need for irrigation in dry spells. Additional examples include the use of swales, terraces, and other land-forms to capture and store water both above and below ground, slowing its flow and allowing it to

---

33  https://www.beyondbuckthorns.com/content/diploma-applied-permaculture-design/catching-rain
34  IBC, Intermediate Bulk Container

seep into the soil to recharge groundwater. At Beyond Buckthorns, ditches and berms on a slope serve to catch and store water[35].

When it comes to rain water I use the 3S rule explained to me by DanMcTiernan[36] during a Permaculture Design Course – which I later adapted to the 4S rule:

1.  **Slow**
2.  **Spread**
3.  **Sink**
4.  **Store**

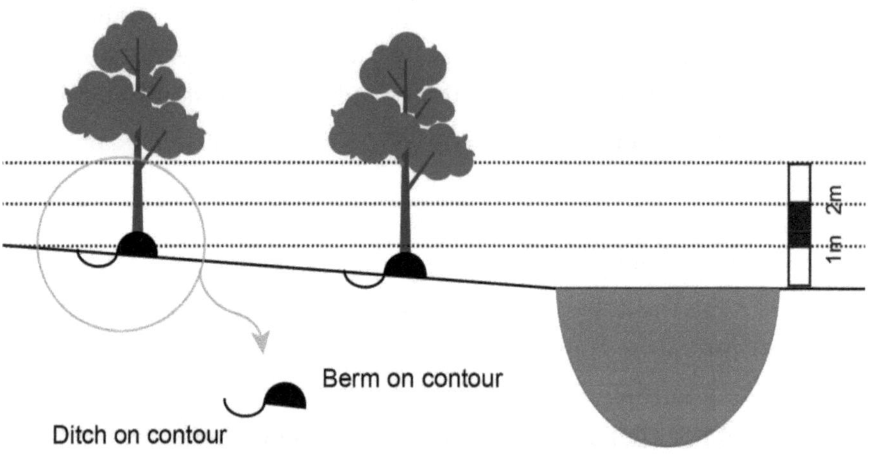


Ditch and berm on contour, slowing down the water run-off, spreading it on the contour and also infiltrating it. The pond at the end acts as storage.

---

35  https://www.beyondbuckthorns.com/content/diploma-applied-permaculture-design/eutopia-borealis
36  https://www.earthbound.fi

Catch and store energy also encompasses greenhouses and other structures for capturing and storing solar energy, along with composting and other techniques to harness and store nutrients from organic waste.

Transitioning this principle to the digital realm requires an understanding of energy. Wikipedia defines energy as "a conserved quantity – the law of conservation of energy states that energy can be converted in form, but not created or destroyed."[37]

Data stored on devices like SSDs (Solid State Drives) or hard drives embody conserved energy, retrievable at a cost. When we generate information and craft knowledge, storing it represents captured and stored energy – a person's work. This work requires energy in the form of sustenance. **We continuously capture various forms of people's work**, such as paintings, essays, and books, constituting caught and stored energy in one form or another. Catch and store energy serves as a nearly universal principle applicable to diverse permaculture designs.

One of our clients at Chase & Snow[38], our marketing company, recently underwent a website redesign with another web development company. However, they soon noticed a decline in their search engine ranking,

---

37  https://en.wikipedia.org/wiki/Energy
38  https://www.chaseandsnow.com/

specifically their position in Google search results. Upon investigation, it became evident that the web development company responsible for the redesign had disregarded the second design principle of permaculture. Rather than taking into account the existing links and structure of the old website, they opted to delete it and create something entirely new. In doing so, they neglected to consider the stored energy and value embedded within the previous site. This is a common occurrence in the digital realm, where changes can be made with just a click. It highlights the importance of applying the principles of digital permaculture, which emphasize the preservation and thoughtful transformation of existing digital assets.

By adopting a digital permaculture approach, we can avoid the unnecessary destruction of valuable digital resources and instead harness their potential to create more sustainable and successful digital platforms. It reminds us that the digital realm, much like the natural world, requires careful consideration, conservation, and regeneration to foster long-term success and resilience. After all the digital world is rooted in the real world.

# 3. Obtain a yield

Obtain a yield emphasizes designing and managing systems to generate benefits or outputs, including food, medicine, materials, and energy. The goal is to create productive, self-sustaining systems that cater to the fundamental needs of the individuals who rely on them.

As Holmgren aptly expressed on his website:

*"You can not work on an empty stomach."*

Cultivating food-producing systems such as gardens, orchards, and aquaculture ensures an abundance of fresh fruits, vegetables, and fish. Designing these systems to be both productive and self-sustaining, we can fulfill our needs and contribute to our communities' well-being.

Bill Mollison wrote:

*"The yield of a system is theoretically unlimited. (or only limited by the knowledge and imagination of the designer)"*

Permaculture design can also encompass the production of non-food yields, such as medicine, materials, and energy. This can involve using plants to create medicine, employing sustainable harvesting techniques for material production, and harnessing renewable energy sources.

In 2017, we made a sustainable investment by installing a 4.7 kW peak solar panel array on our house. This grid-connected system allows us to generate renewable energy, and any excess energy we produce is fed back into the grid and sold. This arrangement ensures a fair share for both ourselves and those in need.

During the sunny summer months when our solar panels are most productive, we generate surplus energy that can be put to the grid. In contrast, during the winter months when solar production is close to zero, we have the opportunity to purchase energy from the grid. This fair share system allows us to access the energy we need while supporting the grid and ensuring equitable distribution.

On the other hand on January the 5th 2024 the price for one kWh spiked to 2,35 € in Finland. And in May 2023 the price for one kWh went into the negative. People got paid for consuming electricity.

In permaculture, obtaining a yield also entails ensuring the yield satisfies the basic requirements of those who utilize the system in a sustainable manner, without exhausting the resources at hand.

To apply the principle of obtaining a yield within the digital realm, we must first determine what constitutes a yield. Wikipedia lists various types of yields[39].

- Yield (chemistry), the amount of product obtained in a chemical reaction
- Crop yield, measurement of the amount of crop harvested, or animal product produced
- Ecological yield, used in forestry and fishery
- Specific yield, a measure of aquifer capacity
- Yield (hydrology), the volume of water escaping from a spring
- Yield (finance), a rate of return for a security

The Cambridge Dictionary defines the verb "to yield" as "to supply or produce something positive such as a profit, an amount of food, or information."[40]

The last part, 'information', is the aspect most relevant for us. Obtaining a yield can be interpreted as gathering valuable information.

---

39  https://en.wikipedia.org/wiki/Yield
40  https://dictionary.cambridge.org/dictionary/english/yield

In general, the "obtain a yield" principle allows for a great deal of creativity. It is up to the designer to decide what constitutes a yield in any given application.

When designing websites for non-profit organizations or personal projects, I ensure that my company's logo is displayed and a link to my company's website is provided. This allows interested individuals to follow the link and easily contact me, representing a yield obtained.

At some of my websites I ask registered members to test new functions. Those functions can later be used in another website. I obtained a digital yield.

## 4. Apply self regulation and accept feedback

This principle speaks to the notion of vigilance in monitoring and adjusting systems to ensure they function as intended and adapt to ever-changing conditions. It involves employing feedback loops to observe the performance of a system and making necessary adjustments to maintain its health and productivity.

In permaculture, techniques like crop rotation, companion planting, and intercropping can be used to preserve soil health and productivity. By carefully observing the success of these methods and modifying them when needed, we can guarantee the vitality and productivity of our food-producing systems.

We can also deploy sensors and data collection tools to monitor the performance of renewable energy systems, making adjustments as required to optimize their efficiency and output.

Applying self-regulation and accepting feedback also means being receptive to new ideas and input from fellow practitioners and experts, and being willing to adapt in order to enhance the performance of the system.

Feedback systems can range in scope, from global issues like climate chaos to smaller matters like the absence of hedgehogs after moving a pile of branches. We are constantly bombarded with feedback, and our response to it is what makes the difference.

Natural systems will self-regulate without human intervention. Consider an Earth devoid of humans – what kind of place it would be?[41]

Bill Mollison noted:

> *"You don't have a slug problem,*
> *you have a duck deficiency."*

In the digital realm, applying self-regulation and accepting feedback can involve using analytics and monitoring tools, conducting user testing and surveys, implementing feedback loops, encouraging

---

41  https://en.wikipedia.org/wiki/The_World_Without_Us

community participation, continuously evaluating the effectiveness
of digital systems, being open to new technologies and ideas, and
incorporating them as needed to improve performance, security, and
sustainability.

Self-regulation can also pertain to our relationship with the web and
digital tools, particularly social media. **How much do we consume?
How often are we online?** Do we crave constant updates, are we
doom scrolling[42]? Self-regulation might manifest as a detox from
social media or setting specific online hours. It's about recognizing
necessary limits. As Paracelsus said, "The dose makes the poison",[43]
and excessive social media is undoubtedly harmful.

Consider the countless apps available in the Google Play Store or
Apple's App Store for plant identification or ruler function apps.
There's an overabundance in the app world, and no one exercises
self-regulation. Questions like, "Does someone actually need this?"
or "Is the existing app good enough?" or "Can I contribute to the
existing app?" go unasked. Imagine the wasted resources due to a
lack of self-regulation and feedback acceptance. Unfortunately we
too often fall for "Not invented here".[44]

---

42  https://en.wikipedia.org/wiki/Doomscrolling
43  https://en.wikipedia.org/wiki/The_dose_makes_the_poison
44  https://en.wikipedia.org/wiki/Not_invented_here

# 5. Use and value renewable resources & services

In permaculture, we strive to design and manage systems that harness resources naturally replenished while providing vital services like pollination, pest control, and soil enrichment. The goal is to create sustainable and resilient systems using resources that regenerate over time, delivering essential services that support the system's health and productivity.

At Beyond Buckthorns, we employ polycultures, a method of cultivating multiple crops together within the same space. This approach includes planting various crops in a single bed, intercropping, and companion planting. By emulating natural ecosystems where diverse plants and animals interact and support each other, essential services such as pollination, pest control, and soil building are provided.

We also utilize renewable energy sources, like wood, solar and biogas[45] to power our homestead. This reduces our reliance on fossil fuels and helps minimize the environmental impact of these systems.

Several years ago, I discovered the concept of Repair Cafés[46]. These delightful gatherings enable people to come

---

45  https://beyondbuckthorns.com/content/biogas
46  https://www.repaircafe.org/en/

together, fixing broken items while enjoying a cup of coffee. Repair Cafés are typically recurring events that take place in the same location. When I resided in Essen, Germany, the Repair Café was an integral part of the local Transition Town initiative[47].

# 6. Produce no waste

In permaculture, the pursuit of producing no waste involves designing and managing systems that minimize waste while maximizing resource utilization. This is achieved through reusing, recycling, and repurposing materials, discovering ways to transform waste into valuable resources, composting and employing other recycling methods, emulating natural ecosystems, reducing synthetic chemical usage, and opting for natural alternatives.

For years, we've had a compost system for our food scraps, and since 2018, we've also implemented a biogas system for usage during the summer months. A DIY biogas

---

47   https://transitionnetwork.org

digester serves as an excellent nutrient cycling system, producing burnable gas and nutrient-rich effluent. Nothing goes to waste.

# "The web is an ocean full of crap."

Gerry McGovern[48]

The digital realm also presents opportunities to apply this principle. We've already explored Open-source and Open-hardware concepts, but there are more strategies worth considering.

We can implement recycling and repurposing programs for digital devices and equipment, such as smartphones, laptops, and servers, to extend their life cycles and curb the demand for new resources. For instance, rather than relying on the standard Android operating system, an older phone might be able to run a custom ROM[49], like LineageOS[50]. Older phones can also be repurposed as security cameras or webcams for 3D printers. Laptops, whether PCs or Macs, can be used with Linux[51], an Open source alternative.

---

48  https://gerrymcgovern.com
49  https://de.wikipedia.org/wiki/Liste_von_Android-Custom-ROMs
50  https://wiki.lineageos.org
51  https://www.linux.org

Designing digital systems that can be easily updated, maintained, and upgraded is another approach that helps reduce the need for new resources and waste generation. As a site builder, I've used Drupal since version 5 – since about 2006. Over the years, most of my earlier sites have been upgraded and now operate on the latest version. Some of the websites I created using a Content Management System (CMS) have transitioned to static websites, such as the 2022 Nordic Permaculture Festival's website.[52] Static websites are pure HTML, they don't need a database and a hypertext pre-processors like PHP. Hence they require less resources.

Using Open-source software and open standards to reduce the amount of proprietary software and lock-in, and to promote the sharing and reuse of digital resources. One of best examples for sharing and reuse of code is **Github**, which is a code repository platform where coders could host their work. According to Wikipedia Github[53] hosted more than 28 million publicly available code repositories[54] in 2023. It might be that the software you like to create or use is already available there. Who knows?

The most important question at the beginning of a product cycle should always be: **Is it necessary?**

And the most important questions when I want to replace something is: **Do I need it – and why?**

---

52  https://2022.nordicpermaculturefestival.org
53  https://github.com
54  https://en.wikipedia.org/wiki/GitHub

Venturing further into the digital world, servers run continuously to host data and facilitate website visits. These servers demand a significant amount of energy, particularly when storing or requesting data. Server farms are notorious for their voracious energy consumption. As servers require energy, they generate heat, which must be dissipated to maintain optimal performance. This heat can be repurposed for other applications, such as heating an algae farm or perhaps a nearby hospital. It's all about the strategic placement of elements. No server farm should squander its heat by releasing it into the environment; it must be harnessed and utilized.

During a discussion in 2010 with the CEO of a hosting company, the topic of "green IT" came up. When I inquired about their approach to environmentally-friendly practices, the CEO responded with a disheartening statement: "Currently not possible." At the time, it seemed that the concept of green hosting was not widely embraced or feasible within the industry.

However, as I embarked on writing this book in 2019, I conducted research on green hosting providers and was pleasantly surprised by the progress made in just a few years. By the time 2024 arrived, the landscape had significantly changed, with a notable increase in the number of hosting companies adopting green practices.

Personally I believe that server farms should be prohibited if they fail to capitalize on their excess heat. Moreover, it is imperative that these facilities operate on renewable energy sources. The push for sustainability in the digital sphere is just as crucial as everywhere.

## 7. Design from pattern to details

This principle highlights the importance of recognizing the underlying patterns and relationships that shape a system, using this understanding to guide the design of intricate elements. This approach employs techniques such as **zone and sector analysis, biomimicry**[55], and a comprehensive understanding of the relationships between different components of the system to create more holistic, efficient, and sustainable designs.

*"Can't see the forest for the trees."*

Proverb by John Heywood

---

55  https://en.wikipedia.org/wiki/Biomimetics

Applying this principle to digital systems is equally crucial. Initially, we must establish the "why" behind a project. For instance, should a website aim to inform, sell, connect people, or achieve a combination of these objectives? **What is its ultimate purpose?** Once the broader perspective is established, we can gradually go deeper into the details, from designing the login page to selecting specific images for the front-page.

Ultimately, effective design requires stepping back and examining the big picture, ensuring that the details align with the overall patterns and objectives. By designing from patterns to details, we create digital systems that are not only functional and user-friendly but also adaptable and sustainable for the long term.

# 8. Integrate rather than segregate

In permaculture, this principle emphasizes the need for designing and managing systems that are interconnected and holistic, as opposed to segmented and isolated. This approach enables permaculture practitioners to establish systems that are more effective, resilient, and sustainable. Within land design, this can manifest as polycultures, companion planting, and food forest design, while in social design, it encompasses inclusiveness, low barriers to entry, and conflict resolution.

Digital permaculture primarily focuses on the social aspects, as most digital tools are developed for and used by humans.

When designing a website, for instance, accessibility should be a top priority. High color contrast, adequately sized fonts, and responsiveness must be in place to accommodate users with different screen formats and abilities and disabilities.[56]

Furthermore, consideration should be given to visitors with limited bandwidth, such as everyone in the Global South. By creating permaculture websites that consume minimal bandwidth, we can ensure that valuable information remains accessible to all. The difference in loading time between a website that requires 20 MB versus 1 MB is significant. Our digital tools and websites must be integrative, with low barriers to entry.

Integrating different digital systems and platforms can be achieved through the use of Application Programming Interfaces (API) and other integration tools.

---

56  https://ec.europa.eu/social/main.jsp?catId=1202&intPageId=5581&langId=en

Although WordPress is Open source, it is from my point of view not the most adequate system. At the European Permaculture Network (EuPN), we encountered difficulties connecting a calendar plugin with a newsletter plugin due to the absence of a standardized API, which would have let the two plugins "talk" with each other.

Creating multi-functional digital systems is also essential, designing features and services that serve multiple purposes rather than having a single function. This adheres to Mollison's ecological principle of **"multiple functions per element"**. For example, the European Permaculture Network[57] website incorporates news, a newsletter, RSS feeds[58] for various categories, user-generated content like events and places, and more.

Designing digital systems that can be easily integrated with other services and systems enhances their functionality and usability. For instance, at the EuPN, we were able to import events from other websites using a

---

57  https://permaculture-network.eu
58  https://en.wikipedia.org/wiki/RSS

feed importer. However, many permaculture community websites do not provide ics/iCal[59] (standardized calendar format) files, either due to a lack of knowledge or understanding of their utility – compounded by the prevalence of WordPress websites. Nonetheless, every event on the EuPN website includes an ics file, which, along with our RSS feed, can be effortlessly integrated with other systems.

The adoption of Open-source software and open standards encourages the integration and sharing of digital resources. As previously discussed, Open-source software allows for the modification and distribution of source code. Open standards, on the other hand, refer to universally accessible standards. The World Wide Web itself is an open standard, with open protocols such as TCP (Transmission Control Protocol) / IP (Internet Protocol) and HTTP (Hypertext Transfer Protocol) forming the backbone of the internet as we know it.

Today, in 2024, we usually only interact with HTTP(S). But the internet once relied on a broader range of protocols,

---

59  https://en.wikipedia.org/wiki/ICalendar

such as POP (Post Office Protocol), IMAP (Internet Message
Access Protocol), and SMTP (Simple Mail Transfer
Protocol). The graphical, visually appealing front-end of
the internet is now predominantly dominated by HTTP(S),
simplifying our online experience. As Albert Einstein once
said, "Make everything as simple as possible, but not
simpler." It seems we have reached a point where
simplicity may have gone too far.

# 9. Use slow & small solutions

In my home, I've employed various techniques that exemplify the
slow and small solutions principle. Sheet mulching[60] and
hügelkultur[61] are two such methods that gradually build soil fertility,
as opposed to resorting to synthetic fertilizers or other quick-fix
solutions. These techniques involve layering organic matter like
leaves, straw, and compost on top of the soil, allowing it to
decompose over time and ultimately enhance soil fertility and water
retention.

Another instance of slow and small solutions is the use of
permaculture design to establish small-scale food production
systems like home gardens and community gardens, instead of large-

---

60  https://en.wikipedia.org/wiki/Sheet_mulching
61  https://en.wikipedia.org/wiki/Hügelkultur

scale industrial agriculture. This approach allows for more efficient resource utilization, less waste, and enhanced system resilience by decreasing dependence on any single component.

Embracing slow and small solutions also entails patience, giving systems the time to develop and mature, rather than anticipating instant results. This method enables systems to adapt, evolve, and respond to shifting conditions.

In the digital realm, change also could take a large amount of time. Consider how long AOL[62] persisted before it ultimately collapsed, or how Meta and its brands, such as Facebook, Instagram, and WhatsApp, have dominated the social application market for an extended period.

When I develop websites, I commit changes to my GIT[63] repositories (Git is a versioning system) incrementally. This technical approach, known as incremental development[64], involves constructing digital systems in small, iterative steps rather than attempting to create everything simultaneously. Incremental development promotes more efficient resource use and renders the system more adaptable and resilient to change.

Using Open-source software and open standards is another example of slow and small solutions in digital permaculture. It allows for small-scale digital system development without reliance on large commercial software vendors, granting more flexibility and control

---

62  https://en.wikipedia.org/wiki/AOL
63  https://en.wikipedia.org/wiki/Git
64  https://en.wikipedia.org/wiki/Iterative_and_incremental_development

over the system's evolution. Implementing slow and small solutions in digital permaculture also necessitates patience, giving systems time to grow and mature, and fostering their ability to adapt, evolve, and respond to changing circumstances.

In stark contrast to Holmgren's permaculture principle of "Use slow and small solutions" stands the prevailing ethos of the startup culture. The startup world often champions a fast-paced, growth-oriented approach, typically characterized by rapid scaling, aggressive market penetration, and a focus on large, immediate impacts. This 'move fast and break things' mentality, popularized by high-tech startups, prioritizes speed and size over sustainability and gradual evolution.

While this approach can yield quick results and significant short-term gains, it sometimes overlooks the long-term implications and sustainability of such rapid growth. This mentality can lead to resource depletion, burnout, and a lack of resilience in the face of challenges, contrasting sharply with the permaculture principle that advocates for small, incremental changes. Permaculture emphasizes building systems that are sustainable, resilient, and adaptable over time, reflecting a deep understanding of and respect for natural processes and cycles.

In the realm of digital technology and sustainability, adopting the "slow and small solutions" approach means valuing long-term effectiveness over short-term efficiency. It involves carefully considering the environmental and social impact of digital projects, focusing on building robust systems that grow and evolve organically, and prioritizing the well-being of communities and ecosystems over rapid expansion. This principle encourages a more thoughtful, deliberate approach to innovation and growth, one that aligns with the sustainable ethos of permaculture and fosters lasting positive change.

Adopting a small and slow approach also implies resisting the temptation to chase the latest trends or succumb to the fear of missing out[65]. In our pursuit of more lasting, sustainable solutions, we must consider the long-term consequences of our choices.

Small and slow solutions sometimes require us to acknowledge that, in many situations, analog tools are simply more effective or convenient. While we could opt for a laser leveler, an a-frame or water level would be just as useful and significantly more affordable. Even today, pen and paper often outperform digital tools.

At Beyond Buckthorns, we prioritize sustainable and self-sufficient practices, including our approach to heating. We rely on wood as our primary source of heat, and what sets us apart is that we harvest the wood from our very own forest. This allows us to have full control over the entire process, from the selection of trees to the careful extraction and preparation of firewood.

---

65  https://dictionary.cambridge.org/dictionary/english/fomo

To align with our sustainable values, we employ traditional and manual methods whenever possible. Hand tools such as kataba handsaws, bucksaws, axes, and a splitting wedge with a sledgehammer play a crucial role in our wood processing. By utilizing these tools, we minimize our reliance on fossil fuel-powered machinery and embrace a more environmentally friendly approach. It is also a slow and small solution compared to a clear cut and using harvesters.

This manual approach not only reduces our carbon footprint but also fosters a deeper connection with the land and a sense of self-sufficiency. It allows us to actively participate in the harvesting and processing of our firewood, gaining a firsthand understanding of the resources we utilize.

Great permaculture solutions tend to be crafted by individuals or communities to serve their own needs, rather than by large-scale corporations catering to smaller groups. Though we frequently gravitate towards industrial-scale tools due to their affordability, they may ultimately create more problems than they solve in the long run. During a Permaculture Design Course (PDC) we often hear about appropriate technology[66] or as I call it: 'human scale' technology. They are usually all slow and small.

# 10. Use and value diversity

Permaculture seeks to establish diverse and resilient systems by incorporating a variety of elements. Here are some examples:

**Polyculture planting:** Instead of growing just one crop in a particular area polyculture involves planting a variety of crops together. This approach provides multiple benefits, such as improved soil fertility, pest control, and increased productivity. In the face of the industrial agriculture that dominates our modern world, there exists an inspiring, age-old planting method that defies the logic of monoculture. Known as the 'Three Sisters,' 'this method' unites corn, beans, and squash in a symbiotic dance of mutual support and nourishment. The corn, standing tall like a natural skyscraper, lends its sturdy stalks to the beans, allowing them to reach for the sky. The beans, in turn, work their magic beneath the soil, capturing nitrogen from the air and infusing the earth with this vital nutrient. Meanwhile, the squash sprawls across the ground, forming a living carpet that keeps the weeds at bay and preserves precious moisture. This harmonious trio of plants, working in concert, exemplifies the wisdom of valuing diversity over the lifeless monotony of industrial farming practices.

---

66  https://en.wikipedia.org/wiki/Appropriate_technology

In stark contrast to the environmentally destructive monocultures that have come to define modern agriculture, the concept of **forest gardening** emerges as an elegant, nature-inspired alternative. By imitating the very structure and function of a natural forest ecosystem, forest gardens weave together an intricate tapestry of life, with plants of varying heights and roles coexisting in a harmonious, productive, and resilient landscape. This ingenious approach not only nurtures a diverse array of flora and fauna, but it also encourages natural pest control and provides a cornucopia of food, fiber, and other resources to support human life. Picture a thriving forest garden, replete with fruit and nut trees, bountiful berry bushes, perennial vegetables, and edible ground covers, all thoughtfully arranged to maximize both space and sunlight.

Chat GPT4 generated image. "The illustration of an eco-friendly urban neighborhood using a restricted color palette"

Similarly, the integration of animals into permaculture systems offers a powerful antidote to the damaging practices of factory farming. By welcoming a variety of animals into the fold, these systems tap into the many benefits that diverse species can provide. Chickens, for instance, serve as natural pest controllers, devouring insects, while also contributing valuable fertilizer in the form of their nutrient-rich manure. Goats, too, play their part, grazing on weeds and aiding in land management. Each animal, in its own unique way, fortifies the resilience and self-sustenance of the permaculture system, underscoring the value of diversity in the face of an increasingly homogenized world. These animals are our companions, deserving of respect and care, rather than just objects of use.

In the digital realm, this translates to fostering diversity and inclusivity in the development and application of digital tools and platforms. "Don't put your eggs all in one basket.". This principles encourages us to:

- Search for alternatives
- Avoid defaulting to popular systems – evaluate your options carefully instead of following the crowd without question.

In my opinion, everyone contributes to shaping the digital landscape, and every user influences the system. It's about behavior, the tools we use and the tools we don't use – the choices we make.

When it comes to troubleshooting software glitches or addressing hardware issues, it matters little who I collaborate with, as long as I don't face discrimination, bullying, or harassment. The same principle applies when I offer assistance to others navigating the digital world.

While writing this book I came across a non trivial bug in Libre Office. I first asked for support and then later opened a Bug report[67] – contributing to the improvement of the software.

# 11. Use & value the marginal

The practice of designing and managing systems that make use of and value the areas or elements that are typically considered unproductive or of little value. This approach allows permaculture practitioners to create systems that are more efficient, resilient, and sustainable.

Take, for instance, the utilization of property edges or garden borders, where diverse microclimates and habitats reside. These often overlooked spaces harbor a richness of plant and animal life, proving to be more productive than their uniform central counterparts. Similarly, employing techniques like terracing, swales, and ponding to manage water on a property can transform areas deemed unproductive or flood-prone into fertile, water-retaining spaces for crops and animals.

**What is marginal in the digital world?**

---

67  https://bugs.documentfoundation.org/show_bug.cgi?id=156384

In the digital realm, the concept of marginal shifts. Here, abundance is the norm. There are plenty of developers available and eager to learn new concepts, eager for a new job, new colleagues, money, etc. But when we apply sustainability on the digital realm we need to look closer. Suddenly we are in the marginal again. Sustainability requires a different mindset, different skills and knowledge.

People who have an in depth understanding of the both, the digital world and a deep understanding of permaculture are marginal, rare, edge cases. A true practitioner of digital permaculture must understand not only how digital tools work, but their impact compared to alternatives, how the software works, the company behind it, is it open-source or proprietary, and so on. Just as a permaculture gardener who lectures on food forests would know what plants will grow well together, but also why and how, and let's also add: how it works on a biological, chemical, biochemical and microbiological level.

It is not good enough to know the way around a Google Drive to make an informed decisions what cloud storage service or software an association or company with hundreds members / employees is going to use. A person making that decision must also know the alternatives available on the same level as they know the Google Drive. And if the decision making process was done using an ethical decision framework like permaculture offers, then we wouldn't end up with a proprietary product in a permaculture association in the first place. If we compare companies like Google to companies in the permaculture realm we would talk about the size of Bayer (Bayer acquired Monsanto in 2018). No one in a permaculture garden would use seeds or fertilizers from Bayer. But when it comes to Google we just use it. We don't value and use the marginal. And our behavior will bite us due to the dependency we create.

In September 2023, the UK Permaculture Association's website was built on Drupal 10. Back in 2017, I offered my assistance with their website and provided some tips, leveraging my professional expertise as a Drupal site builder.

However, I never received any further communication from them. This led me to reflect on the availability of Drupal experts within the permaculture community. Ultimately, I decided to focus on making my own websites sustainable and write this book.

As a community, we should appreciate and support those who freely offer their expertise and passion for specific subjects, even if they may be socially awkward or intensely focused. Embracing the geeks and nerds among us can inject fresh perspectives and knowledge into the permaculture community. To truly live by permaculture principles, we must value and use the marginal, recognizing the potential contributions of individuals from all walks of life.

# 12. Creatively use and respond to change

As permaculture designers we should design and manage systems that are adaptable and resilient and can respond to changing conditions. This approach allows us to create more sustainable, efficient and resilient systems.

Techniques such as observation, experimentation, and adaptation help us to monitor and respond to changing conditions, among them are weather patterns, pest outbreaks, and soil fertility. Using those techniques we can adjust our systems as needed, to ensure that they are meeting our goals and maintaining resilience.

We also aim for systems that are multi-functional and multi-layered, which allows for more efficient use of resources and greater resilience in the face of change. Let's plant more perennials!

But the principle also means being open-minded and flexible, and willing to try new things and to learn from failure. This approach allows us to innovate and to find new solutions to the challenges we face.

**Let's see how it could work in the digital realm.**

If you ever came across software development you might have heard the term agile. Agile software development[68] is a way of developing software that encourages rapid iteration and adaptation to changing requirements. It allows developers to respond quickly to changing

---

68  https://en.wikipedia.org/wiki/Agile_software_development

conditions and to make adjustments to systems as needed. It is based on the Agile manifesto[69] and widely used in software development.

> At my company we use parts of Scrum[70] (Scrum is one of the most popular frameworks that implement Agile principles) to deliver high quality sustainable websites to our clients.
>
> I used methods from Scrum / Agile to get my Diploma in Applied Permaculture Design done in under 2 years.

Creatively use and respond to change also means being open to experimentation and innovation, and being willing to try new technologies and approaches, to find new solutions to the challenges we face.

**It generally follows the "the problem is the solution" attitudinal principle.**

---

69  https://agilemanifesto.org
70  https://www.scrum.org/resources/what-is-scrum

# Conclusion

The three ethics and the principles are the core concepts in permaculture. They are the bread and butter of every permaculture designer. Without ethics there is no permaculture. Also without design there is no permaculture.

Permaculture principles, which include more than just the attitudinal, ecological, and design principles, help us stay on course with our designs. They can be used in multiple ways during the different stages of the design process. I often use design principles as a checklist in the design stage to ensure that I'm on track regarding resilience, sustainability, resourcefulness, and holistic thinking. I also benefit from them as brainstorming tools, simply stepping through each principle to see what ideas emerge

# Patterns

In permaculture, patterns refer to the recurring shapes, forms, or processes found in nature that can be replicated and used in sustainable design. The concept of patterns in permaculture is derived from the observation that certain arrangements and processes occur repeatedly in the natural world, and these can be harnessed to enhance the efficiency and sustainability of human-made systems.

There are certain benefits which come from observing patterns. Observed patterns can be mimicked. A designer could for example create a food forest (also known as forest garden[71]), which mimics the layers of a natural forest, creating a diverse and resilient ecosystem that can withstand pests and climatic chaos better than a single-crop system. One often used pattern is the herb spiral[72]. It allows for efficient resource use by creating varying microclimates within a compact space, each suited for different plants. Patterns are not an exclusive to permaculture. In software development patterns are used as well.

| Aspect | Patterns in Permaculture | Patterns in Software Design |
|---|---|---|
| **Context** | Ecological and agricultural contexts | Software development and engineering contexts |
| **Environment** | Natural systems, landscapes, sustainable living | Creation, maintenance, and optimization of software |
| **Principles** | | |
| Natural Systems | Inspired by nature (spirals, waves, branches) | Not applicable |
| Sustainability | Creating self-sustaining, resilient ecosystems | Reusability, Modularity, Scalability, Efficiency |
| Integration | Integrating elements for mutual benefits | Modular, interchangeable components |
| **Application** | | |
| Design | Layout and management of land, water, plants, animals | Solve recurring design problems, improve code maintainability |
| Examples | Swales, guild planting, keyhole gardens | Singleton, Observer, Factory |
| Goals | Enhance productivity, resource conservation, ecological balance | Enhance reliability, reduce development time, improve code quality |

---

71  https://en.wikipedia.org/wiki/Forest_gardening

72  https://www.permaculturenews.org/2015/04/17/the-magic-and-mystery-of-constructing-an-herb-spiral-and-why-every-suburban-lawn-should-have-one/

While patterns in permaculture and patterns in software design are applied in different domains, they share several similarities in terms of their purpose, structure, and benefits.

Patterns in permaculture and software development

- aim to solve common problems efficiently.
- encourage reusability and modularity.
- promote efficiency and sustainability.
- support adaptability and scalability.
- represent best practices and facilitate education and communication.

While the domains of application differ, the underlying principles of using patterns to create effective, efficient, and sustainable systems are remarkably similar. This similarity underscores why this book is necessary.

Radial
Hexagon
Wave
Meanders
Branching
Webs
Spiral
Scattering
Lobe

# 4. Survey

As SADIM dictates we start our permaculture design with an extensive survey of the subject. In a land based design, where I design for example for my own homestead, I surveyed the land for a two years – and I'm still surveying. In case of this book the survey was extensive as well. Extensive survey of the subject is important, otherwise our outcome will fall short.

The 3 rules for survey are: Carefully, Carefully, Carefully

## Soft- and Hardware

Depending on when you are reading this book, some of the soft- and hardware described here might already be out of date but the derived patterns will remain. The observations made in the following chapters are made from my personal perspective. In this stage of the design I encourage you to start your survey as well!

### Hardware

Over a decade or so I have been part of multiple meetings with different organizations and people – all related to permaculture. Over that period of time I have met the highest amount of Apple users I have ever met. Usually the amount of Apple computers would be at some 20% of all users[73]. In the permaculture and sustainability world I have been part of it was the other way round. I would say about 80% of the people I worked with on permaculture projects were Apple users. No worries if you are using Apple hard- and software. Some things and habits are more difficult to get rid of than others.

Apple Inc., known simply as Apple, became a symbol of market valuation when it reached the unprecedented milestone of a 1 trillion-dollar market cap in 2018. This valuation did not come from curing diseases, eradicating poverty, or resolving the complex issue of climate chaos. Instead, it was about the company's immense success in the technology sector. This moment raised an important questions about our collective priorities and the criteria we use to assign value and prestige in our global economy. It suggests that we may need to reflect more deeply on our ethical frameworks and consider how they align with the challenges facing humanity. It seems we have some ethical decision making to do!

Nearly all their software is closed source (they have some Open-source contributions[74]). Their lock-ins[75] are well known and documented.

---

73  https://www.statista.com/statistics/576473/united-states-quarterly-pc-shipment-share-apple
74  https://opensource.apple.com/projects/
75  https://www.techconstant.com/apples-lock-in/

## Lock-ins

Our culture is consumer-driven. And among our culture a disturbing trend has emerged: the prevalence of technology designed to keep us tethered to a single manufacturer, often rendering products obsolete before their time. This practice, known as vendor lock-in, contributes to an ever-growing mountain of e-waste, as devices are cast aside in pursuit of the latest, seemingly indispensable gadget. It falls upon our legislators to put an end to this wasteful cycle and ensure that companies no longer dictate the lifespan of their products for the sake of appeasing shareholders with impressive sales figures. It is not just about the legislators. As permaculture practitioners, we must resist the siren call of disposable technology and refuse to be complicit in a system that prioritizes profit over the health of our planet. By embracing and advocating for durable, sustainable alternatives, we can challenge the destructive norms of our throwaway culture and help to forge a more responsible path forward.

> *"We live in a world where the funeral matters more than the dead, the wedding more than love and the physical rather than the intellect. We live in the container culture, which despises the content."*

Eduardo Galeano, Uruguayan novelist[76]

---

76  https://en.wikipedia.org/wiki/Eduardo_Galeano

On one project the team members were using Slack (page 132) and one of our members had an old MacBook. His Mac was as old as my Lenovo Thinkpad but he couldn't get into Slack because he couldn't update the MacOS any more. Basically Apple decided that the old MacBook wouldn't get the newest MacOS and therefore the needed libraries where missing. He later installed Linux on his Mac – problem solved.

## Outdated

A common problem that we often face is that outdated software renders still usable hardware unusable. But thanks to clever developers there are alternatives around. Most of the time I was able to switch a software that would get no updates any more for an alternative. Linux is usually my go to software. There are so many now – just to name some: Ubuntu or Mint[77] or sometimes even Arch Linux[78] – chose your flavor.

Why is software for older hardware discontinued?

**Hardware limitations:** Newer software versions often require more advanced hardware specifications, making them incompatible with older devices.

---

77  https://linuxmint.com
78  https://archlinux.org

**Cost:** Developing and releasing software updates for older devices can be expensive, and manufacturers may choose to allocate their resources towards newer models instead.

**Declining user base:** As the number of users with older devices decreases, the incentive for manufacturers to continue updating their software also decreases. It kind of also boils down to costs.

**EOL (End of Life) Policy:** Some manufacturers have a policy to support a device for a certain period of time, after which they stop providing software updates.

## Problems from discontinued software

The problems which come from discontinued software, and by that affect the hardware as well, are multiple:

**Security vulnerabilities:** Without regular security updates, older devices can become more susceptible to cyber threats, such as hacking, malware, and data breaches.

**Compatibility issues:** Newer apps and services may require the latest operating system versions, making them incompatible with older devices.

**Performance degradation:** As newer apps and services require more memory and processing power, an older device may struggle to keep up, leading to slower performance and reduced battery life.

**Missing new features:** Users of older devices will not have access to the latest features, improvements, and bug fixes that are available on newer devices.

**Reduced resale value:** A device that is no longer receiving software updates may have a lower resale value compared to newer devices, which are supported with the latest software.

In 2024, I read a discussion in the International CoLab's Slack workspace. The topic was about the latest update Slack had rolled out, which no longer supported devices with Android 8. The phone that couldn't get the update to a newer Android version was the Shiftphone[79]. It was one of the rare cases where an actually well-thought-out product was rendered useless. I then suggested switching away from Slack.

---

79  https://www.shift.eco

## The problem is the solution

Obsolete hardware can contribute to a significant amount of waste (we will see about e-waste later – page 332). The rapid pace of technological advancement means devices become outdated relatively quickly, and this can result in a large amount of e-waste, which can have negative impacts on the environment.

But luckily we have some options:

**Refurbishment:** Obsolete devices can be refurbished and reused, either by fixing any broken components or updating the software to make them more functional. Refurbished devices can then be sold or donated to those in need. Alternative operating systems like Linux[80] and custom ROMS can help.

**Upcycling:** Obsolete devices can be repurposed or upcycled[81] into new, useful products. For example, an old smartphone can be turned into a smart home device or a digital picture frame. I use my old smartphone as wildlife camera.

**Recycling:** Obsolete devices can be recycled to recover valuable materials, such as rare earth metals[82], and to minimize the environmental impact of e-waste.

---

80  https://en.wikipedia.org/wiki/Linux
81  https://en.wikipedia.org/wiki/Upcycling
82  https://www.visualcapitalist.com/visualizing-the-critical-metals-in-a-smartphone/

**Donating:** Obsolete devices can be donated to schools, non-profit organizations[83], or individuals in need, providing them with access to technology and reducing waste.

**Trade-in programs:** Some manufacturers and retailers offer trade-in programs, where users can trade in their old devices for discounts on new devices, helping to reduce e-waste and provide incentives for consumers to upgrade their technology.

In conclusion there are many options around to extend the life-cycle of computers and telephones. The Open source community is very helpful when it comes to the support of older devices.

## Hardware inventory

Here are some questions we could ask ourselves when we create our hardware inventory:

- What hardware do I own?
- When have I bought that hardware?
- Was it a conscious decision to start / continue using it?
- Which operating software is it running?
  - Licensing model?
- Am I locked in?
- Am I using leased hardware or hardware given to me by e.g. the company I work for?

---

83  https://www.labdoo.org/global/en/

| Hardware Layer | Year | What | OS | Conscious |
|---|---|---|---|---|
| Layer 0 | 2015 | Self build PC | Windows, Linux | Yes |
| | 2012 | E-Book reader | Linux | Yes |
| | 2019 | Smartphone | Google Android | Yes |
| Layer 1 | 2015 | Laptop | Linux | Yes |
| Layer 2 | 2020 | Camera | Proprietary | Yes |
| | inherited | Tablet | Lineage Android | - |
| | inherited | Tablet | Lineage Android | - |
| Layer 3 | 2013 | Raspberry Pi | Linux | Yes |
| Layer 4 | 2018 | Raspberry Pi | Linux | Yes |
| | 2021 | Drone | Proprietary | Yes |
| Layer 5 | 2019 | Gimbal | Proprietary | Yes |

Table of hardware, only some have me locked in. Hardware layers according the frequency and duration of usage.

Once we have our list we could check for energy efficiency, expected lifespan and its repairability, especially of *Zone 0 to 2* devices.

| What | Energy | Lifespan | Repairability |
|---|---|---|---|
| Self build PC | - 115 Watt | open | High |
| E-Book reader | - 3.9 Watt | open | Fair |
| Smartphone | 1.5 – 16 Watt | EOL | Difficult |
| Laptop | - 55 Watt | open | Fair |
| Camera | - | EOL | Difficult |
| Tablet | - 7 Watt | EOL | Fair |
| Tablet | - 6 Watt | EOL | Fair |

Table of hardware – Hardware Layer Zone 0 to 2, energy consumption, lifespan and repairability

The concept of an '**open lifespan**' for hardware is particularly relevant in the context of rapidly evolving technology. For instance, my self-built PC usually runs the latest operating system version, but future iterations of the operating system may impose new hardware requirements, necessitating unforeseen upgrades or solutions. This uncertainty underscores the need for forward-thinking in hardware choices and maintenance.

My e-book reader exemplifies a device with a relatively sustainable profile, benefiting from ongoing firmware updates and a simple battery replacement process. The longevity of its battery is further enhanced by the **energy-efficient** e-ink display, which significantly extends the device's usable life.

The term **'End-Of-Life'** (EOL) marks a critical juncture for electronic devices, indicating the cessation of software updates. While EOL may not significantly impact devices like cameras, it poses considerable risks for network-connected devices such as smartphones and tablets. The absence of updates for these devices, especially for essential applications like web browsers, can expose them to security vulnerabilities.

**Repairability** is another crucial factor in the sustainability equation, which I've categorized as High, Fair, and Difficult. 'High' repairability indicates that I can confidently address maintenance or repair needs, often without needing external guidance. 'Fair' suggests that repairs are manageable with the aid of manuals or resources from platforms like iFixit[84], which provide detailed repair guides. 'Difficult' repairability denotes a significant challenge, often due to the absence of available manuals or the device's design, which may not accommodate easy repair.

---

84  https://www.ifixit.com

I use hardware as long as possible and extend its life by using operating systems like Linux. Linux is knowledge intensive, but so is permaculture. It seems like a perfect fit.

From obsolete computer hardware I create stunning clocks, lamps[85] and art[86].

Tillam clock made of a 3,5" hard drive.

---

85  https://www.tillam.one
86  https://www.dominikjais.com/artwork/hdd

# Software inventory

Let's continue with our survey. For software in particular we have to ask ourselves the following questions:

- What software are we currently using?
- What is the license model? Proprietary or Open-source?
- Why are we using that software?
- Was it a conscious decision to use that software?
- Who is developing that software?
  - If a company → What is their revenue?
- What alternatives are there? Are there any?
- Are we in a locked-in system or can we install software freely from different sources?
- What sectors influenced my decision?
- Does it need an internet connection?

Let's open our computers, tablets and smartphones and check for the software we are continuously using.

As a permaculture designer I have used a lot of different digital tools over the years. It is most of the time about documenting my designs or about managing the homestead.

Below is a list of software run on my PC (*Hardware Layer 0*) categorized into the Software Layers (SL)

| SL 0 | Office, Vector Graphics editor, Raster Graphics editor, Email, Tasks & Projects, Websites & CMS, Code editor, Virtual Machine, |
|---|---|
| SL 1 | Photo RAW editor, Note taking / Wiki, Messenger, Teleconference, Social Media, Calendar / Scheduling |
| SL 2 | CAD & 3D, Forms, Mindmaps, Cloud storage, Online document collaboration, |
| SL 3 | GIS, Website analytics, Collaboration platforms, |
| SL 4 | Video editing, Audio recording, Screen recording, Login providers, Newsletter, Arduino IDE, |
| SL 5 | Virtual Machine, Windows XP, Electronic arts, |

Software Layer Zones 0 to 5 according to the frequency of usage and the duration.

I will now step through most of the software I listed and answer the questions in order to get a detailed overview of the software I'm using. Please do the same for yourself! And please do this for all your hardware. You might get a very extensive list.

## Software Layer 0

The Software Layer *0* – software which I'm using on a daily basis.

## Office

I started with Word 5.0 in 1990. During that time Word run as DOS program – pre Windows. It type with a speed of about 74 words per minute and an accuracy of 99%.[87] Over the years I used different versions of MS Word, Excel and Access. During my studies to become a Brewmaster, I tested different Linux office suites, but non could compete with MS Office during that time. Ten years later I

---

87  https://www.livechat.com/typing-speed-test/#/

switched to Libre Office[88] (successor of Open Office) and I never looked back.

For this book I used Libre Office Writer. I also use Libre Calc for spreadsheet calculations, Libre Base for database applications (I have all my plants stored in a DB), and Libre Presenter for presentations.

I never regret switching to Libre Office and as I wrote before: I'm not going to look back.

- I use Libre Office
- Open-source
- Developed by The Document Foundation[89] non-profit
- Conscious decision
- Sectors: Peers, Economic conditions, Users
- There are alternatives around
- No constant internet connection required

## Vector Graphics editor

A vector graphics editor is a computer software application that allows users to create and edit digital images using vector graphics. Unlike raster graphics, which represent images as a collection of pixels, vector graphics are made up of paths defined by mathematical equations. These paths can consist of lines, curves, and shapes, and they can be filled with colors, patterns, or gradients.

---

88  https://en.wikipedia.org/wiki/LibreOffice
89  https://www.documentfoundation.org

Since vector graphics are mathematically described, they can be scaled up or down infinitely without losing clarity or detail, making them especially useful for design work that might need to be resized to various dimensions – such as logos, icons, illustrations and even maps.

Due to their mathematical approach to graphic vector graphic files could be far smaller than same-sized raster graphic files.

> I have been into vector graphics editors[90] for as long as raster graphics editors. For years I created t-shirt designs for my own t-shirt online shop. I even proofread an Adobe Illustrator book for a university. The signs and info-panels at my homestead Beyond Buckthorns are made by using vector graphics.

On Linux I'm using **Inkscape**[91]. It comes with most of the features I expect from a vector graphic editor. Inkscape is developed by a community of volunteers who contribute their time and expertise to the project. It was originally created by Bryce Harrington, MenTaLguY, Ted Gould and Nathan Hurst in 2003 as a fork of the Sodipodi project. Since then, the project has grown significantly, and many developers and users have contributed to its development.

---

90  https://en.wikipedia.org/wiki/Vector_graphics_editor
91  https://inkscape.org

For some time I also use the non Open source alternative **Affinity Designer** (Serif Europe).

- I'm using Adobe Illustrator, Affinity Designer and Inkscape
- Illustrator and Designer are proprietary, Inkscape is open-source
- Revenue of Serif Europe in 2022 was $29.7 million[92] - they got bought by the Australian company Canva in 2024 for about $380 million
- Revenue of Adobe in 2022 was $17.606 billion[93]
- Conscious decision during that time due to a lack of alternatives. Inkscape is lacking the features I need, Affinity Designer is safe enough to try
- Sectors: Manufacturer, User, Peers, Economic condition
- There are alternatives available
- Affinity Designer and Inkscape don't require a constant internet connection

## Raster Graphics editor

As permaculture designers we often come across photos, illustrations and videos.

For image editing I need a raster graphics editor. The elephant in the room is of course Photoshop. Photoshop was originally developed by Thomas and John Knoll in 1987. It is published by Adobe. They

---


92  https://rocketreach.co/serif-europe-ltd-profile_b5c6e74df42e0d20
93  https://en.wikipedia.org/wiki/Adobe_Inc.

offer a wide variety of creative software – an entire suite used for graphics design, video editing, photography, etc[94].

> I came across Photoshop in 1992 / 1993. I needed a leaflet for a party and a friend of mine was designing advertisement leaflets for an electric appliances company during that time. The clear user interface and the layers made it my choice during that time.

In 2011-12 Adobe switched their licensing model. Customers had to subscribe to their software-as-a-service (SaaS)[95] model instead of buying a product they would then own for a lifetime. Of course using a subscription model means customer have to constantly pay for the service[96]. The roll-out of mass cloud computing allowed for the raise of SaaS. Adobe was probably the most famous one to switch their sales model to it.

It was when Adobe switched their licensing model I went to look into alternatives. As a Linux user I was already aware of **GIMP**[97]

---


94  https://en.wikipedia.org/wiki/Adobe_Creative_Cloud
95  https://en.wikipedia.org/wiki/Software_as_a_service
96  https://www.linkedin.com/pulse/why-adobe-shifted-subscription-model-travis-hardman/
97  https://www.gimp.org

(GNU Image Manipulation Program). It was developed by the GIMP Development Team, a group of volunteers who work to provide a high-quality, free alternative to commercial image editing software. Its original authors are Spencer Kimball and Peter Mattis. GIMP comes with a comprehensive set of tools for photo editing, including support for non-destructive editing, layer masks and color correction. It is available for Windows, macOS and Linux.

Coming from Photoshop I initially had my problems with GIMP. I was never fully satisfied with it, and due to a lack of time never switched fully over. But I was fed up with Adobe's licensing model. After some search and test I was happy when I found **Affinity Photo**. It is developed by Serife Europe[98], a UK based company.  It provides a wide range of features and tools for editing and retouching images, creating composites, and working with a variety of digital imaging files. It can open the Photshop standard file format PSD and it also allows editing of RAW[99] files. What more do I need?

- I use Photoshop CS6 (Released in 2012), Affinity Photo and GIMP
- Photoshop and Affinity are proprietary while GIMP is open-source
- See Vector Graphics editor for revenue
- Photoshop was a conscious decision during the time of decision making, so was Affinity Photo and Gimp.
- Sectors: Manufacturer, User

---

98  https://affinity.serif.com/de/
99  https://en.wikipedia.org/wiki/Raw_image_format

- Photshop CS6, Affinity Photo and Gimp don't require a
  constant internet connection

## Email

Email[100] has been around for forever. It is older than the WWW.
When it comes to communication email is one of our digital
communication backbones. It is universal. It can be used as a one-to-
one as well as one-to-many (multiple recipients, cc, bcc)
communication tool.

In order to find out what email providers people are using I pulled
anonymized data of a permaculture association. 90% of members
used Gmail. I pulled from the same source again one year later and
nearly got the same numbers. It's an unprecedented number. Isn't
that weird? In permaculture you think of the principle "use and value
diversity" yet it is 90% Gmail. How is that even possible?

If you own an Android phone a Gmail address is more or less
mandatory. Last time I checked in September 2023 Android had ~
70% market share[101].

In general, there are more or less two ways to access mail: via an
email client that runs as an app or software on a device, or through a
webmailer – a website. (Of course, you could access emails on a
server within its directory – if they are not encrypted) – after all, an
email is just a text file.

---

100 https://en.wikipedia.org/wiki/Email
101 https://gs.statcounter.com/os-market-share/mobile/worldwide

If you have used a mail client on a computer you either came across Outlook, Outlook Express, Apple Mail[102], or Mozilla Thunderbird[103] or maybe something else. Thunderbird has been around since 2003[104]. It was developed by the Mozilla Foundation and is Open source. One of the benefits since 2020[105] is PGP[106] encryption. (Pretty Good Privacy).

**Let's compare it:** email without encryption is a postcard, while a letter is an encrypted email. Currently we are sending postcards, which could be read by a lot of people – if they want to: "Greetings from Italy. Here is my account login:"

Besides the obvious email providers the simple and sometimes even fast solution towards an email address is **domain & hosting[107]**. A standard hosting packages usually also comes with email hosting and often hosting providers offer a web-mailer. Otherwise you have to use a mail client software / app.

---

102 https://en.wikipedia.org/wiki/Apple_Mail
103 https://www.thunderbird.net/de/
104 https://en.wikipedia.org/wiki/Mozilla_Thunderbird
105 https://blog.thunderbird.net/2020/07/whats-new-in-thunderbird-78/
106 https://de.wikipedia.org/wiki/OpenPGP
107 https://en.wikipedia.org/wiki/Web_hosting_service

If you feel experienced enough you can also run your **own mail server**.

Until 2023, multiple companies have more and more upgraded their mail systems with measures to protect from spam. Most of the bigger players, like Google, Yahoo, Microsoft, etc. have those measures in place. They are called SPF, DKIM and DMARC. Now it gets difficult – but don't worry, as a permaculture designer, you don't need to know it unless you are running a mail server.

The problem is that those big players are continuously coming up with new countermeasures to fight spam. In 2023 Google rate limited emails received by Gmail addresses to a maximum of 5000 mails per day[108]. Meaning that if you for example have a successful email marketing business with a newsletter with more than 5000 subscribers with an Gmail address you have to precisely follow their new rules or you get banned. It is dictatorship according to their terms – they act as if they own email itself.

You can skip the next page to below DMARC if you don't want to read about the technical details of email configuration in order to prevent SPAM.

**SPF** is the Sender Policy Framework and it makes sure that the mail servers IP is authorized to send mails from a given domain.

---

108 https://techcrunch.com/2023/10/03/gmail-to-enforce-harsher-rules-in-2024-to-keep-spam-from-users-inboxes/

**DKIM** is DomainKey Identified Mail and is an important measure against spam. On a server with for example the domain beyondbuckthorns.com two files get generated, a public and a private key. The public key gets added to the domain – with the right tools that key can be read – because it is publicly available.

Every outgoing mail is signed with the private key and when the recipient mail server gets the mail it checks if the keys match.

If you are interested in more details about DKIM read about it at Wikipedia[109]. Last in line of defense is **DMARC**, the Domain-based Message Authentication, Reporting and Conformance. DMARC only makes sense if SPF and DKIM are in place, because with DMARC the DNS record will tell a receiving server how to act. In my case I get a report from the receiving server.

I only gave you an insight into this because as a server owner you kind of have to implement all that stuff – because otherwise Gmail, Yahoo or Microsoft will put mails into the spam folder. The pressure on small hosters or web development companies who run their own mail server has constantly increased over the past decades and it doesn't seem like those 3 measures are the end of it.

It is ridiculous that the big players require all that stuff but the most Spam I get is from existing Gmail addresses.

- I use Mozilla Thunderbird with own Domain

---

109 https://en.wikipedia.org/wiki/DomainKeys_Identified_Mail

- Thunderbird is developed by Mozilla Foundation[110] non-profit
- Open-source
- Conscious decision. I use it since 2010, before I used Outlook, KMail[111], Netscape Navigator[112]
- Sectors: Manufacturer, Culture, Economic condition
- There are alternatives available
- While an internet connection is needed to receive and send mails all my mails are stored locally. With Thunderbird I'm able to read and compose mails while I'm offline.

## Tasks and Projects

In our homesteads, farms or permaculture projects in general the amount of tasks can easily get out of hand. In order to get them organized project management tools can be used.

What I have seen with the projects I have been involved in the majority used Trello[113] for tasks and project management. While they used Trello, which is technically a Kanban board[114], the style of management wasn't that of Kanban[115].

---

110 https://en.wikipedia.org/wiki/Mozilla_Foundation
111 https://apps.kde.org/de/kmail2/
112 https://en.wikipedia.org/wiki/Netscape_Navigator
113 https://en.wikipedia.org/wiki/Atlassian
114 https://en.wikipedia.org/wiki/Kanban_board
115 https://en.wikipedia.org/wiki/Kanban_(development)

A Kanban board more or less requires a different approach to project management than for example Waterfall[116] style. Kanban is often used in combination with Scrum[117] / Agile[118].

In 2022 I helped organize the Nordic Permaculture Festival and we used Trello to manage the tasks. The team had a conversation about the task management and we tagged the tasks with the different sociocratic circles. All was well.
Until someone started the conversation about that we are using the software wrong. We were told that we should create one task and than put all the details into the task instead of breaking everything down in edible parts, which can be then moved from the Backlog into Doing and then into Done – making the progress visible.

Software is only as good as the people using it. You can create the most intelligent piece of software, but someone may still use it in a way that was not intended.

116 https://en.wikipedia.org/wiki/Waterfall_model
117 https://en.wikipedia.org/wiki/Scrum_(software_development)
118 https://en.wikipedia.org/wiki/Agile_software_development

At Chase and Snow we opted for **Kanboard**[119], which is developed
by Frédéric Guillot and released under MIT license. Since it is self
hosted it needs a server.

- Kanboard
- Open-Source & self-hosted
- Developed by Frédéric Guillot
- Available since 2014
- Conscious decision after testing different Kanban boards
- Sectors: Culture, Users
- There are alternatives available

## Websites & Content Management Systems (CMS)

The general need for a website, either personal or business, is clear.
Why people default for WordPress or one of the cloud-based SaaS
platforms is also clear: they're cheap and simple.

Why WordPress? Because it is the market leader. But that would be
too simple. WordPress has been around since 2003 and its
commencement falls into the same time with other developments
around the Web 2.0[120] (participatory web, before that the web was
more static). It was simply at the right place at the right time and
simple enough.

When it comes to WordPress we should know Automattic Inc[121], the
company closely knit with WordPress. Since Automattic is not a

119 https://kanboard.org
120 https://en.wikipedia.org/wiki/Web_2.0
121 https://automattic.com

publicly traded company it is difficult to get numbers. According to
Wikipedia they had 2.029 employees in 2022.[122] But that doesn't
really tell us anything.

How about some other numbers? According to W3Techs WordPress
is installed on 63,6% of websites[123] that use a CMS (a CMS that is
known to W3Techs), which then is 43,2% of the all websites. That's
an impressive number, isn't it?

Let's face it: WordPress is so simple that everyone could build a
website with it. No knowledge needed. And many hosters offer a
one-click-installer – yes it is that simple. Then you choose one of the
ready-made themes, fill in your content and you are done.

In my professional work in my marketing agency we often have to
handle clients which came from WordPress or have a defunct
WordPress site. Because in WordPress everything is just a click
away, new themes, new plugins – everything from the shop. Easy!
And with this "easy" come the problems. As soon as something out
of the ordinary happens the one running the website doesn't know
what to do. You have locked database tables because of CiviCRM
plugin – who you gonna call? Your hoster upgraded the PHP version
and suddenly the whole website is offline – who you gonna call? A
bought plugin is not available any more because the company who
sold the plugin went bankrupt – who you gonna call?

---

122 https://en.wikipedia.org/wiki/Automattic
123 https://w3techs.com/technologies/details/cm-wordpress

I'm afraid of no ghost, and I get asked to fix many of these defunct websites with all those problems. It's always a pleasure to help!

> In 2023, the Finnish Permaculture Association was compelled to transition their website from Drupal to WordPress. The front-page then occupied a staggering size of over 6 MB (MegaBytes), nearly 8 times larger than its previous version. Regrettably, this change also resulted in the forfeiture of many favorable outcomes, like speed, usability, etc.

- I use Drupal
- Developed by the Drupal community
- Open-source and self-hosted
- Conscious decision after months of evaluation and testing several CMS. I evaluated WordPress, Joomla and Typo3 during that time.
- Sectors: Users, Culture
- There are alternatives available

## Internet Search

Before there were any search engines we had to rely on curated directories, most notably the Yahoo! Directory[124] (1994) and

---

124 https://en.wikipedia.org/wiki/Yahoo!_Directory

DMOZ[125] (1998). Altavista (1995) was during its day the most used search engine – before it lost relevancy against Google or let's just say: "hasta altavista baby".

> During a visit to my colleague's office, I asked him to open up my website. I gave him the URL. He opened the Firefox browser and typed the URL into the Google search bar, effectively conducting a search for my website. The sustainable way is to put the URL into the browser's address bar which brings us directly to the desired page. Less energy used!

Of course, an internet search engine makes our lives easier but what would we as users actually demand from a search engine of our choice besides the obvious search results?

**Respect for privacy**

Search engines should prioritize our privacy by implementing robust data protection measures and transparent data collection practices.

---

125 https://en.wikipedia.org/wiki/DMOZ

## Clear distinction between advertisement and content

Search engines shouldn't mix search results and advertisement. More than 90% of users never go to the 2nd page of search results[126]. Advertisement usually happens before the first results in order to lead the users to mistake the advertisement as search results. "When it is first it is best" got stuck in our heads and entire industry was formed[127] around that belief.

## Fair competition

Have you ever noticed that when you run a search on Google and then visit other sites, you suddenly see advertisements from the sites you previously visited, delivered by Google? For example, if I went to Google.com and searched for solar panels, then went to an IT website to read an article about solar panels, I would suddenly see advertisements from the solar panel website I visited earlier – of course delivered by Google. This tracking occurs across multiple websites. I hardly see any fair competition in that. They intertwine their advertising and search engine businesses to use our data against us. We traded our freedom in order to use a free products. And this trade is always the same when it comes to free products.

- I use Google Search and Ecosia
- Google Search is operated by Google a subsidiary of Alphabet Inc.. Alphabet Inc. had a revenue of $ 282.8 billion

126 https://moz.com/blog/google-organic-click-through-rates-in-2014
127 https://en.wikipedia.org/wiki/Search_engine_optimization

in 2022[128]. Ecosia is run by Ecosia GmbH. In 2022 they had a
revenue of 34.5 million €[129].

- Google was a technical innovation during their time. Hence
  there weren't any alternatives available. Ecosia was a
  conscious decision
- Sectors: Technological Innovations and Advancements,
  Culture
- There are alternatives available

## The browser

The inception of web browsers dates back to the early 1990s when
Sir Tim Berners-Lee developed the first browser, 'WorldWideWeb'
(later Nexus), laying the groundwork for the internet as we know it.
The browser landscape saw its first significant shift with the
introduction of Mosaic in 1993, which popularized the web with its
graphical interface. This set the stage for Netscape Navigator's
dominance, a browser that introduced many to the Internet's
potential. However, the browser scene was soon disrupted by
Microsoft's Internet Explorer (IE), bundled with Windows, leading
to widespread adoption due to its operating system integration,
despite the controversies over anti-competitive practices.

The subsequent years saw a resurgence of innovation and
competition with the advent of alternative browsers like Mozilla
Firefox in 2004, emphasizing security and customization, and
Google Chrome in 2008, known for its speed and minimalistic

---

128 https://en.wikipedia.org/wiki/Alphabet_Inc.
129 https://en.wikipedia.org/wiki/Ecosia

design, which quickly rose to prominence. Today, the browser ecosystem is marked by diversity, but also by new challenges, such as Apple's restrictive policies that limit browser engines on iOS devices to Safari or its Webkit engine, sparking debates around competition and user choice in the digital age. In 2024 Apple was forced by the European Union to open up their software for alternative browsers. Opera saw a huge influx of users[130] after that happened.

- I use Chrome, Chromium, Firefox, Brave and Opera
- Chromium, Firefox and Brave are Open-source
- Opera and Chrome are proprietary freeware
- Sectors: Technological Innovations and Advancements
- There are alternatives available


## Software Layer 1

## Photo raw editor

If you are into photography you might have used the RAW photo format[131] of your camera. RAW is an unprocessed image file format that contains the raw sensor data captured by a digital camera. Unlike compressed image formats like JPEG, which apply in-camera processing and compression, RAW files preserve all the original data captured by the camera's sensor. This includes information about the color, exposure, white balance, and other image parameters. And

---

130 https://press.opera.com/2024/03/18/opera-jump-in-new-eu-users-after-ballot-
    screen/
131 https://en.wikipedia.org/wiki/Raw_image_format

since RAW files retain more detail in highlights and shadows it allows for better recovery of overexposed or underexposed areas.

As digital cameras evolved in the late 1990s and early 2000s, major manufacturers like Canon, Nikon, and Sony each developed their proprietary RAW formats, such as .CR2, .NEF, and .ARW, respectively. Over time, the advantages of RAW in terms of editing latitude and image quality led to its widespread adoption among professional photographers and serious enthusiasts, cementing its place as a cornerstone format in digital imaging.

Nowadays, most digital cameras, including smartphones, offer the option to capture images in RAW format alongside other file formats like JPEG. This allows photographers of all skill levels to take advantage of the benefits of RAW and have more control over the final image results. Downside is that the files are larger and use up more storage space.

During the process of writing this book, I initiated the transition from Adobe software to explore alternatives such as Darktable or RawTherapee for my image editing needs.

- I'm using Photoshop
- Proprietary
- Conscious decision during that time due to a lack of alternatives
- Sectors: Manufacturer, Users,
- There are now several alternatives available which need to be checked

# Note taking / Personal Wiki

For me note taking apps are more or less useful. It mostly depends on the use-case. I have been using ZIM, which is a personal Wiki, for a very long time but recently checked out others. I also installed Notion, but since it required an online connection and an account was mandatory I deleted it after some days.

> Usually note taking apps use markdown[132] and store their documents as easy readable files, which can then be imported in other note taking apps. It took some 5 minutes to get all my documents from ZIM to Obsidian.

- I use ZIM
- Developed by Jaap Karssenberg
- Open-source
- Conscious decision
- Sectors: Culture, Peers
- There are alternatives available
- No constant internet connection required

---

132 https://en.wikipedia.org/wiki/Markdown

## Messengers

In a non-representative poll in 2023 I asked the members of a
Finnish permaculture Facebook group[133] about the messengers they
use.

When I look at the chart it is clear that WhatsApp and Facebook
messenger more or less dominate the Finnish permaculture
community – with 61%. The statistic is also backed by other
sources[134]. Both messengers belong to the Meta company.

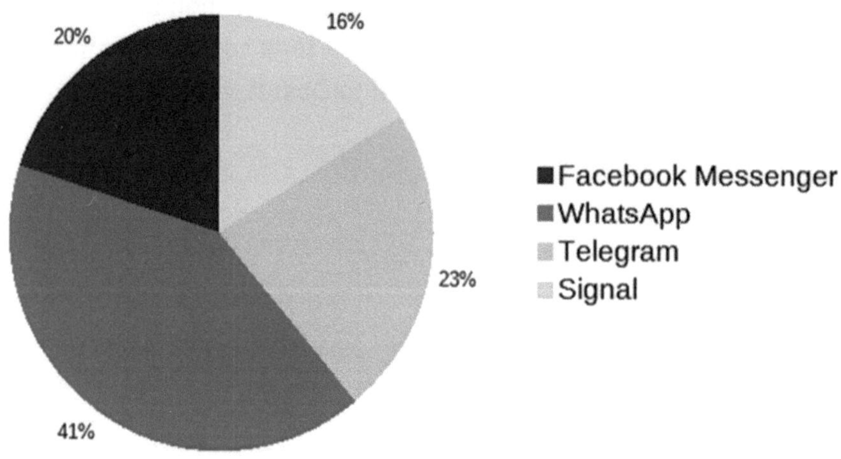


---

133 https://www.facebook.com/groups/110622338125
134 https://www.statista.com/statistics/258749/most-popular-global-mobile-
    messenger-apps/

Messengers are standard communication tools that can be seen as the successors to phone-based services like SMS (Short Message Service) or the more advanced MMS (Multimedia Messaging Service). While these two are dinosaurs compared to modern smartphone and web messengers, they used to fulfill the same need: to communicate and connect. Today, we have group chats, hopefully end-to-end encryption, and whatever features the company developing the software comes up with next.

The first messenger I used was ICQ[135] and the IRC[136] (Internet Relay Chat – not really a messenger per se) and other chat systems with messenger function.

Messengers should generally come with **end-to-end encryption** which can be verified. We don't want others to snoop in into our conversations no matter how ordinary they are. The software needs to be available for different operating systems and/or run in a web browser. If possible the received files should be stored encrypted as well.

**Encryption is not about hiding something. It is about privacy.**

- I use Signal, WhatsApp, Telegram
- Signal is developed by Signal Foundation[137] no-profit
- WhatsApp is developed by Meta Platforms Inc. (Facebook) and had a revenue of $116.609 billion in 2022

---

135 https://en.wikipedia.org/wiki/ICQ
136 https://en.wikipedia.org/wiki/Internet_Relay_Chat
137 https://en.wikipedia.org/wiki/Signal_Foundation

- Telegram is developed by Telegram FZ LLC, I was unable to get any financial information – their headquaters are in Dubai and Tortola[138]
- Signal was a conscious decision, I use WhatsApp and Telegram because of other people
- Sectors: Culture, The manufacturer, Legislation/Policies, Other Users
- There are alternatives available

## Social media platforms

Compared to email social media, especially social media platforms are rather young. It started with Friendster[139] (2002), MySpace[140] (2003) and LinkedIn[141] and then took of when Facebook[142] (2004), YouTube[143] (2005) and Twitter[144] (2006) entered the market.

For years this category was more or less split between a few companies. Probably best known is Meta[145] for Facebook, Instagram[146] and WhatsApp. Then there is of course Alphabet[147] which owns Google LLC, which owns Youtube. Then there is

------

138 https://en.wikipedia.org/wiki/Telegram_(software)
139 https://en.wikipedia.org/wiki/Friendster
140 https://en.wikipedia.org/wiki/Myspace
141 https://en.wikipedia.org/wiki/LinkedIn
142 https://en.wikipedia.org/wiki/Facebook
143 https://en.wikipedia.org/wiki/YouTube
144 https://en.wikipedia.org/wiki/Twitter
145 https://en.wikipedia.org/wiki/Meta_Platforms
146 https://en.wikipedia.org/wiki/Instagram
147 https://abc.xyz

ByteDance[148], with its brand TikTok[149]. Though there are others, we'll concentrate on the huge players.

I often argue, in permaculture we shouldn't actually use any of those platforms, but none of the bigger permaculture associations in Europe is not using Facebook or Instagram. Some of them even advertise their events, means they pay the social media platform money. I asked some of their representatives why they use it and the argument is always the same: "We do this because the users are there". And yes, that's right. Facebook had over 2,9 billion users in 2022[150].

Here are my general concerns regarding social media:

**Privacy concerns:** Social media platforms often collect vast amounts of personal data, raising concerns about privacy[151] and data security. Users' information can be misused or exposed to unauthorized parties. Who can guarantee me that my personal information isn't sold and I'm not a subject of social profiling?[152]

**Cyberbullying and harassment:** Online harassment, cyberbullying[153], and trolling have become prevalent on social

---

148 https://www.bytedance.com/en/
149 https://en.wikipedia.org/wiki/TikTok
150 https://www.shacknews.com/article/131576/facebook-had-293-billion-
    monthly-active-users-maus-in-q2-2022
151 https://en.wikipedia.org/wiki/
    Privacy_concerns_with_social_networking_services
152 https://en.wikipedia.org/wiki/Social_profiling
153 https://www.unicef.org/end-violence/how-to-stop-cyberbullying

media. This can have severe emotional and psychological effects on victims.

**Fake news and misinformation:** Social media can be a breeding ground for the rapid spread of fake news and misinformation[154]. False information can go viral and mislead users.

**Addiction and mental health issues:** Excessive use of social media has been linked to addiction and mental health problems[155], including anxiety, depression, and feelings of isolation.

**Filter bubbles and echo chambers:** Algorithms used by social media platforms can create filter bubbles[156], where users are exposed only to information and opinions that align with their existing beliefs. This can lead to polarization and a lack of exposure to diverse perspectives.

**Loss of productivity:** Time spent on social media can reduce productivity at work or in daily life[157]. It's easy to become distracted by notifications and endless scrolling.

---

154 https://www.coe.int/en/web/campaign-free-to-speak-safe-to-learn/dealing-with-propaganda-misinformation-and-fake-news
155 https://www.theguardian.com/global/2021/aug/22/how-digital-media-turned-us-all-into-dopamine-addicts-and-what-we-can-do-to-break-the-cycle
156 https://www.nbcnews.com/better/lifestyle/problem-social-media-reinforcement-bubbles-what-you-can-do-about-ncna1063896
157 https://link.springer.com/article/10.1007/s43546-022-00335-x

**Comparative living:** Seeing idealized versions of others' lives on social media can lead to social comparison and feelings of inadequacy[158].

**Political polarization:** Social media has been linked to increased political polarization, as users engage with like-minded individuals and may not be exposed to diverse political viewpoints. (Echo Chambers). The system acts like the sorting hat in Harry Potter. Once you have been sorted into a house you stay with it. Bridging the gap to the other houses becomes more and more difficult and the confirmation bias[159] pushes us further into one direction.

**Data manipulation and election interference:** Social media platforms have been criticized for allowing the spread of disinformation[160] and for their role in election interference and manipulation[161].

**Online scams and phishing:** Users are vulnerable to online scams, phishing attempts[162], and identity theft on social media platforms.

---

158 https://www.researchgate.net/publication/
    363028726_Social_Comparison_and_Well-
    being_under_Social_Media_Influence
159 https://en.wikipedia.org/wiki/Confirmation_bias
160 https://online.maryville.edu/blog/social-media-influence-on-elections/
161 https://demtech.oii.ox.ac.uk/research/posts/industrialized-disinformation/
162 https://www.trendmicro.com/en_za/what-is/phishing/social-media-
    phishing.html

**Environmental impact:** The data centers and energy consumption required to support social media platforms contribute to environmental concerns[163].

On the other hand only few permaculturists support decentralized applications, or even know that alternatives exists. The user base in the permaculture **Matrix** channel[164] is very low. There are hardly any permaculturists at **Mastodon**[165] (though the number is growing), a decentralized alternative to Twitter which uses the **Fediverse** protocol. In general the Fediverse[166] isn't really in use. Perhaps **ActivityPub**[167], which is a protocol, could solve the general non-compatibility between the different social media platforms in the times to come.

It's concerning that permaculture associations rely heavily on social media channels to engage new members, a practice that seems at odds with core permaculture principles. This approach is neither a reflection of the 'slow and small solutions' ethos, nor does it embrace the value of diversity or the marginal. It's paradoxical that organizations, which thrive on principles of sustainability and mindful living, align themselves with platforms that might not withstand the scrutiny of a permaculture design analysis due to their expansive digital footprints and potential for fostering uniformity rather than diversity. This alignment raises questions about the

---

163 https://earth.org/how-social-media-habits-are-contributing-to-internet-pollution/
164 https://app.element.io/#/room/#freenode_#permaculture:matrix.org
165 https://en.wikipedia.org/wiki/Mastodon_(social_network)
166 https://en.wikipedia.org/wiki/Fediverse
167 https://en.wikipedia.org/wiki/ActivityPub

compatibility of such digital strategies with the foundational values of permaculture.

I do understand the argument that the user base determines the tools used, but shouldn't we create the tools needed for our communities? It's a difficult topic as it is more or less a hen & egg problem. Do we find new members for an association at Facebook or do we actually help Facebook sell more advertisement? Do we actually need the social media channels to constantly grow our movement? Or to go further – do we need national permaculture associations? Shouldn't we go back to our drawing board and create a Digital Permaculture communication design? At least we should evaluate our current usage and check for the alternatives. The developers out there could be of help!

Tristan Harris[168] from the Center of Human Technology used the term "race to the brain stem" and "attention economy"[169] in conjunction with social media. He claims that social media and the algorithms they are using are made to addict us, to grab our attention as much and often as possible, hence they are bad for human consumption.

---

168 https://medium.com/@HumaneTech_/technology-is-downgrading-humanity-lets-reverse-that-trend-now-893fb9f6e580
169 https://en.wikipedia.org/wiki/Attention_economy

For my Diploma in Applied Permaculture Design I crafted a design about the communication in the Finnish Permaculture Association[170]. According to my tutors it is very difficult to read but you might want to give it a try anyway. It is one of the few (value the marginal – publicly available permaculture communication designs.

The concept of Zones can also be applied to our intended recipients – to the zones of communication. Social media platforms which more or less disrupted our understanding of Zones, should represent Zone 3 to 5 (furthest away from the center of action). This Zone typically consist of the wider public and individuals we may never personally encounter. Despite this, they often hold greater significance to us than Zone 0 or 1. Social media has forced its way into our Zone 0 and 1. It seems as it is more important to please strangers and get likes than be with family and friends.

Instead of allocating resources to Zone 5, our energy could be better utilized within the intermediate Zones. Responsibility for message delivery into Zone 5 should not solely rest on our shoulders. If society functioned as intended, the posts of friends and colleagues would effectively fulfill this role, yet the only messages that go round are bad news and gossip.

---

170 https://beyondbuckthorns.com/content/diploma-applied-permaculture-design/communications-finnish-permaculture-association

*Nothing travels faster than the speed of light, with the possible exception of bad news, which obeys its own special laws.*

Author Douglas Adams

- I'm registered at Facebook, Instagram, X, TikTok, Mastodon
- I use Facebook, Instagram, Mastodon
- Facebook, Instagram, X and TikTok are proprietary
- Meta Platforms Inc. (Facebook) had a revenue of $116.609 billion in 2022[171]
- Twitter had a revenue of $4.4 billion in 2022[172]
- ByteDance had a revenue of $85.2 billion in 2022[173]
- Mastodon is open-source
- Facebook was during the time of decision making a conscious decision, due to lack of alternatives. Instagram, X and TikTok weren't. TikTok was a typical Fear of missing out (Fomo) decision. Mastodon was conscious.

---

171 https://www.macrotrends.net/stocks/charts/META/meta-platforms/revenue
172 https://www.businessofapps.com/data/twitter-statistics/
173 https://nypost.com/2023/10/03/tiktok-owner-bytedances-revenue-growth-has-slowed-sharply-report/

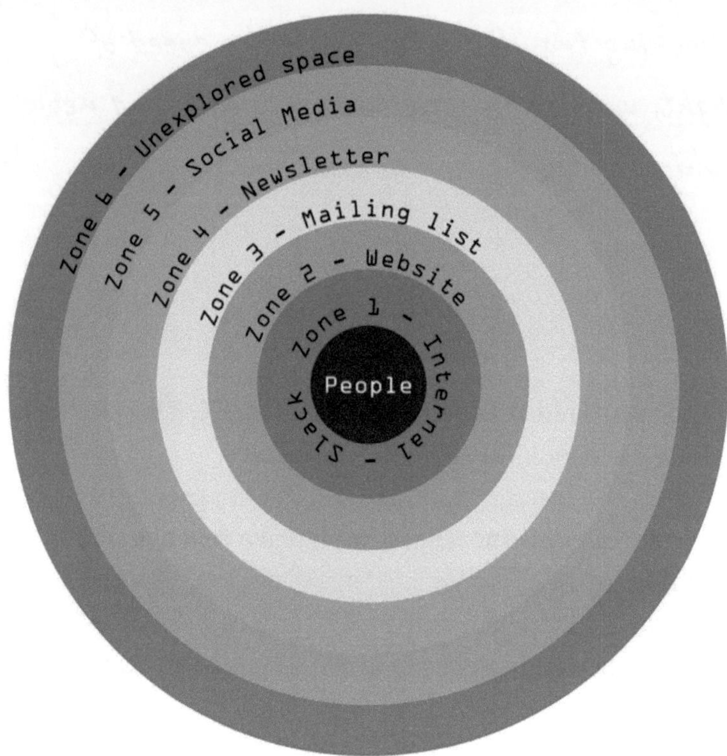


The illustration shows the concept of permaculture zones used for the dissemination of information from the perspective of a permaculture association. It was used in 2021 for the Finnish Permaculture Association[174].

## Calendar / Scheduling

Digital calendars have been around since 1979[175]. They usually come with the operating system but are also available as standalone application or integrated in a suite.

---

174 https://www.beyondbuckthorns.com/content/diploma-applied-permaculture-design/communications-finnish-permaculture-association
175 https://en.wikipedia.org/wiki/Digital_calendar

**What we should require from them is interoperability.** No matter what calendar application we are using the format should be compatible with the application another person is using. This makes sure we are not pressured into using a specific product because of peer pressure or because of vendor lock-ins.

- I use Mozilla Thunderbird[176] and Google Calendar
- Thunderbird was a conscious decision. Google Calendar was more or less forced as it is so deeply integrated into the Android device and often scheduling of team calls happened via Google Calendar
- Sector: Decision makers, Peers, Other users

It should be clear by now how what is required in surveying the software we are using. For the sake of a careful survey I step through all Software Layers on my PC. I suggest you follow and do the same.

## Software Layer 2

## CAD & 3D

CAD (Computer-Aided Design) software is an incredible tool that helps designers, engineers, and architects bring their ideas to life in the digital realm. It's like having a virtual drafting table where you can create precise and detailed models of objects, structures, or systems. With CAD software, you can easily visualize and explore

---

176 https://en.wikipedia.org/wiki/Flarum

your designs, making it easier to plan, analyze, and communicate your ideas.

CAD software is also used to create precise 3D models for example for 3D printing.

If you want to dive into 3D mesh modeling, animation and games you want to check out **Blender**[177]. It is FOSS and maintained by the Blender Foundation[178].

- I use Sketchup
- Proprietary
- Developed by Trimble Inc.
- Their revenue was $3.757 billion in 2022[179]
- Conscious decision during the time due to simplicity of the software
- Sectors: Culture, Peers, Economic Conditions
- There are alternatives available

---

177 https://www.blender.org
178 https://en.wikipedia.org/wiki/Blender_(software)
179 https://www.macrotrends.net/stocks/charts/TRMB/trimble/revenue

I used Sketchup[180] to visualize our Poop Palace[181] and also for creating STL files[182] which can be used in slicer[183] software in order to create G-code[184] for a 3D printer. Some time ago I designed a permaculture  pocket stencil template[185] for 3D printing. The file is available for free[186].

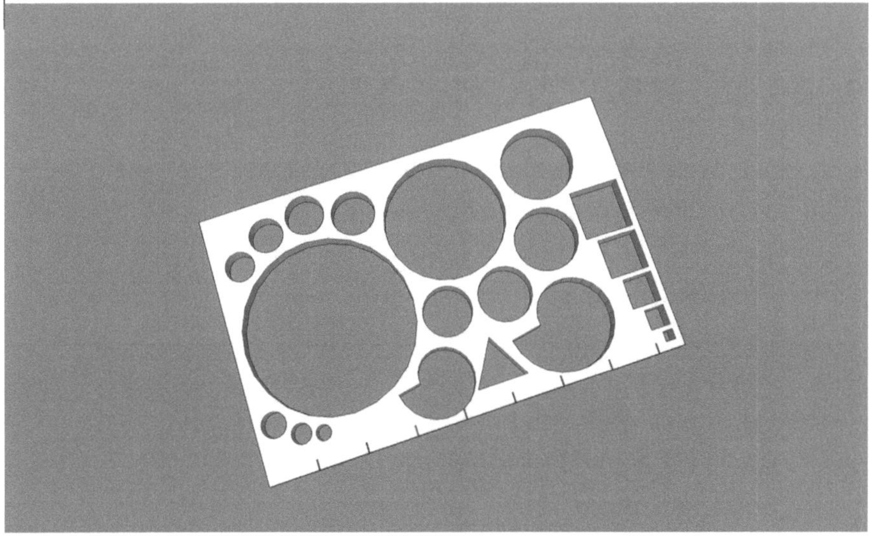

Pocket stencil template for permaculture designers, designed using Sketchup.

180 https://en.wikipedia.org/wiki/SketchUp
181 https://beyondbuckthorns.com/content/zone-1/building-poop-palace-
    integrated-composting-area
182 https://en.wikipedia.org/wiki/STL_(file_format)
183 https://en.wikipedia.org/wiki/Slicer_(3D_printing)
184 https://en.wikipedia.org/wiki/G-code
185 https://beyondbuckthorns.com/content/ndapd/permaculture-pocket-stencil-
    template
186 https://www.thingiverse.com/thing:3736275

## Mindmaps

Mindmaps, either analog or digital, are a helpful tool – of course also for permaculture design. The technique of mapping is around for a very long time. For me mind maps offer several benefits, particularly in enhancing learning, creativity, and organization. They visually represent ideas and concepts, making it easier to understand and remember information. Mind maps encourage brainstorming, allowing for the exploration of relationships between different thoughts and fostering creative problem-solving.

In most of my designs I extensively use mind maps. They help me navigate complex topics or teaching lessons.

- I use Freeplane[187]
- Developed by Dimitry Polivaev, et al.[188]
- Open-source
- Conscious decision. I used Freemind before but the last stable release of Freemind was in 2014[189]
- Sectors: Culture
- There are alternatives available

## Forms

Within the permaculture community there is a need to create different forms for different purposes. What I have often came across were forms for Erasmus+ calls for participants, event sign-ups and

---


187 https://docs.freeplane.org
188 https://en.wikipedia.org/wiki/Freeplane
189 https://en.wikipedia.org/wiki/FreeMind

also feedback forms. The great majority of these forms were made with Google Forms.

Forms are useful as they offer a structured way of data collection. Fields can be set to be mandatory. The collected data can be parsed into a spreadsheet. Results can be send by Email and/or stored in a database.

More advanced form software offers complex forms for example where fields can be set dependent on answers in other fields.

- I use Drupal Webforms
- Developed by the Drupal community, especially Jacob Rockowitz[190]
- Open-source and self-hosted
- Sectors: Peers, Other users, The manufacturer, Culture
- Conscious decision

## Cloud storage

The need for a cloud drives is simple: We want to exchange files. Let's say we want to exchange hundreds of photos of different size from a permaculture festival. Sending them by email might not work if there is a limit on the mailbox of 50MB per mail. Exchange on a physical drive might be possible if the recipient wouldn't be 1000 km away. A cloud file storage saves the problem – easily.

---

190 https://www.drupal.org/u/jrockowitz

> I had a discussion with a member of CoLab[191] and our topic
> was the Google Drive and its alternatives. I got told that
> the UK permaculture associations dependency on Google
> Drive is huge, it is hundreds of thousands of ten thousands
> of files – with multiple inter-linking between documents.
> The CoLab member said: "the dependency is that huge, it
> is close to impossible to migrate away"

But besides the obvious need there are of course more. We might
want to collaborate on documents and edit them simultaneously with
our co-creators. We want no limit regarding amount of files or size.
Ideally there is an automatic versioning system happening to files we
edit and there is of course an automated backup. What we also want
is simplicity – we'd rather not to think about anything. AND we
want all that for free. That's why we usually end up at one of the big
cloud drives. But for free has its price and the price is as always:
freedom.

**The interlinking problem**

Imagine a large association with thousands of files. It is not the files
itself which make the migration so difficult. Within our GDrive we
can create Google Doc files and within those files we can link other
files. If we have thousands of files using interlinking between
documents, or linking into the document structure of the Google

---

191 https://www.perma.earth/colab/

drive itself we have some work, possible headaches, ahead of us. While migrating the files itself is easy, re-linking is a different kind of work – and who is going to pay for that?

**Let's open a Whatever drive©**

The deeper I got into the permaculture community the more GDrive links and shares I got. It went always like "we have this Google Drive here" or "you will be invited to our GDrive". I never came to a project where I heard or could say: "Hey let's open a Whatever drive©". It can't be that difficult to either use an alternative or set one up.

- I use Nextcloud | Google Drive
- Nextcloud is developed by Nextcloud GmbH and the community | Google Drive is developed by Alphabet
- Nextcloud is open-source and self-hosted | Google Drive is proprietary
- Nextcloud was a conscious decision | Google Drive was forced due to multiple permaculture groups, teams and associations using it
- Sectors: Legislation/Policies, Culture, Decision Makers, Peers, Other users
- There are alternatives available

## Document collaboration

You remember the Google Drive and its Google Docs integration? If not then just go back some lines. It is more or less the holy grail when it comes to cloud office suites. Of course you can switch to another big cloud office solution but that would be to fight one evil with another equally bad or worse one. Google Docs has been available since March 2006 and it is deeply integrated into their GDrive.

But it is not just Google Docs, its Sheets, Slides and Forms and so on. And together with the Drive they make you a master of Google Office.

**What do we need from an online document collaboration?**

If we could formulate our needs it would be as simple as the category itself: Online document collaboration, usually on text files. Additionally the ability to work on the same document simultaneously, able to comment on words / sentences and a version history in order to see changes and checkout revisions. Ideally we have an automated backup.

Of course there are plenty of alternatives around. The question remains: **why don't we use them?** What keeps us back from doing so? Knowledge? Money? Both?

- I use Nextcloud Office (Collabrora)[192] | Google Docs

---

192 https://en.wikipedia.org/wiki/Collabora_Online

- Collabora Productivity Ltd. | Alphabet
- Open-source | Proprietary
- Nextcloud Office was a conscious decision, Google Docs was forced
- Sectors: Legislation/Policies, Culture, Decision Makers, Peers, Other users

## Video- and teleconferencing

When the Blueprint Alliance, a permaculture charity I was a part of in the 2010's, started in the portuguese ecovillage Tamera, we needed a tool to continue work after everyone returned to their home countries. We used **Mumble**[193] to connect the members. It is Open source and voice only. Many of the members didn't like it and even I had some trouble using it. Sooner than later we switched to Zoom.

Zoom is in the permaculture community – at least when it comes to UK and the Nordic countries – the standard. At the Finnish Permaculture Association we used **Jitsi Meet**[194], which is Open source, for 6 years, before a new board decided that "Jitsi is playing tricks" and Zoom has to be used. The group reverted back to the known and seemingly easy solution instead of choosing to learn something new. The result was losing their freedom and even paying a monthly fee for it. How stupid is that?

**The need to connect is clear.** While the telephone itself is a superb connection device, the smartphone and wireless transmission opened

---

193 https://www.mumble.info
194 https://jitsi.org/jitsi-meet/

up a whole new world. From file transfers to video conferencing, suddenly everything was in our pocket. And then the video call became the new normal: **"Let's zoom"**.

For me a letter is as good as a phone call or a video conference. Each of them has their own benefits and I acknowledge that a video call brings us closer. But to be honest, if we constantly need to rely on just one of our senses, the eyes, we are doomed. Besides, video calls use up a lot of bandwidth, hence energy. Go write a letter!

> I participated in one conference call with the camera turned off and one of the participants constantly insisted, even nagged me, to turn on my camera – "he otherwise wouldn't trust me".

Let's not let our communication style become a monoculture, only relying on images and video. Time to change!

- I use Jitsi Meet, Zoom and Signal
- Jitsi is developed by 8x8 with a revenue of $638 million (2022),
- Zoom by Zoom Video Communications with a revenue of $4.1 billion (2022)[195]
- Jitsi is open-source, Zoom is proprietary
- Jitsi was conscious decision, Zoom was forced due to project involvement and demand from decision makers
- Sectors: Culture, Decision Makers, Peers, Other users

---

195 https://www.macrotrends.net/stocks/charts/ZM/zoom-video-communications/

## Software Layer 3

## Digital mapping and GIS

GIS stands for Geographic Information System. It is a system
designed to capture, store, manipulate, analyze, manage, and present
all types of spatial or geographical data.

In simpler terms, a GIS is a digital mapping tool that allows users to
create and view maps and data layers that are tied to real-world
locations. It can be used for a wide range of applications – and of
course permaculture design.

GIS combines the use of maps, statistics and databases to provide a
better understanding of relationships, patterns, and trends in
geographic data. It helps us to visualize, analyze, and understand
data in a spatial context, which can provide valuable insights that
might not be apparent from traditional data analysis methods.

It can be a valuable tool in permaculture design by helping designers
and planners understand the existing conditions on a site and
evaluate different design options. It can be used to create maps of the
existing vegetation, topography, soil types, and other environmental
factors that are important in permaculture design. This information
can then be used to develop site-specific designs that maximize the
use of resources and minimize waste.

The software can also be utilized to monitor the progress of
permaculture projects over time and to assess the success of different

design elements. This can help to identify areas for improvement and to make informed decisions about future designs.

> I use GIS for our permaculture homestead Beyond Buckthorns. It allows me to pull maps from different sources, like OpenStreetMap[196], which is an open geographic database updated and maintained by the community of volunteers[197], and overlay it with information from for example the Finnish service Karttapaikka[198]. They offer elevation profiles, property boundaries, etc. Additionally to the publicly available OpenData[199] I have added information about the trees, bushes, etc. which I have planted over the years. The data is then exported from GIS and imported into the Beyond Buckthorns website to show an interactive map of plants, mainly trees and bushes.[200]

196 https://www.openstreetmap.org/
197 https://en.wikipedia.org/wiki/OpenStreetMap
198 https://asiointi.maanmittauslaitos.fi/karttapaikka/?lang=en
199 https://en.wikipedia.org/wiki/Open_data
200 https://www.beyondbuckthorns.com/plants

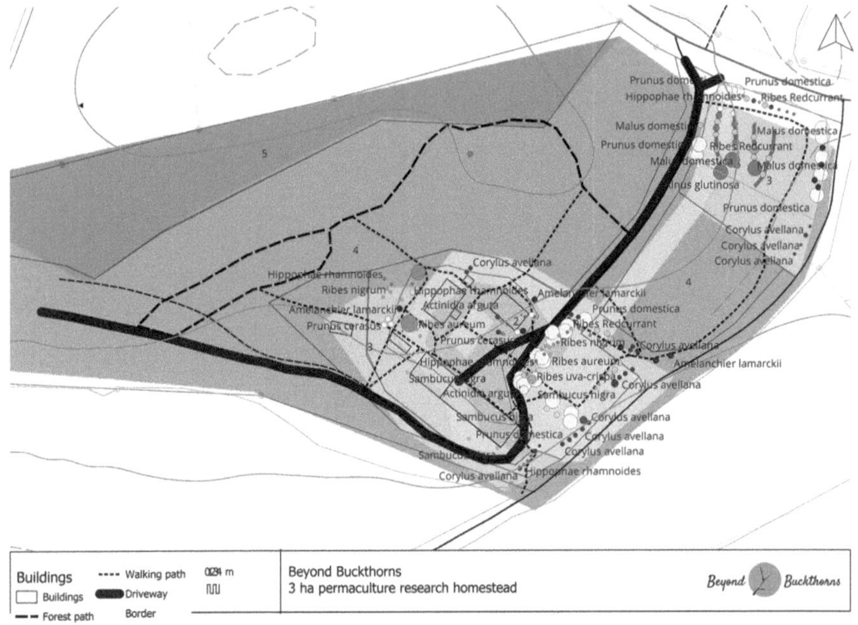


A map of Beyond Buckthorns made in QGIS, showing contour lines, forest areas, orchard, etc.

## Website analytics

Since the inception of websites owners wanted to track visits, which page visitors stayed on, which links they used, etc. Back in the old days we actually put counters[201] on our websites which showed others how many people have visited our page. Looking back: Hilarious!

---

201 https://en.wikipedia.org/wiki/Web_counter

At Chase and Snow we use **Matomo**[202] **(former Piwik)**. It offers a pretty neat dashboard, an overview of all connected websites and enough information about visitors to be able to optimize the website in question.

> For the 2021 online European Permaculture Convergence the UK permaculture association was offered Matomo but instead they chose Google Analytics.

- I use Matomo
- Developed by the community
- First release in 2007
- Open-source and self-hosted
- Conscious decision due to privacy concerns with Google Analytics
- Sectors: Other users, Peers, Culture, Legislation/Policies
- There are alternatives available

## Collaboration platforms

Collaboration platforms emerged around they early 2010s. They are designed for real-time, synchronous communication. They are ideal for instant messaging, team collaboration, and quick exchanges.

---

202 https://en.wikipedia.org/wiki/Matomo_(software)

Those platforms can be used to connect and engage permaculture practitioners and enthusiasts from all over the world, creating a global community of people sharing ideas and knowledge. They can also be used for local or national groups.

Slack[203], established in 2013, is widely used in the permaculture community. Every associations and projects I have been so far used Slack in one way or another. It also often gets used for some time and then abandoned, and then after some years someone remembers the long lost Slack workspace and of course no one has any clue who the admin was. Usually its just dead space when not embraced.

The Finnish Permaculture Association found great value in utilizing Slack as a communication tool between board meetings. The platform's channels and notification features allowed for continuous and efficient discussions, enabling prompt decision-making and streamlined communication within the group. Whenever a decision needed to be made, I could simply reach out on Slack and seek approval to proceed, ensuring transparency for all members. Of course, transparency often depends on the leaders applying it.

---

203 https://en.wikipedia.org/wiki/Slack_(software)

For smaller groups with a limited number of members, a full-fledged collaboration platform like Slack may not always be necessary. In many cases, a traditional forum and/or mailing list can adequately serve the communication needs of the community. It needs some research and some feedback from the members to determine the tools used – observe and interact.

- I use Slack | Element (Matrix client)
- Slack is developed by Slack technologies[204] with revenue of $5967  million (2023[205])
- Matrix is developed by The Matrix.org Foundation non-profit
- Element is developed New Vector Limited
- Slack is proprietary, Element is FOSS
- Slack was forced | Element was conscious
- Sectors: Decision Makers, Other users, Culture, Peers
- There are alternatives available

## Software Layer 4

## Video editing

While the standard is more or less Adobe Premier or Final Cut Pro (Mac), there is other video editing software around – unfortunately I don't have any experience with any of them.

---

204 https://en.wikipedia.org/wiki/Slack_Technologies
205 https://www.demandsage.com/slack-statistics/

I'll come to video as a file format later, in the "Data Spectrum" on page 206.

- I use Adobe Premiere
- Proprietary
- Conscious decision during that time due to a lack of alternatives
- Sectors: The manufacturer
- There are alternatives available

## Audio recording / editing

On rare occasions, I need to record a lecture, such as the permaculture lecture series PermaPuheet[206], and then edit it later. When I need to record something, I usually use Audacity[207]. It is free and open-source software (FOSS), maintained by the Audacity team[208], and available for many operating systems.

- I use Audacity
- Open-source
- Conscious decision
- Sectors: Culture, Peers
- There are alternatives available

---

206 https://permapuheet.fi
207 https://www.audacityteam.org
208 https://en.wikipedia.org/wiki/Audacity_(audio_editor)

# Screen recording / streaming

For screen recording I use OBS Studio[209]. It is FOSS and maintained by Lain Bailey[210]. The software is easy to use. It allows several different sources to be layered and then switched between. I recorded some of the PermaPuheet with it.

- I use OBS Studio
- Open-source
- Conscious decision
- Sectors: Culture, Other users
- There are alternatives available

# Forums

These platforms can be used to connect and engage permaculture practitioners and enthusiasts from all over the world, creating a global community of people sharing ideas and knowledge. They can also be used for local or national groups.

The best known permaculture forum is probably **permies.com**. There is no other channel which unites more members and has more topics per month than permies.com. It was founded by permaculturist Paul Wheaton[211] in 2000.

The term 'forum', sometimes called a 'bulletin board' or simply a 'board', refers to software that can be installed on servers. Many of

---

209 https://obsproject.com
210 https://en.wikipedia.org/wiki/OBS_Studio
211 https://paulwheaton.com

these forums are available as open source. With the so-called 'one-click installers' offered by many hosting providers, nearly anyone can install and run a forum. It does take time to get used to the settings, configuration, and behavior, but that's the case with any software.

<blockquote>

During a conversation with a retired salesperson, an interesting perspective was shared regarding the perceived obsolescence of forums in favor of social media platforms like Facebook. This statement prompted me to reflect on whether this individual had considered evaluating social media platforms through the lens of permaculture ethics and principles.

</blockquote>

- I use Flarum[212]
- Developed by Franz Liedke and Toby Zerner
- It is open-source and self-hosted
- Conscious decision after testing different forum software
- Sectors: Culture, Peers,
- There are alternatives available

---

212 https://en.wikipedia.org/wiki/Flarum

# Mailing lists

Mailing lists[213] have been around forever, or basically back since the time of the ARPANET[214]. The Linux Kernel's developer communication[215] is still running on a mailing list.

The purpose of mailing lists is pretty simply. It's a one-to-many mailing where the sender doesn't need to know all the recipients. All the sender needs to know is the address of the mailinglist and be subscribed to it. By sending a mail to that mailing list the mail gets distributed to all subscribers. Everyone subscribed to a list usually also can send mails.

When we got Web 2.0[216], we suddenly also got fancier mailing lists and thanks to Google we ended up with one of their products again, this time with Google Groups, which is a place for multiple mailing lists and an easy to use web GUI (Graphical User Interface). In the permaculture world I actually haven't come across many mailing lists other than those hosted at Google Groups.

- I use Google Groups
- Owned by Google
- Forced decision as other members of the group used it and set it up
- Sectors: Peers, Decision Makers
- There are alternatives available

213 https://en.wikipedia.org/wiki/Mailing_list
214 https://en.wikipedia.org/wiki/ARPANET
215 https://lkml.org
216 https://en.wikipedia.org/wiki/Web_2.0

# Newsletters

Newsletters are a go-to tool with which we can reach a lot of people and can bring forward our message. From the permaculture perspective it spans from communication Zone 1 to 5. It relies on email to function.

For several of my projects I integrated the newsletter system directly into the website, making it possible to send already published articles out via newsletter. (Multiple functions for important elements)

> Before the European Permaculture Network website was migrated from WordPress to Drupal we used MailPoet to send mails. But due to a badly implemented newsletter sign-up form, which didn't have good spam protection, the form was used to subscribe e-mail addresses of persons who didn't sign up for it. Therefore the people who received the double opt-in[217] (which is essential when it comes to newsletters) put their mails into the spam folder. Now you have to remember the 3 spam measures in mail: SPF, DKIM, and DMARC. When someone signs up someone else for a newsletter and that newsletter subscription mail for the double opt-in gets put into the spam folder the reviving server sends a notification to the sending server

---

217 https://en.wikipedia.org/wiki/Opt-in_email

(ours), and notifies us of sending too much spam. Let's imagine someone who subscribed another person like 1000 times. And that person put the subscription mail into spam a 1000 times. As a result our server got a bad reputation, thanks to a person who abused the system.

But luckily now all our newsletter systems come with protection and we have SPF, DKIM and DMARC in place. Our mails usually score a 10 out of 10 at Mail tester[218]. Thanks to DMARC we would immediately discover an abuse of newsletter sign-up forms.

- I use Drupal Simplenews
- Developed by the community, especially Berdir[219] and Miro Dietiker[220]
- Open-source & self-hosted
- Conscious decision, especially due to the simplicity of the software and the always good tone of voice in their issue queue
- Sectors: The manufacturer, Culture, Other users, Peers

---

218 https://www.mail-tester.com
219 https://www.drupal.org/u/berdir
220 https://www.drupal.org/u/miro_dietiker

# Software Layer 5

## Login providers

The concept of social login, also known as Single Sign-On (SSO),
has evolved over time as the internet has grown and social networks
have become more prominent.

The concept of Single Sign-On began to take shape in the late 1990s
and early 2000s. Initially, it was focused more on enterprise settings,
allowing employees to log in to multiple services within an
organization using a single set of credentials. An example would be
LDAP[221], the Lightweight Directory Access Protocol.

In 2005, OpenID[222] was introduced as an open standard for user
authentication, allowing users to log in to different sites using a
single digital identity.

As social networks like Facebook and Twitter became more popular,
they started to offer their own login services. In 2008, Facebook
launched Facebook Connect[223], allowing users to log in to third-party
websites using their Facebook accounts.

In addition to Facebook, Google, and X (formerly known as Twitter),
other services like LinkedIn, and even Amazon began offering their
own login options.

---

221 https://en.wikipedia.org/wiki/Lightweight_Directory_Access_Protocol
222 https://en.wikipedia.org/wiki/OpenID
223 https://en.wikipedia.org/wiki/Facebook_Platform#Facebook_Connect

Today it is often possible to choose from several login providers when login into a website / web-service.

Looking especially at Google you might imagine how convenient a single login for all their services, from Gmail to YouTube, GDrive, etc. is.

For those of us who run websites this becomes a problem, especially regarding data security. We don't want share our or our users' data with any social media company. Yet we want our sites to be as usable as possible. In the end it often means looking the other way. Which we shouldn't.

Luckily a lot of platforms besides the usual big ones offer login provider functionality. For example there is a **Mastodon** module for Drupal[224] and WordPress[225] and other software available.

The other way round is also possible: **create our own login provider**. Many software offer modules which allow websites to function as their own login provider.

SSOs play a pivotal and sensitive role in the infrastructure of countless websites and applications. Their convenience might obscure the significant implications they carry. By centralizing access through a single provider, we inadvertently deepen our reliance on these services, complicating any potential departure from them. Once more, we find ourselves exchanging a measure of our

---

224 https://www.drupal.org/project/social_auth_mastodon/
225 https://plugins.miniorange.com/wordpress-social-login-providers

autonomy for the convenience of streamlined access, satisfied by the simplicity of needing to recall just one password. We trade our freedom for a for free product.

*One service to rule them all, one service to find them, one service to bring them all, and in the darkness bind them.*

- I hardly use any Login providers not run by myself or colleagues
- Sectors: Legislation/Policies, The Manufacturer

## Electronic arts

In the world of art mixed with technology, there are these cool types of art called electronic, interactive, and generative art. Imagine artworks that can change based on things happening around them or even create new patterns all by themselves, thanks to computer codes. These aren't just your regular paintings or sculptures; they're like living pieces that can involve you in the art or keep transforming over time, making each moment with them unique and surprising. It's like art getting a techy upgrade, inviting us to explore creativity with a modern twist.

Processing[226] is a super handy tool for artists diving into this tech-art mashup. Think of it as a digital art kit that's really easy to use, even

---

226 https://processing.org

if you're not a computer whiz. It's made specifically for people who want to create cool digital art or interactive pieces without having to learn a bunch of complex programming. Whether it's a simple digital drawing or a more elaborate setup that people can interact with, Processing is the go-to for creative folks playing around at the edge of art and technology.

I occasionally dip into creating this type of art myself, usually spending about a week on a project before moving on to other things. That's why I've placed it in Zone 5 of my digital world – it's not something I use all the time, but it's there when I want to get creative in a techy, artsy way.

- I use Processing
- Developed by the Casey Reas and Benjamin Fry
- Open-source
- Conscious decision
- Sectors: Culture, Technological Innovations and Advancements

## Alternative operating systems

I started making T-shirts back in 2005, combining my love for art with the joy of making something you can wear. Instead of the usual way of printing, I use a knife plotter[227] and then another machine to press them onto the shirts. It's a cool method to create unique prints. But things got tricky when the new Windows 7 came out because my

---

227 https://en.wikipedia.org/wiki/Plotter

printing machine didn't work with it anymore, and it didn't work with Linux either.

To solve this, I had to use an old version of Windows, Windows XP, on a special computer program that pretends to be another computer (called a Virtual Machine[228]). It was a bit of a hassle to set up with all the specific cables and stuff, but it was the only way to keep making my T-shirts. This whole situation shows how sometimes you have to get creative with technology to keep doing what you love, mixing old and new tools together. I avoided buying a new plotter.

Because setting up for printing takes quite a bit of effort, I wait until I have a bunch of T-shirt designs ready to go before I start. That's why I consider this activity as part of Zone 5, something I don't do every day but is still important to me.

- I use Windows XP in a Virtual Box
- Conscious decision
- Sectors: Technological Innovations and Advancements

## The internet

Zone 5 also takes us into the endless world of the Internet. Just like a vast forest full of life, the Internet offers us endless chances to learn new things, find out about different cultures, and dive deep into a sea of ideas and creativity. It's like opening a door to a maze of connected stories, facts, and people from all around the globe.

---

228 https://en.wikipedia.org/wiki/Virtual_machine

But lately, the way we explore this vast digital world is changing. More and more, we're using apps on our phones to get to the Internet's treasures. While handy, this 'appification' might be making our journey through the Internet's wilderness a bit too predictable, as if we're walking down a well-trodden path instead of wandering freely.

Then there's the mysterious side of the Internet, known as the Dark Web[229], which you need special tools like the Tor browser[230] to visit. While it might sound a bit scary and is often talked about for the wrong reasons, the Dark Web is also a place where people go to speak freely, away from prying eyes, showing just how diverse the Internet can be.

Thinking about the Internet as part of Zone 5 reminds us to keep this digital wilderness wide open and full of variety. It encourages us to be mindful of how we navigate the online world, making sure we stay curious and open, much like the way we aim to live our lives following permaculture's guiding principles.

## Conclusion

As we wrap up our exploration of Soft- and Hardware *Layers,* I hope my examples have illuminated how to assess and categorize the software and hardware we interact with daily. It's your turn now. Your inventory might look different from mine, and that's perfectly

---

229 https://en.wikipedia.org/wiki/Dark_web
230 https://en.wikipedia.org/wiki/Tor_(network)

fine. The key is to understand what tools you're using, how often they're in use, and the factors influencing these choices. I encourage you to review the applications on your devices and the cloud services you rely on. By asking the right questions, you'll end up with a detailed map of your digital landscape. For those looking to dive deeper, consider tracking how much time you spend with each application for even richer insights.

This exercise is universally applicable, whether you're evaluating personal use, professional tools for your business, or software for an organization you're part of. The concepts of *Zones*, *Sectors* and *Layers* are your guides in this journey.

I want to extend my heartfelt thanks for staying engaged through this comprehensive chapter. Your willingness to go into the intricacies of your digital environment is the first step towards more mindful and sustainable tech use.

Now, let's transition to a pressing issue in the digital age — the "Zone 0 dilemma". The omnipresence of the internet has blurred the lines between our traditional Zones, challenging our perceptions and strategies. In the following chapter, we'll tackle how the digital world reshapes our concept of proximity and influence, and what it means for our digital permaculture practice.

# The zone 0 dilemma - the Internet

In Finland, there's a term called 'Kalsarikänni'[231] (which translates to 'PantsDrunk'). It describes someone drinking alcohol at home in their underwear, with no intention of going out. This unique Finnish concept is more than just a quirky term; it's a reflection of the country's culture that values personal freedom, relaxation, and the joy of unwinding in one's own space. 'Kalsarikänni' is about finding comfort and contentment in solitude, and it speaks to a broader appreciation for moments of peace and self-care. In a world that often values constant connectivity and socializing, 'Kalsarikänni' represents a conscious choice to disconnect, relax, and enjoy one's own company in the most comfortable and unpretentious way possible.

To paint a picture let's imagine a fictional, beautiful homestead somewhere in Finland. Our protagonist, whom we'll call Pekka – a common Finnish name – has just returned from Helsinki airport after one of his many business trips:

After a long and successful business trip, Pekka, a well-accomplished Finnish entrepreneur, returns to his homestead. He's just clinched a major deal, expanding his business to China. The village around him is quiet tonight – no party.

Choosing to celebrate this personal victory in his own unique way, Pekka decides on a 'Kalsarikänni'. It's his preferred mode of

---

231 https://fi.wikipedia.org/wiki/Kalsarikänni

relaxation – a quiet evening in the comfort of his home, away from the hustle of business life. In his spacious living room, with a view of the Finnish landscape, he pours himself a drink, appreciating the solitude that allows him to unwind and reflect.

Settling on his couch, he casually browses through various websites, a habit that keeps him informed and connected to the world beyond his immediate surroundings. When he comes across an article criticizing aspects of the Finnish meat export industry – the very industry he's part of – his emotions stir. The article challenges not just his business practices but his personal and professional values.

In the heat of the moment, emboldened by the anonymity the internet offers and the comfort of his home, Pekka finds himself typing out a sharp response. This response, fired off into the digital world, is a departure from his usual demeanor, highlighting the complex interplay between our private and public selves, especially in the digital age.

As we see with Pekka, the comfort and anonymity of our personal digital spaces can lead to behaviors online that we might not exhibit in more public or formal settings. This disparity between our private and public digital personas underscores the need for a set of guidelines to navigate these complex interactions. This is where the concept of netiquette becomes crucial. But before we enter into the world of netiquette we will check the 'Zones of Communication'

# The Zones of communication

In permaculture, the concept of *Zones* is used to organize elements of a landscape based on the frequency and duration of visit. We already used it to sort through our soft- and hardware Layers – but *Zones* are a universal concept. They can intriguingly be applied to the realm of communication, offering a framework for understanding and organizing our interactions based on their proximity and frequency in our lives.

At the core of this model is **Zone 0**, representing ourselves. This is our personal space of thoughts, feelings, and self-expression. It's where our communication is most introspective and personal.

Expanding outward, **Zone 1** encompasses our closest relationships, typically our family members. Here, communication is frequent, intimate, and forms the foundation of our support system.

In **Zone 2**, we find our friends. These are people with whom we share strong bonds and communicate regularly, but perhaps with less intensity and frequency than with family.

*Zone 3* encompasses individuals you interact with on an occasional basis or in specific contexts. These might include neighbors, parents of your children's friends, or members of community groups you're involved with. The communication in this zone is typically less frequent and more casual or context-specific than with closer relationships.

Moving outwards to **Zone 4**, this zone includes colleagues and regular professional contacts. These are people you interact with regularly due to work or professional activities. While these interactions are ongoing, they usually remain within the realm of professional settings and tend to be less intimate than the interactions found in the inner zones.

**Zone 5** represents strangers – individuals with whom we have no existing relationship. Interactions in this zone are typically brief, incidental, and based on immediate needs or circumstances.

By viewing communication through the lens of *Zones*, we gain a structured perspective on the various levels of our interpersonal interactions, aiding us in navigating them with greater awareness and intention.

Since the internet is just a browser-opening away, we have access to all communication *Zones* right from our physical *Zone 0*. The comfort of our *Zone 0* extends into these other *Zones*, effectively erasing traditional barriers. The only things separating us from this expansive digital world are pieces of hardware and software, along with links and search engines. This ease of access transforms our perception and interaction with these spaces, blending the boundaries between our private sanctuary and the vast, interconnected online world.

The spatial and temporal distinction between *Zones* collapses. The internet allows instantaneous access from *Zone 0* (one's personal digital space like a home computer or smartphone) to *Zone 6* (areas of the internet that are less frequently visited or more 'wild' and unstructured). This immediacy of access changes the dynamics of interaction:

**No physical distance:** Unlike physical permaculture *Zones*, the internet doesn't have physical distances, allowing immediate transition from personal spaces to global networks.

**Instantaneous interaction:** Actions and interactions that would normally take time and effort in physical space (like traveling to a distant location) are instantaneous online.

**Blurring of boundaries:** The distinct functions and experiences of different zones in traditional permaculture are blurred in the digital context, as personal, social, and public domains merge.

**Challenge in time management and prioritization:** The ease of moving between zones in the digital realm can lead to challenges in managing time and prioritizing activities, as the boundaries that physically separate different areas of life in traditional permaculture do not exist.

In this digital era, where the barriers between different *Zones* collapse, our online interactions become a seamless extension of our personal space. The ease of transitioning from one *Zone* to another in the digital realm challenges us to be mindful of how we communicate and interact across these diverse and interconnected spaces.

Returning to the scenario illustrated with 'Kalsarikänni' as an example, it becomes evident that with the immense power of communication at our fingertips, the establishment of some guiding rules became necessary. This leads us to the concept of netiquette[232], a framework essential for navigating the complex and instantaneous world of online interactions.

## The Netiquette

In the 1980s, the emergence of online bulletin board systems (BBS) and Usenet newsgroups marked the infancy of widespread digital communication. This era necessitated the creation of informal rules of conduct, as users began interacting through text-based messages in a shared virtual space. The absence of visual cues and the novel nature of digital communication led to the early formation of what would become known as netiquette, laying the groundwork for respectful and effective online interaction.

With the internet becoming more accessible to the public in the 1990s, there was a growing need for a standardized set of etiquette guidelines. This period saw a surge in the number of people communicating online, particularly through email, forums, and emerging online communities. The term 'netiquette' gained popularity during this time, symbolizing the evolving culture of online communication and the need for guidelines to navigate this new social landscape[233].

---

232 https://en.wikipedia.org/wiki/Etiquette_in_technology
233 https://www.britannica.com/topic/netiquette

A significant milestone in the formalization of netiquette was the publication of Virginia Shea's book "Netiquette" in 1994. This book provided a comprehensive set of guidelines for online behavior, covering a wide array of digital interactions. Shea's "Core Rules of Netiquette" played a crucial role in defining standard practices for online communication, influencing how people interacted on the internet.[234]

The late 1990s and early 2000s saw the rise of social media platforms and instant messaging, broadening the scope of digital communication. Netiquette adapted to these new forms, addressing the unique styles and norms of these platforms. This era underscored the dynamic nature of netiquette, as it evolved to encompass an ever-growing range of online interactions.

The netiquette as of Virginia Shea's book[235] with some amendments[236]:

**Be respectful and courteous:** treat others as you would like to be treated. Respect different viewpoints and refrain from personal attacks or offensive comments.

**Avoid 'shouting':** Writing in ALL CAPS is perceived as shouting or expressing anger.

234 https://www.encyclopedia.com/science-and-technology/computers-and-electrical-engineering/computers-and-computing/netiquette
235 http://www.albion.com/netiquette/corerules.html
236 https://www.rasmussen.edu/student-experience/college-life/netiquette-guidelines-every-online-student-needs-to-know

**Use clear and concise language:** Online communication often lacks context, so it's important to be clear and concise to avoid misunderstandings. Sarcasm will backfire.

**Remember the human:** Behind every screen is usually a real person. It's important to communicate online with the same respect and kindness as you would in person.

**Respect privacy:** Do not share personal or confidential information without consent.

**Stop … grammar time:** Make an effort to use correct spelling, punctuation, and grammar. However, be reasonable about others' mistakes and avoid being the grammar police. In a German forum I read a signature which translates to "the person who finds typos can keep them".

**Think before you type:** Remember that online communications can be part of a permanent digital record. Be guarded with personal information and respectful in your interactions.

**Don't spam or abuse communication tools:** Avoid sending unsolicited messages or irrelevant or off-topic discussions.

**Read and research before responding or asking:** In discussions, read previous comments before responding to avoid repetition. Try to find answers to questions on your own before seeking help - RTFM[237] - Read The F*cking Manual

---

237 https://en.wikipedia.org/wiki/RTFM

**Acknowledge sources:** Give credit where it's due. Cite sources and give proper attribution for content that is not your own.

**Follow specific group or platform rules:** Adhere to the specific rules of the online platforms or communities you are part of. This includes submission guidelines for assignments and respecting naming conventions and file formats.

As we continue to navigate this ever-evolving digital world, embracing and practicing good netiquette is key to fostering positive and respectful online communities. It is through these guidelines that we can bridge the gap between our private and public digital selves, creating a harmonious and inclusive digital environment.

## Quantity and quality

Since we are in the survey stage of the design there is now some work ahead of us. It is time to survey our communication.

This is more difficult than our soft- and hardware survey. There are several tools that will help us getting through this.

Let's start with quantity to get an overview of the current communication zones:

**Time tracking applications:** If not part of your phones / tables Operating System (OS) then there is an app available that allows usage time tracking. Those applications are very helpful to see how much time your spent on your phone / tablet for example for specific social media applications.

For different OS there are even applications available which track the entire usage of whatever software is used.

**Application diary:** this is the old school variant. We track our time by writing on a sheet of paper or in a spreadsheet what communication tools we are using when.

| 13.01.2024 16:30 | https://www.wolframalpha.com |
|---|---|
| 13.01.2024 16:35 | https://apps.apple.com/ba/app/attentive-digital-wellbeing/id1559421907 |
| 13.01.2024 16:37 | https://support.google.com/android/answer/9346420?hl=en |

Simple application diary in a spreadsheet

**Browser history:** Your browser history is also a valid tools that allows to iterate through the websites you have surfed to.

**E-Mail and message archive:** Look at your email or messaging app history. Many email clients and apps categorize conversations, which can help you identify which zones you communicate with most frequently.

**Feedback from peers and family:** Sometimes, external perspectives can be enlightening. Ask family members, friends, and colleagues about their perception of your communication frequency and style.

**Reflective questions:** Engage in self-reflection with questions like: Which communication Zones do I interact with most? Are there *Zones* I neglect? How balanced is my communication across different *Zones*? This can be an insightful, qualitative approach to understanding your communication habits.

What we are looking for at the end of our survey is something like this:

| Communication Zone | What | Time |
|---|---|---|
| **Zone 0** | Meditation, Yoga, | 45 min |
| **Zone 1** | Talking with family<br>Messages with Mother, Brother, Aunt, etc. | 120 min |
| **Zone 2** | Messages with Friends | 20 min |
| **Zone 3** | Mails with Acquaintances | 15 min |
| **Zone 4** | Mails with other professionals | 10 min |
| **Zone 5** | Strangers, comments on social media | 4 min |

Quantity: Communication Zones and the time spent per day

Once we got the quantity and we know our *Zones* we can evaluate our communication against the Netiquette and map these to the *Zones.*

| Zone | What |
| --- | --- |
| **Zone 0** | Talked too harshly to myself. Still haven't been able to forgive myself for certain topics. Encouraged myself to commit to more yoga. |
| **Zone 1** | Why was I so angry with my brother after the last call? I helped my aunt with a tax problem |
| **Zone 2** | I could have listened better to what Alexis said. Jon made some very interesting points about CSA. |
| **Zone 3** | That sarcasm in my mail wasn't really appropriate. One of my clients send me a 'thank you' mail. |
| **Zone 4** | Aimee, Doug and Leo have valid points but I still often don't think before I type. It is good to get feedback from colleagues. |
| **Zone 5** | The group I posted in didn't appreciate my off-topic discussion |

Quality: Where did my communication go right, where wrong?

We will later, during the analysis stage, use our findings to evaluate them.

# Digital permaculture in education and outreach

## Online courses and tutorials

The realm of permaculture education has embraced the digital era, offering a plethora of online courses and tutorials. From introductory courses to specialized training, the world of permaculture education has expanded beyond traditional classrooms, especially during and after the COVID-19 pandemic[238]. This shift has not only made permaculture education more accessible but has also diversified the ways in which we can engage with these sustainable practices.

During the COVID-19 years, there was a significant surge in the number of online permaculture courses. What was once a niche offering became a mainstream necessity, paralleling the trend in remote work[239]. This period marked a transformative shift in attitudes towards online education, as both educators and learners adapted to the new digital normal, exploring innovative ways to share and absorb knowledge.

Platforms like Udemy[240] allow anyone to create and publish a course, democratizing the field of education. This has led to a wide range of permaculture-related content being available to a global audience. On the other hand, platforms like Mighty Networks[241] offer a more

---

238 https://en.wikipedia.org/wiki/COVID-19
239 https://en.wikipedia.org/wiki/Remote_work
240 https://www.udemy.com
241 https://www.mightynetworks.com/

tailored approach, enabling individuals, companies, and associations to create closed learning communities. For example, the UK Permaculture Association utilizes Mighty Networks since 2023 to provide specialized learning experiences for its members.

Another significant player in the field of online education is open-source software. **Moodle**[242], a robust learning management system, stands out for its flexibility and self-hosting capabilities. It provides educators with the tools to create customizable and interactive online learning environments, further enriching the landscape of permaculture education.

> A friend of mine once ran a bakery in the UK for some years. He developed a baking course and published it on Udemy. According to him the course still makes him money every month.

In this digital era, the incorporation of interactive and practical components in online permaculture education is paramount. These elements help bridge the gap between theoretical knowledge and the hands-on, experiential learning that is at the heart of permaculture practice. Interactive assignments, virtual simulations, and collaborative projects not only engage learners but also foster the development of practical skills crucial for sustainable living. By

---

242 https://en.wikipedia.org/wiki/Moodle

simulating real-life scenarios and encouraging active participation, online courses can mirror the dynamic and immersive nature of permaculture, making learning both effective and enjoyable.

As we look towards the future, the landscape of online permaculture education appears bright and promising. With technological advancements and a growing global interest in sustainable practices, online platforms are poised to play a pivotal role in spreading knowledge and fostering a community of environmentally conscious learners.

But while online education offers unparalleled accessibility and convenience, it's crucial to acknowledge its environmental footprint, particularly regarding video content. Video-based learning, which has become increasingly popular, consumes significant bandwidth and energy. Each video streamed or downloaded over the internet requires data centers to work harder, consuming more electricity, much of which is still generated from non-renewable sources.

We need to ask ourselves: Is video-based learning the only way it works, especially in the permaculture community?

If you have been part of any online course recently please note them:

| Course | Date | Hours |
|---|---|---|
| Introduction Permaculture for Deep Adaption | 01.2023 | 10 |
| PermaPuheet | 01-03.2023 | 14,5 |
| Assessment tutor training | 01.03 – 29.03.2023 | 12 |

# Online documentations, blogs, vlogs, podcasts

Online documentations such as blogs, podcasts and vlogs can be a great way to document the progress, challenges, and learnings of a permaculture project, and share it with the community. They are a valuable source of information and inspiration for others who are interested in permaculture.

At Beyond Buckthorns, my journey through the diploma in applied permaculture design has been meticulously documented.[243] This effort has not only been a personal chronicle but has also resonated with others, sparking discussions, offering guidance, and serving as a source of inspiration for similar projects.

In 2022, we initiated the translation of our content into Finnish, underscoring our commitment to making permaculture knowledge accessible across linguistic barriers. This step is pivotal in broadening the reach of permaculture principles and ensuring inclusivity in environmental education.

Regularly publishing new designs is crucial for permaculture tutors[244]. It demonstrates not just ongoing engagement but also a commitment to evolving with the field. A tutor active in design work is more likely to bring current, practical insights to students, enhancing the learning experience.

---

243 www.beyondbuckthorns.com/content/dapd
244 https://permaculture-network.eu/permaculture-teachers

The surge in **vlogs** can be attributed to their visual appeal and the immediacy with which they convey information. While they have overtaken blogs and podcasts in popularity, it's important to maintain a balance of content forms to cater to different preferences and learning styles.

While video content is engaging, its higher data and energy requirements call for mindful creation and consumption. Content creators can help by optimizing video lengths and encouraging lower-resolution streaming. Simultaneously, integrating text-based content can provide a more sustainable alternative for sharing information.

I encourage content creators in the permaculture community to cultivate a digital presence that reflects our core ethics of sustainability and mindfulness. This means being conscious of the environmental impact of our digital activities and striving for a balance that respects both our educational goals and our planet's resources.

Thoughtfully created content has the power to not just educate but also to inspire and connect. By sharing our experiences, challenges, and successes, we foster a vibrant community of learners and practitioners. This collaborative space becomes a crucible for innovation and growth in permaculture, where ideas are exchanged, and collective wisdom flourishes. Let's continue to nurture this community, making each piece of content a meaningful contribution towards a sustainable future.

If you are concerned regarding your media consume you might want
to get clarity. You could write a **media diary**:

| What? | When? | How long? |
| --- | --- | --- |
| Zeit.online | 31.01.2024 | 10 minutes |
| Heise.de | 31.01.2024 | 5 minutes |
| Facebook.com | 31.01.2024 | 2 minutes |

# Online marketplaces / E-Commerce

Online marketplaces can be used to connect permaculture
practitioners with customers, allowing them to sell their produce,
seeds, and other products directly. This can also be an opportunity to
educate customers about permaculture practices, and how they can
apply these principles in their own life.

Setting up one's own web-shop is a time consuming procedure even
for web developers, depending on the type of products, countries to
ship to, tax settings, etc. It is often easier for permaculturists to use
one of the established market places instead of running their own
shop.

Permies Market[245] is an online marketplace integrated it the well
known permies.com forum, focused on permaculture, homesteading,
and sustainable living. It offers a wide range of products, including
seeds, plants, tools, books, and courses, all related to permaculture
practices.

---

245 https://permies.com/f/323/digital-market

# The Need for Easier Solutions

There is a need for easier solutions, and it is perhaps not entirely a question of software but also of social design. It is about moving away from big supermarkets towards regenerative food-sharing platforms, local initiatives, and decentralized food production. Software could play an enabling role in this transformation.

## Environmental Impact of E-Commerce

Online shopping can lead to increased consumption and transportation, which can have a negative impact on the environment.

The relentless march of e-commerce has taken its toll on the environment, with the dark side of convenience becoming increasingly evident. Rapid delivery schedules and our insatiable appetite for online shopping have given rise to more frequent, less efficient shipping methods, spewing out an ever-growing cloud of greenhouse gas emissions.

In 2023 the world wide market for e-commerce was estimated at \$ 6.3 billion[246] and the growth seems to not have ended – yet.

In response, a new wave of eco-conscious consumers, businesses, and policymakers must rise to the challenge, spearheading sustainable packaging alternatives, championing green shipping

---

246 https://www.statista.com/statistics/379046/worldwide-retail-e-commerce-sales/

options, and pioneering a circular economy within the realm of e-commerce. AND we simply have to consume less. (<sarcasm>oh no, probably the whole economy will now collapse</sarcasm>)

## Overconsumption

The convenience of online shopping has unintentionally led to a culture where buying too much has become all too easy – we over-consume[247]. Every day, we're surrounded by ads that seem to know exactly what we might like[248], making it tough to resist just adding one more thing to our cart. This endless cycle can lead to buying things on a whim, spending more than we planned, and ending up with a pile of things we don't really need or that don't last, contributing to a growing problem of waste.

You might have heard of the **Earth Overshoot Day**[249], which is the date in every year where all our biological resources that our planet can regenerate during the year have been used up. In 2023 it was August 2nd, while in 1977 it was November 17th.[250]

We need to break free from the shackles of overconsumption. As consumers we must awaken our inner mindfulness, focusing on procuring only the items we truly need.

At the same time, businesses and policymakers need to work together to encourage sustainable use of resources. They should

---

247 https://en.wikipedia.org/wiki/Overconsumption_(economics)
248 https://en.wikipedia.org/wiki/Microtargeting
249 https://www.overshootday.org
250 https://www.overshootday.org/newsroom/past-earth-overshoot-days/

promote long-lasting, environmentally friendly products and make
the effects of the items we use on the environment and society more
transparent. We need to know the true environmental cost[251].

## Returns and waste

Online shopping, while convenient, lacks the hands-on experience of
in-store buying, leading to a significant rise in returns. This adds to
emissions from shipping products back and forth and results in more
waste, as returned items sometimes end up being discarded. Online
stores need to provide detailed product information, accurate sizing
guides, and reliable reviews to help shoppers make better choices.

Efficient reverse logistics systems, incentivized in-store returns, and
a shift towards refurbished or repurposed products can help mitigate
the environmental impact of this rampant return culture. According
to a report by ZDF Germany[252] from November 2022, the e-
commerce giant Amazon is shredding tonnes of returns, reflecting a
product-to-waste mentality. In contrast, permaculture advocates a
garden-to-fork practice.

## Loss of cultural identity:

As the behemoths of e-commerce continue their relentless conquest,
local products and storefronts find themselves on the brink of
extinction[253], struggling to compete against the homogenization of

---

251 https://www.investopedia.com/terms/t/truecosteconomics.asp
252 https://www.zdf.de/politik/frontal/amazon-retouren-vernichtung-geht-weiter-
100.html

consumer culture[254], or hypersumer culture – a culture were consumerism is at its maximum and seen as the most important to achieve – goods before gods – or money and wealth as more important than intact nature or human lives.

This synchronized economy threatens to leave a permanent mark on communities, severing their ties to their own sense of identity.

To defend the rich tapestry of cultural diversity and bolster local economies, consumers must embark on a journey of rediscovery, seeking out and championing the cause of local businesses and artisans.

In parallel, governments and organizations must become the vanguards of cultural heritage, preserving and promoting our unique identities through policy, education, and innovative marketing strategies.

Permaculture principles such as "use and value diversity" or "use and value the marginal" and "use and value renewable resources" can be used to design for a reduction in environmental impact of online consumption.

253 https://www.theguardian.com/business/2013/may/28/local-shops-to-close-online-retail
254 https://en.wikipedia.org/wiki/Cultural_homogenization

# Gamification

Gamification[255] is the process of adding game-like elements to non-game activities in order to make them more engaging, fun, and motivating. The goal of gamification is to encourage participation, motivate behavior change, and enhance learning and problem-solving.

One of the key benefits of gamification is that it can help increase engagement and motivation. By making activities more fun and interactive, gamification can encourage people to participate in activities that they might otherwise find boring or tedious.

Gamification can also help people develop new skills and knowledge by providing them with instant feedback and rewards for their progress.

In digital permaculture it can also be used to make the learning process more engaging, fun and interactive through the use of games, quizzes, and challenges.

A few years ago, I developed the DesignCamp[256], a two-day intensive permaculture design course at Beyond

255 https://en.wikipedia.org/wiki/Gamification
256 https://www.beyondbuckthorns.com/content/diploma-applied-permaculture-design/permablitz-designcamp

Buckthorns. Participants start with surveying, then move swiftly to analysis and initial design on the first day, followed by presenting their designs, including implementation and maintenance plans, on the second day.

What sets DesignCamp apart is its gamified challenge aspect. Participants are given specific permaculture design constraints and must craft innovative and sustainable solutions within these parameters. This approach fosters creativity, problem-solving, and teamwork, making the learning experience both engaging and effective.

## Sneakernet

A 'sneakernet'[257] is a humorous term used to describe a method of transferring digital information or files between computers using physical means, such as carrying storage devices like USB flash drives or external hard drives. The term is a play on 'sneaker' (referring to shoes) and 'network', highlighting the manual nature of the transfer.

---

257 https://en.wikipedia.org/wiki/Sneakernet

In a sneakernet, data is physically moved from one computer to another, typically because there's no direct digital connection or network infrastructure available. This method was more common in earlier times when network connectivity was limited or slow, and it's still occasionally used today in situations where online connectivity is unreliable or security concerns make online transfers less desirable.

Sneakernets can be as simple as someone walking from one computer to another with a USB drive, an external hard drive, or even a printed copy of a document. The transferred files are physically carried and delivered to the recipient, and the data is then manually copied onto the receiving computer.

While sneakernets are considered a low-tech method of data transfer, they are reliable and can be useful in scenarios where online communication isn't feasible. However, they are limited by the physical distance that someone can cover, making them less practical for transferring large amounts of data over long distances.

In 2017, I presented at Tamera in Portugal on the concept of 'The Living Manual'.[258] The focus was on refugee camps and permaculture. Our team of three each discussed their perspective on what a 'Living manual' meant to them.

258 https://www.beyondbuckthorns.com/sites/default/files/Living-manual.pdf

My presentation centered around introducing education to refugee camps using Raspberry Pi computers loaded with a localized version of Wikipedia. This setup would create a local network where refugees could connect with their own devices or borrowed devices to access sustainability-related educational resources.

Considering the limited data bandwidth often found in refugee camps, accessing large video content for multiple individuals is not feasible. Instead, we proposed creating an ISO image containing relevant data, which could be physically transported to the camps by aid workers— a sneakernet.

Regrettably, my idea was not realized. Some decision-makers had reservations about using Wikipedia, while others were focused on introducing 3D printers to the refugee camps instead.

# Other platforms and tools

## Crowdfunding

Crowdfunding is a method of raising funds for a project, business, or cause by collecting small amounts of money from a large number of people, typically via the internet. This approach allows individuals and organizations to garner financial support from a diverse pool of backers, who often contribute in exchange for rewards, equity, or simply to support a project they believe in.

Various crowdfunding platforms, such as **Kickstarter**[259], **Indiegogo**[260], and **GoFundMe**[261], each catering to different types of projects and fundraising goals. Often there are also specific national crowdfunding platforms, like for example **Mesenaatti**[262] in Finland.

Crowdfunding campaigns can be used for a wide range of purposes, including launching new products, supporting creative endeavors, aiding charitable causes, and helping individuals facing financial hardships. The success of a crowdfunding campaign often depends on effective marketing and communication, as well as the ability to inspire potential backers and demonstrate the value and potential impact of the project or cause.

I haven't yet used crowdfunding to fund one of my projects but I have supported some campaigns. My first one was the Craftbot[263] 3d printer, which I'm still using. Crowdfunding can be sometimes nerve-racking, especially if the people managing the fundraiser are not communicative. Members of the Finnish permaculture

---

259 https://www.kickstarter.com
260 https://www.indiegogo.com
261 https://www.gofundme.com
262 https://mesenaatti.me/
263 https://craftbot.com

community ran a successful crowdfunding campaign to translate a book from Swedish into Finnish.

# Citizen science

It is about the involvement of non-professional scientists or volunteers in the collection, analysis, and dissemination of scientific data. This collaborative approach allows individuals without formal scientific training to contribute to scientific research, often by participating in large-scale projects that require extensive data collection and observation.

In the context of permaculture, citizen science can play a crucial role in expanding knowledge and understanding of sustainable practices, ecosystem dynamics, and resource management. Here are some ways citizen science can be used in permaculture:

Biodiversity monitoring: Volunteers can contribute to biodiversity studies by monitoring and recording the presence of various plant and animal species in permaculture systems. This data can help track changes in species populations and inform the designer of more resilient and diverse ecosystems.

Soil health assessment: Citizen scientists can collect and analyze soil samples from permaculture sites to evaluate soil health, fertility, and microbial activity. This information can be used to improve soil management practices and promote sustainable agriculture.

Climate change adaptation: By monitoring and documenting local weather patterns, and data, citizen scientists can help track the impacts of climate change on permaculture systems. This data can inform the development of adaptive strategies and practices to enhance the resilience of permaculture systems in the face of changing environmental conditions.

In Finland there is the Pähkinäkasvien Kasvatuskokeilu ran by Mustila[264] and Vakka-Taimi[265] - a nut growing trial. This trial allows people to connect with the breeders and purchase nut plants for their gardens. As part of the trial, the gardeners are required to provide reports about the progress and outcomes of their nut-growing experiences.

---

264 http://mustila.fi
265 https://www.vakkataimi.fi

Some Citizen sciences projects (there are of course a lot more[266]):

| Name | Description |
| --- | --- |
| eBird[267] | A platform for birdwatchers to report and track bird sightings |
| iNaturalist[268] | Record and share observations of plants and animals |
| Foldit[269] | Solve puzzles to contribute to scientific research |
| GLOBE Program[270] | Collect environmental data to help scientists understand the Earth |
| MyShake[271] | Use your phone's sensors to detect earthquakes |
| NoiseTube[272] | Measure and map noise pollution levels |
| CoCoRaHS[273] | Report daily precipitation measurements |
| Opal[274] | Observe, record, and protect nature in the UK |
| Zooniverse[275] | Participate in a wide range of research projects across various disciplines |
| Cicada Safari[276] | Help document and track cicada populations during their emergence |
| Pl@ntNet[277] | Identify and contribute observations of plant species |
| Mosquito Alert[278] | Report mosquito sightings |

266 https://en.wikipedia.org/wiki/List_of_citizen_science_projects

267 https://en.wikipedia.org/wiki/EBird

268 https://en.wikipedia.org/wiki/INaturalist

269 https://en.wikipedia.org/wiki/Foldit

270 https://en.wikipedia.org/wiki/GLOBE_Program

271 https://en.wikipedia.org/wiki/Earthquake_warning_system#MyShake

272 https://www.noisetube.net

273 https://en.wikipedia.org/wiki/
    Community_Collaborative_Rain,_Hail_and_Snow_Network

274 https://www.imperial.ac.uk/opal/

275 https://en.wikipedia.org/wiki/Zooniverse

276 https://cicadasafari.org

277 https://en.wikipedia.org/wiki/Pl@ntNet

278 http://www.mosquitoalert.com/en/

From 2014: Arduino connected to a sensor measuring the soil humidity. If the soil is to dry the pump will start automatically, watering the plant.

## Virtual reality and Augmented reality

**Virtual reality (VR)** is a computer-generated, immersive technology that simulates a three-dimensional environment, enabling users to interact with and explore this digital world in a seemingly realistic way. Users typically wear a VR headset, which tracks their head movements and presents stereoscopic images to create the illusion of depth and spatial awareness. In some cases, additional accessories such as gloves, handheld controllers, or haptic feedback devices may be used to enhance the sensory experience and enable more natural interactions with the virtual environment.

**Augmented Reality**[279] **(AR)** is a technology that overlays digital information, such as images, videos, or 3D objects, onto the real-world environment, enhancing the user's perception and interaction with their surroundings.

The general term for AR and VR is **spatial computing**[280].

VR and AR have applications across various domains, including gaming, entertainment, education, training, healthcare, and architecture. By offering an immersive experience, both can create realistic simulations that help users develop new skills, visualize complex concepts, or simply enjoy interactive storytelling and gaming experiences.

Advancements in computing power, graphics rendering, and sensor technology continue to drive the development of increasingly sophisticated and realistic virtual reality experiences, blurring the line between the digital and physical worlds.

In permaculture design we can use spatial computing too:

**Visualization and planning:** VR can help designers create accurate and detailed 3D models of permaculture projects, allowing them to explore different design options and visualize how the system will function and evolve over time.

---

279 https://en.wikipedia.org/wiki/Augmented_reality
280 https://en.wikipedia.org/wiki/Spatial_computing

**Education and training:** spatial computing can be used to create interactive educational experiences that help teach permaculture principles, techniques, and best practices. By immersing students in a virtual permaculture system, they can learn by exploring and interacting with different elements, observing how they function, and experimenting with different design strategies.

Dalle AI. Prompt: VR equipment worn by a gardener, gardener seen from the side, standing in the middle of his flower garden, painting by Monet @dominikjais

# Data visualization and analysis

**Data visualization** refers to the graphical representation of data, using visual elements like charts, graphs, and maps to display complex information in an easily understandable and digestible format. Data visualization helps users identify patterns, trends, correlations, and outliers within large datasets, enabling them to draw meaningful insights and make informed decisions based on the data.

**Data analysis,** on the other hand, is the process of examining, cleaning, transforming, and modeling data to extract useful information, draw conclusions, and support decision-making. Data analysis involves various techniques and tools that can be applied to uncover hidden patterns, relationships, and insights within the data. This process often includes descriptive statistics, exploratory data analysis, and inferential statistics or predictive modeling.

Data visualization and analysis often go hand-in-hand, as visualization tools can be used during the data analysis process to help better understand the data and communicate findings to others. By combining effective data analysis with clear and concise data visualization, complex information can be presented in a way that is both accessible and actionable.

> At Beyond Buckthorns we visualize the temperature data
> coming from our biogas digesters and the greenhouse to
> make decisions regarding feeding the digesters.

# Internet of Things (IoT)

The **Arduino** project[281] originated in 2005 as a collaboration
between a group of students at the Interaction Design Institute Ivrea
(IDII) in Ivrea, Italy. They sought to create an easy-to-use and
affordable platform for artists, designers, and hobbyists to develop
interactive projects.

The initial idea was to design a simple microcontroller board that
could be programmed using a user-friendly software development
environment. The team aimed to provide an accessible platform that
didn't require extensive knowledge of electronics or embedded
systems. They focused on making the hardware and software Open
source, allowing others to modify, improve, and build upon their
work.

The first Arduino board, named the Arduino NG (Next Generation),
was introduced in 2005. It featured an Atmel ATmega8
microcontroller, USB connectivity, and a simplified programming

---

281 https://www.arduino.cc

interface. The board gained popularity quickly due to its affordability, ease of use, and extensibility.

In subsequent years, the Arduino team continued to refine and expand the Arduino platform, releasing new board variations with enhanced capabilities. They introduced the Arduino Diecimila in 2007, which included automatic power switching and a USB interface chip. The Arduino Uno, released in 2010, became one of the most widely used Arduino boards and solidified Arduino's position as a dominant platform in the maker community.

The Open source nature of Arduino played a crucial role in its success. It fostered a vibrant community of users who shared projects, tutorials, and libraries, contributing to the growth and development of the platform. Arduino's simplicity and versatility attracted users from various backgrounds, ranging from artists and hobbyists to professionals in fields like engineering and industrial design.

Over time, Arduino expanded its product lineup to include boards with different form factors, capabilities, and specialized applications. The platform has been widely adopted for prototyping, education, and developing commercial products across a diverse range of fields, including robotics, home automation, wearables, and Internet of Things (IoT) applications.

But the Arduino had a problem in its early days (back in 2014): connectivity. While there was an Ethernet shield available it was bulky and difficult to use.

Luckily in 2014 Espressif Systems[282], a Chinese semiconductor company, released their **ESP8266[283]** microchip.

When the ESP8266, and especially the ESP-01, developed by Ai-Thinker[284], was first introduced, it received relatively little attention, due to its Chinese documentation. However, the Open source community quickly recognized its potential and started exploring its capabilities. Developers discovered that the ESP8266 was not only a Wi-Fi module but also a powerful microcontroller with an integrated TCP/IP (Transmission Control Protocol/Internet Protocol[285]) stack.

As news of the ESP8266's capabilities spread, enthusiasts and developers began experimenting with the module, adapting it for a wide range of projects. The ESP8266's affordability, small form factor, and ease of use made it particularly attractive for IoT applications, such as home automation, sensor networks, and remote monitoring.

Its integration with the Arduino IDE (Integrated development environment[286]) allowed makers and developers to easily create projects that could communicate over WiFi, opening up a world of possibilities for home automation, sensor networks, and more.

282 https://www.espressif.com
283 https://en.wikipedia.org/wiki/ESP8266
284 https://ai-thinker.eu
285 https://en.wikipedia.org/wiki/Internet_protocol_suite
286 https://en.wikipedia.org/wiki/Integrated_development_environment

Today, the ESP8266 and its successor ESP32[287] remain a widely used and respected platform for adding WiFi connectivity to projects of all sizes. Its affordability, ease of use, and extensive community support have made it a favorite among makers, enabling them to create innovative and connected devices in a cost-effective manner.

> When I experimented with Arduino to log temperature of a DIY biogas system I never liked the additional amount of parts needed to get the data logged: SD-card module and a real time clock.
>
> With the ESP-01 I switched to remote data logging using a Raspberry Pi[288] (small single-board computer), rendering the SD-card module and the real time clock obsolete.

IoT, especially the Arduino and the ESP8266, changed the availability and affordability of sensors that we can use today.

---

287 https://en.wikipedia.org/wiki/ESP32
288 https://en.wikipedia.org/wiki/Raspberry_Pi

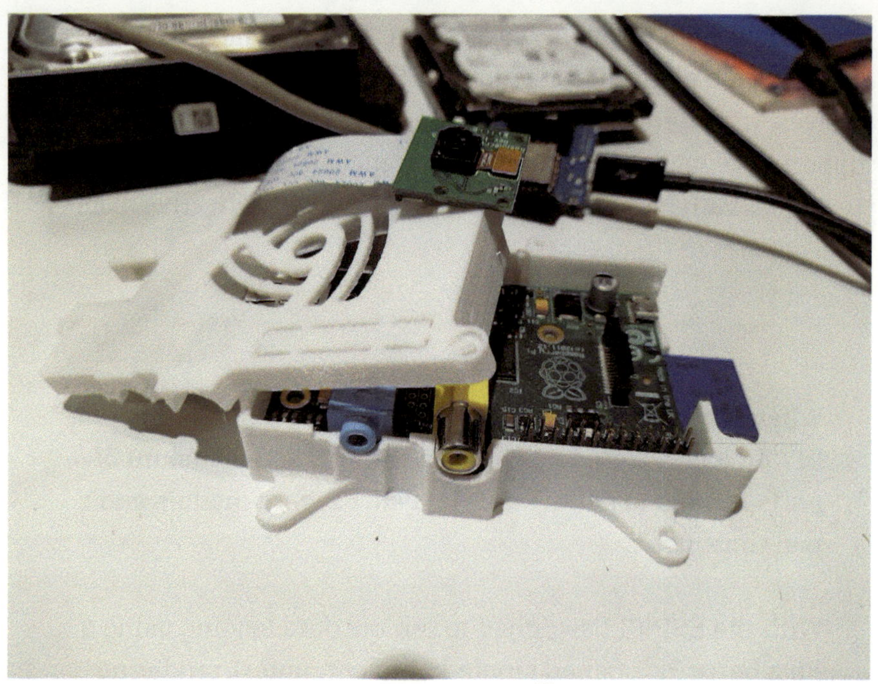

Raspberry Pi Model B with camera and 3d printed case[289]

# Practical applications of IoT in permaculture

There is a wide rang of what we now can do:

**Data collection and analysis:** IoT devices can gather real-time data from various sensors, such as soil moisture, temperature, humidity, and sunlight levels. This data provides valuable insights into the conditions of the permaculture system, helping farmers and

---

289 https://en.wikipedia.org/wiki/ImageMagick

gardeners make informed decisions about irrigation, pest control, and plant health.

In our greenhouse, we have implemented soil sensors to monitor the temperature of the soil. By comparing the soil temperature with the ambient temperature, we can precisely determine the ideal timing for planting and watering. These sensors provide us with accurate data that allows us to make informed decisions about when to initiate planting activities and irrigation. By synchronizing our actions with the optimal soil temperature conditions, we can ensure better plant growth, improved water efficiency, and overall success in our greenhouse operations.

**Automation and control:** IoT technology enables automation and remote control of various processes in a permaculture system. For example, irrigation systems can be programmed to water plants based on real-time sensor data, ensuring optimal moisture levels without manual intervention. Or the data can be used for automated weeding using the sunlight[290].

---

290 https://www.tomshardware.com/news/raspberry-pi-weed-burning-robot

I experimented with an automated solar air floor heating. The purpose of this system is to utilize the heat generated by the solar air heater effectively. When the air heater reaches a temperature higher than the ground, the fan automatically activates and starts blowing the hot air into the pipes placed beneath the greenhouse. This allows the warm air to circulate and effectively warm the soil, creating a favorable environment for plant growth. By automating this process, we can harness the solar heat efficiently and promote optimal conditions for the greenhouse, contributing to enhanced plant health and productivity.

**Resource optimization:** IoT technology can help optimize resource usage in permaculture systems. By monitoring and analyzing data, farmers can precisely adjust water and nutrient inputs, minimizing waste and reducing environmental impact.

One of my ongoing projects involves automating the winter heating of the water line. In colder climates, the point where the water line enters the house is susceptible to freezing. To prevent this, I have installed a well-insulated pipe and added a heating cable. However, rather

than running the heating cable continuously, it would be
more efficient to have an automated system that activates
the heating only when the temperature
drops below -20°C. This intelligent automation would save
resources in the long run by providing targeted and
efficient heating exactly when needed, ensuring the water
line remains unfrozen while minimizing energy
consumption.

As much as IoT brings convenience and efficiency, it also raises
significant environmental and social concerns. The energy
consumption[291] of constantly connected devices, the generation of
electronic waste[292], and issues related to data privacy and security are
just a few of the challenges posed by the widespread adoption of
IoT. Additionally, the production and disposal of these devices have
implications for resource use and environmental sustainability.

Aligning IoT implementation with permaculture principles such as
"produce no waste" and "use and value renewable sources" can
guide us in mitigating negative effects. This introduction sets the
stage for a deeper exploration of IoT's role in our lives, its benefits,
and the challenges it presents, particularly in the context of
sustainability and permaculture.

---

291 https://ntnuopen.ntnu.no/ntnu-xmlui/handle/11250/2458157
292 https://spectrum.ieee.org/the-internet-of-trash-iot-has-a-looming-ewaste-
    problem

# Intranet of Things

In my journey with digital technology at Beyond Buckthorns, I've embraced a unique approach known as the **'Intranet of Things' (InoT)**, which stands in contrast to the more commonly known Internet of Things (IoT). While IoT typically involves devices connected to the broader internet, enabling remote access and control, InoT confines the connectivity of devices to a local intranet. This distinction has significant implications, particularly in terms of data privacy and network usage.

The key difference with InoT is that the data collected by various sensors and devices remains within our local network. Unlike conventional IoT, where data is often sent to cloud servers or external platforms, InoT ensures that all information stays on-site. This approach offers enhanced privacy, as the data is not exposed to potential vulnerabilities on the internet. It also allows for greater control over the data, as it is not subject to the policies and practices of external service providers.

At Beyond Buckthorns, our InoT setup includes a variety of devices, such as temperature sensors in the biogas digester, light sensors in the solar air heater, and weather stations tracking multiple environmental parameters. These devices collect data crucial for decision-making in our permaculture practices, but instead of transmitting this data over the internet, it circulates and is utilized only within our local network.

Using InoT, we can monitor and manage our permaculture systems with a high degree of precision while maintaining the confidentiality of our data. This setup aligns with permaculture principles by fostering a self-sufficient and secure digital environment. The data remains accessible to us for analysis and application but shielded from the broader digital world, reducing risks related to data breaches or unauthorized access.

Furthermore, InoT contributes to efficiency in network usage. By keeping data transmission confined to the local network, we avoid the bandwidth and energy consumption associated with cloud computing and external data storage. This not only makes our digital infrastructure more sustainable but also ensures that our systems are resilient and less dependent on external internet connectivity.

In practice, this means that our InoT devices, like the temperature sensors in the greenhouse or the weather station, send updates every 30 minutes and then enter a deep sleep mode. This method significantly reduces energy usage as the devices are only active for a fraction of the time. The data packets they send are small, minimizing the load on our network and contributing to overall energy efficiency.

In adopting InoT at Beyond Buckthorns, I've found a harmonious balance between leveraging advanced technology and adhering to the permaculture ethos of sustainability and self-reliance. This approach demonstrates that technology, when thoughtfully implemented, can be an ally in sustainable living, enhancing our ability to interact with and understand our environment without compromising our values or the integrity of our data.

## Concerns with IoT

I'm actually not that big a fan of IoT, especially commercially available IoT. Here are some concerns:

**Security:** IoT devices could have weak security measures, making them vulnerable to cyber attacks. This can lead to unauthorized access, data breaches, or even the ability to take control of the devices themselves.[293] [294] [295]

In November 2016 the city of Lappeenranta, Finland, was target of a cyber attack[296] which disrupted a home automation systems of two buildings. The attack resulted in the loss of the heating system during winter time.

293 https://securityscorecard.com/blog/internet-of-things-threats-and-risks/
294  https://unit42.paloaltonetworks.com/iot-supply-chain-cve-2021-28372/
295 https://www.zdnet.com/article/critical-iot-security-camera-vulnerability-
     allows-attackers-to-remotely-watch-live-video-and-gain-access-to-networks/
296 https://yle.fi/a/3-9278770

- **Privacy:** As IoT devices collect and transmit a vast amount of data, privacy concerns arise[297]. The risk of data leaks, unauthorized access, or misuse of personal information is a constant concern for users.

- **Data overload:** The sheer volume of data generated by IoT devices can be overwhelming, posing challenges in data management, storage, and analysis. In 2021 the IDC[298] estimate for 2025 55.7 billion connected IoT devices, which could result in 80 zettabyte (1 ZB = $10^{21}$ byte) of data.

- **Reliability:** The performance and stability of IoT devices can vary, leading to concerns about their reliability. A failure in one device can have a cascading effect on other connected devices or systems.

- **Interoperability:** IoT devices from different manufacturers and platforms often lack standardization, making it difficult for them to communicate and work together seamlessly. Thanks that ISO has already thought about that[299].

- **Energy consumption:** As the number of IoT devices increases, so does the demand for energy to power them.

297 https://en.unesco.org/inclusivepolicylab/analytics/data-privacy-and-internet-things
298 https://blogs.idc.com/2021/01/06/future-of-industry-ecosystems-shared-data-and-insights/
299 https://www.iso.org/standard/83752.html

- **Environmental impact:** The production, use, and disposal of IoT devices can have negative environmental impacts, such as increased electronic waste and resource depletion.

- **Ethical concerns:** IoT technologies raise ethical questions[300] around surveillance, consent, and the potential misuse of personal data.

- **Digital divide:** The IoT has the potential to widen the digital divide[301], as those who can't afford or access IoT technologies may be left behind in terms of the benefits they offer.

In light of these concerns, it's imperative that they are not just acknowledged but actively addressed in any permaculture design. My approach with InoT is a step in this direction, offering a more controlled and secure way of integrating digital technologies within our permaculture practices. However, there is always room for improvement, and the journey towards a more sustainable and secure digital environment is ongoing.

IoT is undeniably here to stay, and it holds immense potential for enhancing the efficiency and effectiveness of our farms, homesteads, and various projects. The onus is on us to harness this technology thoughtfully, ensuring that it is used sustainably and in ways that

---

300 www.letstrack.com/the-ethical-considerations-of-using-iot-devices?
Blogid=244
301 https://www.researchgate.net/publication/
356433981_IOT_A_NEW_DIMENSION_OF_DIGITAL_DIVIDE

align with the core principles of permaculture. By doing so, we can leverage IoT not just as a tool for convenience, but as a means to foster more resilient and ecologically harmonious living spaces.

# The use of digital technology in regenerative agriculture

I'll briefly look into where the digital world intersects with regenerative agriculture.

## Precision farming

Precision farming, also known as precision agriculture, is an advanced farming approach that utilizes modern technologies, such as GPS, remote sensing, and data analysis, to optimize crop production and resource management. The primary goal of precision farming is to enhance agricultural efficiency, productivity, and sustainability by making more informed decisions based on accurate, site-specific data.

Digital technology such as sensors, drones, and GPS can be used to gather data about soil conditions, weather patterns, and crop health. This data can be analyzed to optimize planting, irrigation, and other agricultural practices, leading to more efficient and sustainable farming.

While precision farming's primary focus may not align perfectly with permaculture's core principles, some of its tools and approaches can be adapted to support permaculture objectives. By integrating appropriate precision farming technologies and practices, permaculture practitioners can enhance their system's efficiency, productivity, and sustainability.

## Hydroponics

Hydroponics is a soilless method of growing plants, where nutrients are delivered directly to the plant roots via a nutrient-rich water solution. Plants in hydroponic systems are usually grown in inert substrates like coconut coir, perlite, or rockwool, which provide support but don't supply nutrients. Hydroponic systems can be highly controlled, allowing for the optimization of nutrient levels, pH, temperature, and lighting, which can result in faster growth and higher yields compared to traditional soil-based growing methods.

Digital technology is used to create and control the conditions in hydroponic systems, such as temperature, light, and nutrient levels. This allows for year-round crop production in controlled environments, reducing the need for large amounts of land and water.

It has to be noted that hydroponics often relies on synthetic nutrient solutions and energy-intensive lightning. As permaculturists we have to consider how we can incorporate it into our existing system. If I would integrate hydroponics into my existing system I would combine it with the effluent from my biogas plant, removing the need for synthetic nutrient solutions.

196

Kathy Puffer showed me her hydroponic greenhouse when
I shot the documentary about the Solar C³ITIES DIY biogas
community in the USA in 2016. She showed me how she is
using the
effluent from her biogas digester to grow vegetables
indoor in a vertical hydroponic garden.
You can watch the video for free on Youtube:
https://youtu.be/9sIR-aNPXRc

## Vertical gardening

Vertical gardening is a space-saving approach to growing plants by
utilizing vertical structures, such as walls, trellises, fences, or
specialized vertical garden systems, to maximize the use of available
space in both indoor and outdoor settings. By growing plants
upwards, vertical gardening allows gardeners to cultivate a larger

number of plants within a limited area, making it an ideal solution for urban environments, small gardens, or balconies where space is limited.

Vertical gardens may require specialized irrigation systems to ensure even and consistent water distribution to all plants. Digital irrigation controllers and sensors can help automate and optimize watering schedules, reducing water waste and ensuring that plants receive the necessary moisture.

Digital tools, such as temperature and humidity sensors, can help you monitor and maintain the ideal growing conditions for your vertical garden. This information can be particularly useful for indoor vertical gardens or green walls, where environmental factors may need to be carefully controlled.

## Robotics and automation

Robotics and automation can be used to perform tasks such as planting, harvesting, and weeding, reducing the need for human labor and increasing efficiency.

**Fruit-picking:** These robots are designed to pick fruits such as apples, oranges, and strawberries. They use cameras, sensors, and machine learning algorithms to identify ripe fruits, grasp them gently, and detach them from the plant without causing damage.

Examples include FFRobotics[302]' apple harvester and Dogtooth Technologies[303]' strawberry-picking robot.

**Vegetable harvesting:** These robots can harvest vegetables like lettuce, cucumber, and bell peppers. They use similar technologies as fruit-picking robots, with specialized gripping mechanisms to handle different types of vegetables. An example is the Vegebot[304], developed by researchers at the University of Cambridge, which can harvest iceberg lettuce.

**Vineyard robots:** These robots can perform tasks like pruning vines, removing leaves, and harvesting grapes in vineyards. Wall-Ye[305] and Vitirover[306] are examples of vineyard robots that use advanced technology to navigate the vineyards and perform various tasks.

**Specialty crop harvesters:** Some robots are designed for specific crops, such as asparagus, tomatoes, or mushrooms. These robots use specialized harvesting mechanisms and algorithms to identify and harvest their target crop. Examples include the Asparagus Harvester by Cerescon[307] and the sweet pepper harvesting robot SWEEPER[308].

The question remains in what way those robots fit in permaculture.

---

302 https://www.ffrobotics.com
303 https://dogtooth.tech
304 https://www.cam.ac.uk/research/news/robot-uses-machine-learning-to-harvest-lettuce
305 http://www.wall-ye.com
306 https://www.vitirover.fr/en-home
307 https://cordis.europa.eu/project/id/811469
308 https://www.wur.nl/en/project/sweeper-the-sweet-pepper-harvesting-robot.htm

# Smart irrigation

Smart irrigation is an innovative approach to watering crops and landscapes that uses advanced technologies, including sensors and weather data, to optimize water usage and increase efficiency. The main aim of smart irrigation is to provide plants with the optimal amount of water at the right time, while reducing water waste and minimizing the environmental impact of irrigation.

Traditional irrigation methods often involve watering plants on a fixed schedule, regardless of the actual water needs of the plants or weather conditions. Smart irrigation systems, in contrast, use data from sensors and weather stations to adjust watering schedules based on factors such as **soil moisture levels, temperature, humidity, and precipitation**. This results in more precise and efficient watering and can lead to significant water savings.

Smart irrigation systems can be remotely monitored and managed through a central control system. Some systems incorporate machine learning algorithms, which can analyze data over time and make predictions about future water needs based on patterns and trends.

There are several types of smart irrigation technologies, including soil moisture sensors, weather-based controllers, evapotranspiration-based controllers, and flow meters. These technologies can help reduce water waste, improve crop health and yield, and increase the sustainability of agricultural and landscaping practices.

It is actually fairly easy to create a smart system for a homestead or permaculture farm. The components are widely available and all it takes is some pieces of code. At Beyond Buckthorns we have created a simple prototype of smart irrigation. All it does is measure the soil moisture level and based on that, starts irrigating only when needed.

# Energy consumption and e-waste

In our rapidly evolving digital age, the pervasive use of technology – from smartphones to computers – has become a fundamental aspect of daily life. However, this convenience and connectivity come with an often-overlooked cost: **energy consumption**. The environmental impact of digital technology is significant, extending beyond the direct usage of devices to encompass the entire life-cycle, including manufacturing, operation, and disposal. As the digital landscape continues to grow, so does its energy demand, leading to increased greenhouse gas emissions and other environmental impacts.

The use of digital technology, such as computers and smartphones requires energy. More usage and more devices can lead to increased greenhouse gas emissions and other environmental impacts. Permaculture principles such as use and value sustainable resources and services and designing for efficiency can be used to reduce the energy consumption associated with digital technology.

We treat the digital landscape as infinite, yet it is rooted within a finite system, bound to the availability of resources. **We have to treat our digital landscape as we should treat our planet – with uttermost care!**

## Hardware

In the pursuit of reducing the environmental impact of our digital habits, one effective strategy lies in understanding and utilizing energy ratings for hardware[309]. These ratings, often found on devices ranging from LED light bulbs to washing machines, provide crucial insights into the energy efficiency of the products we use daily. In the European Union and many other regions, energy ratings are standardized, giving consumers a clear and accessible way to assess the energy consumption of their devices.

These ratings, typically ranging from A (most efficient) to G (least efficient), are more than just labels; they are tools empowering

---

309 https://en.wikipedia.org/wiki/European_Union_energy_label

consumers to make environmentally conscious choices. By opting for products with higher energy efficiency ratings, consumers can significantly reduce their energy consumption. This not only leads to lower electricity bills but also contributes to a broader effort to reduce greenhouse gas emissions.

Understanding energy ratings is particularly important when selecting digital hardware. For instance, choosing an A+ rated computer or monitor over a lower-rated model can result in substantial energy savings over the device's lifetime. This is especially relevant considering the continuous and often intensive use of such devices in our daily lives.

Moreover, energy ratings also give an indication of the overall environmental impact of a product. Energy-efficient devices typically consume less power, which means they exert less strain on energy resources and, by extension, on the environment. This is crucial in our efforts to combat climate chaos, as the energy used by our devices still often comes from non-renewable sources that contribute to carbon emissions.

As consumers, it's vital to not only look at the upfront cost of a device but also consider its long-term energy implications. By choosing energy-efficient hardware, we take a step towards a more sustainable digital lifestyle. This approach aligns with the core permaculture principle of valuing and using renewable resources, reminding us that our choices in the digital domain have real-world environmental consequences.

When I began experimenting on some artwork with
Arduino in 2009 I started to look into LED lighting.

In 2011 I built 3 lamps out of old hardware parts, mostly
hard drives and printed circuit boards. You can find some
of them at Tillam.one[310]. In 2023 those lamps still have the
same LED bulbs they were build with.

I still design those lamps and create unique pieces on
commission basis.

Tillam lamp made of PCBs from 3,5" hard drives

---

310 https://www.tillam.one

# Software

When it comes to digital sustainability, the energy efficiency of software is a critical yet often overlooked aspect. Unlike hardware, where energy consumption can be more directly measured and mitigated, software energy efficiency involves a more complex set of considerations. It's about how the software is coded, optimized, and run, which can significantly impact the overall energy consumption of the devices it operates on.

Efficient software design plays a crucial role in reducing the energy footprint of our digital activities. For example, a well-optimized application or operating system can minimize the processing power required, thereby reducing the energy demand of the device. In contrast, software that is poorly optimized or unnecessarily resource-intensive can lead to higher energy consumption, even on energy-efficient hardware.

This becomes particularly relevant in the context of large-scale software systems and cloud-based services. The servers hosting these services consume substantial amounts of energy, and the way software is designed and managed on these platforms can have a sizable impact on their overall energy efficiency. Developers and companies are increasingly recognizing this and are adopting more energy-efficient coding practices, such as streamlining code, optimizing algorithms, and reducing unnecessary data processing.[311]

---

311 https://media.ccc.de/v/bitsundbaeume-19349-green-coding-measuring-energy-use-of-arbitrary-applications-and-software-stacks-en-

For consumers, understanding the energy implications of the software they use can be challenging, as there aren't standardized energy ratings like those for hardware. However, they can make informed choices by preferring software known for its efficiency, checking for energy-saving features, and keeping their applications updated, as updates often include optimizations.

Moreover, the type of software and its intended use also matters. For instance, a video editing software inherently requires more processing power and, consequently, more energy, compared to a simple text editor. Users should be mindful of the nature of the software they use and consider alternatives that offer similar functionality with lower energy demands.

Incorporating energy efficiency into software design and usage aligns with permaculture principles of creating sustainable systems and designing for efficiency. By prioritizing energy-efficient software, we contribute to reducing the digital carbon footprint, ensuring that our embrace of technology is in harmony with our commitment to environmental stewardship

## Data richness, file size, and energy consumption: a crucial correlation

Data is typically defined as a collection of facts, statistics, or information that can be in various forms such as numbers, text, images, or other formats. It can represent anything from

measurements and observations to records, documents, or even
digital content. Data, in its raw form, lacks context and meaning but
can be processed and analyzed to extract useful information and
insights. It serves as the foundation for decision-making, research,
analysis, and numerous applications in various fields including
science, business, technology, and more. Data can be stored,
retrieved, manipulated, and transmitted using different methods and
technologies, making it a fundamental component of the modern
information age.

With the progression from text to video not just the size increases
but also the richness of the content. Content richness encompasses
the depth and breadth of the sensory experience that it provides.
When we think of text-based content, it's primarily a medium of
words and symbols. While it's incredibly efficient for conveying
information and ideas, it lacks the visual, auditory, and emotional
dimensions found in other forms of media. Text, in essence, is the
foundation of the digital world, serving as the backbone of
communication and knowledge exchange.

As we move along the spectrum of digital content, we encounter
images – a fusion of text and visuals. Images can convey complex
ideas, emotions, and stories with a single glance. Yet, with this
increase in richness comes an expansion in file size. Images consist
of thousands or millions of pixels, and the higher the resolution, the
more data is required to represent them accurately. This increase in
data translates into larger file sizes.

Audio content takes us into another sensory immersion. It adds the auditory dimension, which also can evoke emotions, provide context, and enhance storytelling. However, audio files, whether music, podcasts, or soundscapes, are more substantial than images – contributing to their larger file sizes compared to images or text.

Video represents the zenith of content richness in the digital realm. It combines text, images, and audio into a seamless, time-based experience. Video can transport us to different places, engage our emotions, and deliver complex narratives. Yet, this richness comes with a considerable cost in terms of storage space and bandwidth.

This progression from text to video illustrates the trade-off between content richness and file size.

In the context of reducing energy consumption, choosing more efficient data formats can have a substantial impact. Opting for lower-resolution images or compressed video formats, where appropriate, can reduce the file size without significantly compromising the quality. Similarly, when creating digital content, considering the necessity of high data richness can lead to more energy-efficient choices. For example, choosing a simple infographic over a video for conveying similar information can save a considerable amount of energy.

Have you ever wondered why everything needs to be in video format? Do we really need to see something in motion to understand it, or could text, a thoughtfully designed image, or spoken word suffice? From an energy efficiency perspective, we should also consider the production process. Creating videos consumes significantly more energy than producing audio, photography, or text. Additionally, videos require much more storage space. While my entire digital permaculture library fits on a 20 GB stick, I wouldn't be able to fit even one 4K movie on it.

A colleague of mine recorded a meeting with his smartphone for me. The video was about 1.5 hours long, and he complained that he couldn't upload it. The video was recorded in 4K and was approximately 20 GB in size. He had no clue about the amount of data and how to configure his phone. He was totally unaware and just using the device.

Additionally, optimizing existing content can also contribute to energy efficiency. Techniques like data compression, which reduce file size without losing significant quality, are essential tools in this effort. Efficient coding and formatting of digital content not only save storage space but also reduce the energy required for data transmission and processing.

By understanding the relationship between data richness, file size, and energy consumption, we can make strides in aligning our digital activities with permaculture principles. It allows us to use and value renewable resources and services, ensuring that our digital footprint is as sustainable as our physical one.

KB = Kilobyte = 1000 bytes

MB = Megabyte = 1000 KB = 1.000.000 bytes – 1 Million

GB = Gigabyte = 1000 MB = 1.000.000.000 bytes – 1 Billion

TB = Terabyte = 1000 GB = 1.000.000.000.000 bytes – 1 Trillion

**The file size for data formats**

1. **Text,** like this book, needs only little space. Without any pictures, just text, this book is some 200 KB

2. **Images.** Photos, stored in compressed format take some 100 KB to 40 MB per image (depends on resolution). This book with images is ~ 10 MB

3. **Audio.** Compressed MP3 audio is about 1 MB per minute

4. **Video**

   1. Low video resolution (240p): 300 MB / hour
   2. Medium Video resolution (480p): 0.7 GB / hour
   3. High Definition (1080p): 3 GB / hour
   4. Ultra-High Definition (4K): 7 GB / hour[312]
   5. Spatial Video (3D Video in 1080p) 7.8 GB / hour[313]

There is an open end to video as the resolution of the screens keeps increasing.

---

312 https://www.gvec.net/streaming-video-data-usag

313 https://www.digitaltrends.com/mobile/how-to-use-spatial-video-recording-iphone-ios-17-2

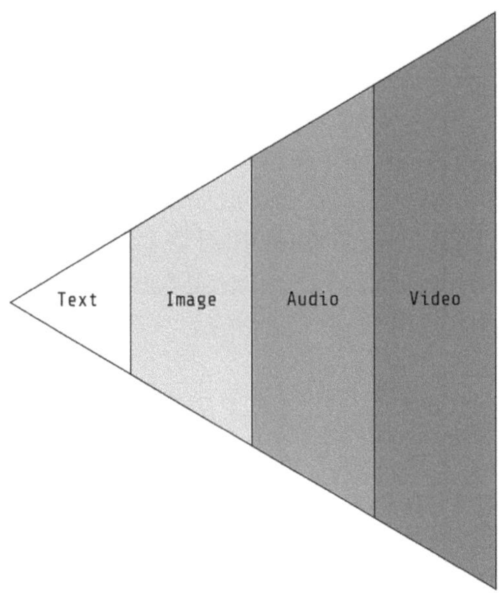


Data spectrum showing the size of data, video is largest. What is next? Maybe spatial video? Higher resolution means more data, means more energy needed.

According to the Sandvine Global Internet Phenomena Report (GIPR)[314] 53,72% of the total internet traffic is video. When it comes to downstream it is YouTube leading the space with a total volume of 16.37% and then Netflix with 10.61%. Roughly 57% of all traffic can be attributed to the brands Google, Netflix, Facebook, Apple, Amazon and Microsoft. They also noted that more people become what they call 'power users' people who consume more than 1 TB / month. (Terabyte = 1000 Gigabyte = 1.000.000 Megabyte – ~ One million floppy disks) - Remember how much text that could be.

---

314 https://www.sandvine.com/phenomena

On websites embedded videos in headers, videos in general, and large scale images became the standard for industry scale websites. And as designers we to often follow the industry's lead. But actually our websites don't need any of that superfluous stuff. If you strip it all away you end up with good looking, well functioning websites serving the need of their visitors.

## Websites

In order to see what my permaculture colleagues are doing I checked their website using the Developer Tools which come with many web browsers.

The table below is from March 2023 and shows a list of websites, most permaculture related and often national permaculture associations, and their transferred amount of data in MB (MegaByte).

| Link | Transferred (MB) |
| --- | --- |
| https://solar.lowtechmagazine.com | 0.292 |
| https://dominikjais.com * | 0.395 |
| https://www.chaseandsnow.com * | 0.393 |
| https://www.seppholzer.at/english | 0.435 |
| https://permaculture-network.eu * | 0.466 |
| https://www.beyondbuckthorns.com * | 0.534 |
| https://nordicpermaculture.org * | 0.718 |
| https://www.perma.earth | 0.874 |
| https://www.permakultura.si | 0.926 |
| https://asso.permaculture.fr | 0.946 |
| https://en.wikipedia.org/wiki/Permaculture | 1 |
| https://www.permacultura.it | 1.1 |
| https://www.permaculture.org.uk | 1.1 |
| https://www.permakultur.no | 2.5 |
| https://www.ridgedalepermaculture.com | 2.7 |
| http://www.permakultura.hr | 2.8 |
| https://www.permaculturenews.org | 3.7 |
| https://permakultur.se | 3.8 |
| https://permakultur-danmark.dk | 3.8 |
| https://www.permaculture-formation.org | 4 |
| https://www.permakulttuuri.fi | 6.2 |
| https://www.permakultur-akademie.com | 14.1 |
| https://ecovillagegathering.org | 16 |
| http://permakultur.ch | 17.3 |
| https://www.permakultur.de | 27.7 |

- Those marked with * are my own.
- Everything below 500 KB is perfect
- Everything below 1 MB is good.
- Everything below 1 MB and 2 MB is acceptable
- Everything above 2 MB is questionable
- Everything above 4 MB is unacceptable / unnecessary

**The more data that we transfer the more energy is consumed**. Hence it is imperative to lower the amount of data, especially on websites that get hit more often than others and especially the front-page of those sites.

In case you want to check your website's transferred data you could use the browser's developer tools – the DevTools. Usually all browsers have them. Within them there is a tab called 'Network'. Open your website with the DevTools Network tab open and reload your page. In the list of elements you can see all the transferred files and their size, as well the total amount transferred.

Amount of data isn't the whole picture: it also is about the speed the data arrives with.

In order to determine the amount of resources a website draws from the server and the network I created a quotient and called it the Website Efficiency Ratio:

$$\frac{Loading\ time\,(ms)}{Data\ transffered\,(MB)} = Website\ Efficiency\ Ratio\,(ms/MB)$$

If you have a low loading time but a lot of data transferred means that the server is pretty quick. On the other side, if you pull just some few KB of data but have a slow loading time, you have bottlenecks along the line.

That's why the Website Efficiency Ratio is an "in between value". A low number, let's say below 1, means you have a pretty fast server. If you go above 3 it means you have high loading time for just a tiny bit of data, which actually isn't that bad, it might be just annoying for those waiting for the site to load.

## Internet infrastructure

The internet, an indispensable part of modern life, is underpinned by a complex and expansive infrastructure that is largely invisible to its everyday users. This infrastructure consists of a vast network of data centers, network routers, servers, and other critical components that work in unison to keep the digital world interconnected and operational.

Data centers are at the heart of this infrastructure. They house the servers that store, process, and disseminate the vast amounts of data we interact with daily, from emails and web pages to videos and cloud-based applications. These centers are operational round the clock, ensuring constant access to data and services. However, this continuous operation requires substantial amounts of energy, not only to power the servers themselves but also to maintain optimal environmental conditions, such as cooling systems to prevent overheating.

Network routers and servers also contribute significantly to the internet's energy consumption. Routers direct traffic across the internet, a task that requires continuous data processing and connectivity.

The energy consumption of internet infrastructure is further amplified by the need for reliability and speed. Redundancy is built into these systems to prevent data loss and downtime, meaning more equipment is running simultaneously than might be necessary for immediate data processing needs.

Understanding the components of internet infrastructure and their energy demands is crucial. It highlights the environmental impact of our digital activities and underscores the importance of designing and using this infrastructure responsibly.

A friend of mine told me that Google's Finnish data center is using up the entire amount of energy produced from an 81 MW (MegaWatt) wind park.[315], 81 MW is the capacity that system can produce in an hour.

The calculation goes like this: 81 MW x 365 days x 24 hours x 25% efficiency = 177.390 MWh / year, that is 177.390.000 KWh.

An average dwelling in Finland uses about 7216 kWh per year. From the wind park Google is running their data center from, 24.582 dwellings could be supplied with energy for 1 year. And that is just one wind park, or let's put it this way: This is just Google, and just one of their data centers. And if you ask: "How many Google data centers are there?" Then Google will answer: "The company has 35 data centers". Which results according to speculations in about 2.5 million servers[316].

There is a lot of speculation of how many servers make the internet. In 2016 and some years after the guess was 80 to 120 million[317]. It is estimated that in 2018 were over 1.5 billion websites online[318].

315 https://www.windpowermonthly.com/article/1492443/wind-power-googles-finnish-data-centre
316 https://www.datacenterknowledge.com/archives/2017/03/16/google-data-center-faq
317 https://www.quora.com/How-many-physical-servers-connected-to-the-Internet-are-there-in-the-world
318 https://www.internetlivestats.com/total-number-of-websites/

To sum up what the energy is used for:

1.  Server operation
2.  Cooling system
3.  24/7 Uptime Requirements
4.  Infrastructure and Maintenance

Data centers use a concept called Power Usage Effectiveness (PUE)[319]. PUE is a measure used to determine the energy efficiency of a data center. It is calculated by dividing the total amount of energy used by a data center by the energy used by its ICT (Information and Communication Technology) equipment alone. The formula can be expressed as:

$$PUE = \frac{Total\ Facility\ Energy}{ICT\ Equipment\ Energy}$$

**Total Facility Energy:** This includes all the energy used by the data center, encompassing IT equipment, cooling systems, power distribution, lighting, and other support infrastructure.

**ICT Equipment Energy:** This is the energy used specifically by the IT equipment, such as servers, storage systems, and network devices.

The ideal value of PUE is 1.0, indicating that all the energy used by the data center goes directly to the ICT equipment, without any loss to cooling, power distribution inefficiencies, or other ancillary systems. However, achieving a PUE of 1.0 is extremely difficult in

---

319 https://en.wikipedia.org/wiki/Power_usage_effectiveness

practice. Most data centers have a PUE greater than 1.0, with varying degrees of efficiency based on their design and management.

A lower PUE means a data center is more energy-efficient, as a greater percentage of its energy consumption is being used directly for computing tasks rather than auxiliary systems. Improving PUE is a key goal for data center operators, as it signifies more efficient use of energy, reduced operational costs, and a lower environmental impact.

Data centers with advanced cooling systems, energy-efficient hardware, and smart management practices typically achieve better (lower) PUE scores. It's also a useful metric for comparing the energy efficiency of different data centers[320].

But PUE is just one part of story, the other WUE.

The Water Usage Effectiveness (WUE)[321] metric is another important measurement used particularly in data centers. Similar to Power Usage Effectiveness (PUE), which focuses on energy efficiency, WUE is a metric designed to assess the water efficiency of a data center. WUE is calculated by dividing the total site water usage by the IT equipment energy usage. The formula can be expressed as:

$$WUE = \frac{Total\,Water\,Used\,(liters \vee gallons)}{ICT\,Equipment\,Energy\,(kWh)}$$

320 https://www.nature.com/articles/s41545-021-00101-w
321 https://en.wikipedia.org/wiki/Water_usage_effectiveness

**Total Water Used:** This includes all the water consumed by the data center for various purposes, such as cooling systems, humidification, and facility maintenance.

**IT Equipment Energy:** This is the same as used in the PUE calculation, referring to the energy consumed by the IT equipment like servers, storage, and network devices.

A lower WUE value indicates greater water efficiency, meaning the data center is using less water per unit of electricity consumed by the IT equipment. This is particularly important in areas where water is a scarce resource, or for companies aiming to reduce their environmental impact.

Water efficiency in data centers is becoming increasingly important, given the substantial amount of water that canbe used in cooling processes and other operations. Implementing water-saving strategies and technologies, such as air-cooled systems, using non-potable water for cooling, or employing advanced cooling techniques that reduce water usage, can significantly improve a data center's WUE.

By focusing on both PUE and WUE, data center operators can work towards comprehensive sustainability, addressing both energy and water efficiency. This holistic approach is crucial in reducing the environmental impact of these facilities and aligns with broader goals of sustainability and resource conservation.

My suggestion is that data centers should only get building permits if they are integrated into the local district heating[322]. Excess heat should never be wasted.

If we search for a number how much energy the internet consumes we will notice that number is pretty difficult to come by. There is not one general number that would state "the internet consumes xy GW / year". There are only estimates. And even those differ widely. That's why I don't want to generalize. What I found interesting though is that the rise in the amount of data transferred doesn't necessarily result in a higher energy consumption[323] as the technology has gotten more efficient.

But I would suggest something similar to the 4R approach (page 332): **R**efuse to use, **R**ethink (is it necessary?), **R**educe (do I need to watch every Netflix series?) and **R**euse (I could play Monkey Island[324] this year again.)

The whole system is designed as a digital trophic level[325] where we are the demand creators. If we consume less, then the whole chain will follow accordingly:

**Less consumption of digital products and services → Less transfer → Less data centers → Less energy consumed**

---

322 https://en.wikipedia.org/wiki/District_heating
323 https://www.nytimes.com/2021/06/24/technology/computer-energy-use-study.html
324 https://en.wikipedia.org/wiki/Monkey_Island
325 https://en.wikipedia.org/wiki/Trophic_level

# Electronic waste

Electronic waste, commonly referred to as e-waste, is a rapidly growing environmental challenge in our increasingly digital world. E-waste includes a wide array of discarded electronic devices and components such as smartphones, computers, televisions, and household appliances. As technology advances and consumer demand for new and upgraded devices continues to rise, the lifecycle of these electronic products becomes shorter, leading to a significant increase in e-waste.

E-waste is particularly concerning due to its composition and the disposal practices often associated with it. Many electronic devices contain a variety of hazardous materials, including heavy metals like lead, mercury, and cadmium, as well as chemicals like brominated flame retardants. These substances are safe when contained within the devices but become dangerous when the devices are discarded improperly.

**Environmental hazards:** When e-waste is dumped in landfills or processed informally, toxic substances can leach into the soil and groundwater, posing serious environmental risks. This pollution can lead to the degradation of ecosystems and harm to wildlife.

Incineration of e-waste, a practice used in some waste management processes, releases toxic fumes and greenhouse gases into the atmosphere, contributing to air pollution and climate change.

The extraction of raw materials for new devices, driven by the discarding of old devices, leads to further environmental degradation, including habitat destruction and resource depletion.

**Health risks:** The informal recycling of e-waste, common in many developing countries, exposes workers to hazardous materials. Without proper safety measures, these workers face increased risks of respiratory diseases, skin conditions, and other long-term health problems.

Communities near e-waste processing sites are also at risk. They can suffer from health issues related to exposure to toxic substances, either through contaminated water supplies, polluted air, or direct contact with hazardous waste.

The global nature of e-waste disposal, often involving the movement of waste from developed to less regulated regions, amplifies the health risks and makes it a worldwide concern. This transboundary movement of e-waste creates a disparity in health impacts, disproportionately affecting poorer communities.

Addressing the challenges of e-waste requires a multifaceted approach, grounded in permaculture principles such as 'produce no waste' and 'use and value renewable resources.' It's imperative to foster a culture of repair, reuse, and responsible recycling to reduce the generation of e-waste. This approach not only alleviates the environmental and health impacts but also conserves valuable resources and energy that would otherwise be used in the production of new electronic devices.

Furthermore, promoting the design and production of more sustainable, durable, and easily recyclable electronics can contribute significantly to reducing e-waste. Consumers, manufacturers, and policymakers all play crucial roles in this endeavor. By making informed choices, advocating for environmentally friendly practices, and supporting regulations that ensure responsible e-waste management, we can collectively work towards a more sustainable and less wasteful digital future.

The manufacturing of electronic devices necessitates substantial quantities of energy, water, and raw materials, such as precious metals and rare earth elements[326]. Obtaining and processing these resources can result in environmental harm, pollution, and the loss of natural habitats. Moreover, the production process itself can generate toxic waste[327], which must be appropriately handled to reduce its detrimental effects on the environment.

One of the standard components which can be found in nearly every electronic device, from smartphones to household appliances to cars, is a printed circuit board (PCB)[328]. A PCB is a thin board made of a non-conductive material, such as FR-4 fiberglass[329], with conductive copper traces etched onto it. These copper traces form pathways that connect electronic components, like resistors, capacitors, and microchips, allowing them to communicate and work together.

---

326 https://www.weforum.org/agenda/2021/08/this-visualization-breaks-down-the-metals-in-a-smartphone/
327 https://www.theverge.com/2024/2/3/24058476/tesla-hazardous-waste-suit-settlement-california
328 https://en.wikipedia.org/wiki/Printed_circuit_board
329 https://en.wikipedia.org/wiki/FR-4

A rough estimate of the standard materials used in a PCB (without electronic components):

| Material | Approximate % |
| --- | --- |
| Fiberglass (e.g., FR-4) | 30-40% |
| Copper | 20-30% |
| Epoxy resin | 20-30% |
| Solder mask | 5-10% |
| Silkscreen | 1-2% |

Components of a PCB

We have to keep in mind that these percentages are approximate and can vary depending on the specific PCB design and materials used. Other materials, such as gold, tin, nickel, or palladium might be present in small amounts as surface finishes or in specific components. Additionally, some PCBs may contain small quantities of heavy metals, flame retardants, or other chemicals, which are not included in the table above.

Recycling PCBs is crucial for protecting the environment and human health by preventing pollution from hazardous substances, conserving valuable natural resources, and reducing energy consumption associated with mining and refining raw materials. Moreover, recycling contributes to effective e-waste management, supports the economy by creating a secondary market for recovered materials, and generates employment opportunities in the waste management sector.

Recycling PCBs involves several steps[330] - this is the short version:

1. Dismantling: Electronic devices are disassembled, and PCBs are separated from other components.
2. Shredding and grinding: PCBs are mechanically shredded and ground into small particles.
3. Metal recovery: Various methods, such as magnetic separation, air classification[331], and electrostatic separation, are used to separate and recover metals like copper, gold, and aluminum from the non-metallic material.
4. Chemical treatment: Some processes, like hydrometallurgy[332], use chemical treatments to extract valuable metals from the remaining material.
5. Residual waste treatment: The remaining non-metallic material may be thermally or chemically treated to recover additional materials / energy.

This is just for a PCB without any components. The components need to be recycled separately.

According to statista.com global e-waste is more than 50 million metric tons per year (can you imagine that amount?). The amount of e-waste to be collected and properly recycled is 17.4%[333]. One can only speculate what the dark digit looks like.

330 https://www.epa.gov/sites/default/files/2014-05/documents/handout-10-circuitboards.pdf
331 https://en.wikipedia.org/wiki/Air_classifier
332 https://en.wikipedia.org/wiki/Hydrometallurgy
333 https://www.statista.com/topics/3409/electronic-waste-worldwide/#topicOverview

The per capita amount of e-waste is constantly rising; as of 2023 at 8 kg per person and is projected to reach 9 kg per person in 2030[334].

This is far too little material being recycled and far too much e-waste per person. We need to find strategies to counteract e-waste.

# Start-up culture

Let's start this chapter with an imaginative story about a Startup.

In the bustling tech hub of Helsinki, a new startup named EcoTech Innovations emerged with a mission to revolutionize the green technology sector. Founded by a charismatic entrepreneur, Jukka, and a small team of visionaries, EcoTech promised to bring sustainable solutions to everyday problems. With an innovative idea for a solar-powered, smart irrigation system designed to conserve water and maximize crop yield, the team was confident they were on the brink of something big.

Initial excitement led to a successful first round of funding. Investors were captivated by Jukka's pitch and the potential market impact. The influx of cash fueled rapid expansion: a sleek office space, a growing team of top-tier talent, and an aggressive marketing campaign. EcoTech was the name on every tech enthusiast's lips.

---

334 https://www.mdpi.com/2071-1050/15/3/1837

As months passed, the pressure to deliver tangible results mounted. The development of the smart irrigation system faced technical challenges, delaying the launch. Despite this, spending continued unabated. Lavish tech conferences, extravagant networking events, and costly promotional materials further drained EcoTech's reserves.

Internally, the focus shifted from product development to maintaining the startup's image and visibility in the industry. The team worked tirelessly, but progress was slow, hampered by a lack of clear direction and an increasing disconnect from the initial mission.

Investor patience began to wane as EcoTech missed milestone after milestone. The burn rate was unsustainable. Yet, the allure of becoming the next big tech unicorn kept the team chasing more funding instead of reassessing their strategy.

Finally, the inevitable happened. After a series of unsuccessful pitches for additional funding, EcoTech's cash reserves dried up. The groundbreaking product that promised to redefine sustainable agriculture remained unfinished. The once-buzzing office was now silent, a stark reminder of the startup's unfulfilled potential.

EcoTech Innovations vanished as quickly as it had appeared, leaving behind a trail of unmet expectations and a cautionary tale of the startup world's volatile nature. The dream of making a significant impact on sustainability through technology remained just that – a dream.

And while this was just a story to portrait the modern problems with startup culture there is of course more to it than just the obvious problems.

Startup culture is renowned for its dynamic, fast-paced environment, driven by innovation and a relentless focus on rapid growth, scalability, and the disruption of traditional industries. Embracing the "move fast and break things" philosophy, startups often prioritize development speed and market penetration, sometimes at the expense of detailed planning and long-term sustainability. This culture is underpinned by a strong emphasis on entrepreneurship, risk-taking, agile development, and an ongoing pursuit of venture capital to fuel expansion.

| Aspect | Startup Culture | Traditional New Businesses |
| --- | --- | --- |
| Growth | Prioritizes rapid growth and scalability | Focuses on steady, sustainable growth |
| Market approach | Focus on innovation and disrupting existing markets | Builds upon existing market structures and demands |
| Funding | Heavy reliance on venture capital funding | Relies more on traditional financing methods (loans, personal savings) |
| Mentality | "Move fast and break things" mentality | Emphasizes thorough planning and risk management |
| Organizational structure | Often emphasizes a flat organizational structure | Typically follows a hierarchical organizational structure |
| Approach to change | Embraces risk-taking and pivoting as necessary | More cautious approach to change and innovation |
| Key metrics | Product/market fit and user growth are key metrics | Profitability and revenue are key metrics |

| Aspect | Startup Culture | Traditional New Businesses |
| --- | --- | --- |
| **Work culture** | Work culture characterized by agility and flexibility | Work culture often characterized by stability and predictability |
| **Working hours** | Frequent long working hours and potential for burnout | Standard working hours with clearer work-life boundaries |
| **Work environment** | Tends to foster a dynamic, informal work environment | Tends to have a more formal and structured work environment |

The appeal of startup culture lies in its significant contributions to innovation and economic growth. It creates a fertile ground where creativity and groundbreaking ideas thrive, leading to the development of technologies and solutions that tackle complex challenges in new ways. The agility and flexibility of startups enable quick adaptation to changing market demands, positioning these companies as pioneers in their fields. Startups are also crucial in fostering entrepreneurship and generating a wide array of job opportunities, particularly in emerging sectors. The inclusive and collaborative nature of many startups promotes a sense of shared purpose and enhances employee engagement and satisfaction. For those involved in successful ventures, the potential for significant financial and personal rewards provides a sense of achievement that transcends traditional employment.

However, startup culture is not without its criticisms, particularly regarding sustainability and work-life balance. The high-risk nature of startups, characterized by a notable failure rate, can lead to financial instability and significant stress for both entrepreneurs and employees. The prevalent "always-on" mentality risks compromising work-life balance, leading to burnout due to excessive work hours. Furthermore, the intense focus on rapid growth can sometimes overlook environmental and social responsibilities, raising sustainability concerns. The startup ecosystem also faces challenges related to diversity and inclusivity, with disparities in representation and funding opportunities. Ethical issues, such as compromising labor standards and data privacy in the race to outperform competitors, pose serious questions about the broader societal and environmental impact of startup culture.

Indeed, the landscape of successful startups that have transitioned into influential companies is vast and diverse. These trailblazers have not only transformed the industries they operate in but have also fundamentally changed our daily lives. From revolutionizing how we rent accommodations with platforms like Airbnb to altering the way we make payments with services like Stripe, these companies have set new standards and expectations.

The way we consume music has been redefined by Spotify, turning the music industry on its head with its streaming service. Similarly, Netflix has reshaped our television and movie-watching habits, offering a vast library of content on demand, fundamentally altering the entertainment landscape.

These companies, once small startups, have proven the power of innovative ideas combined with the right execution. They've shown that with a clear vision and perseverance, it's possible to disrupt traditional markets and create entirely new ways of doing things, making our lives more connected, convenient, and enjoyable.

Their success stories serve as a testament to the potential of startups to not just succeed commercially but to also make a lasting impact on society and culture at large. They remind us of the boundless possibilities that await when creativity, technology, and entrepreneurial spirit converge, inspiring a new generation of innovators and disruptors to dream big and aim high.

As we celebrate the innovations and transformations brought about by these now-iconic companies, it's crucial to pause and reflect on their alignment with the core ethics of permaculture: care for the earth, care for people, and fair share. Have these companies integrated practices that honor and sustain our planet and its inhabitants? Do they contribute to equitable distribution of resources and opportunities? While their achievements in revolutionizing various sectors are undeniable, it prompts us to question whether their growth and operations reflect a commitment to the holistic well-being of our world and its diverse communities.

Spotify has faced significant criticism since its launch in 2006, particularly regarding artist compensation. Unlike traditional sales, which pay artists a fixed price per song or album, Spotify's model is based on the artist's "market share" of total streams, resulting in variable royalties. This has led to dissatisfaction among artists, with notable figures like Taylor Swift and Thom Yorke temporarily withdrawing their music from the platform[335]. Criticisms extend to Spotify's free service tier, which has been associated with delayed or withdrawn major album releases, and the company's "pay-for-play" practices, where money from labels influences playlist placement.

---

335 https://en.wikipedia.org/wiki/Criticism_of_Spotify

Additionally, Spotify CEO Daniel Ek faced backlash for donating to military AI research[336].

Airbnb has faced criticism on various fronts, including legality, ethics, and community impact. In some cities, Airbnb and similar services operate in a legal gray area or outright violation of local laws. Airbnb listings may not always adhere to local laws. For instance, nearly half of the holiday rentals in Barcelona are unlicensed[337], making them illegal. In 2016, Barcelona fined Airbnb 600.000 € for advertising unlicensed properties despite local regulations.

It is not just Barcelona. Cities around the world have been addressing the issue of Airbnb and short-term rentals due to concerns such as the depletion of local housing for residents and noise disturbances. The surge in short-term rentals, partly fueled by the COVID pandemic, led to an increase in properties being used for Airbnb, causing local governments to take action. Residents and officials in various locations have raised issues about short-term rentals consuming housing stock that could have benefited local people. Consequently, cities in the U.S. and Canada have implemented measures to make it harder to own or manage short-term vacation rentals[338]. Among these cities are New York City, Aspen, Atlanta, Montreal, and Palm Springs, indicating a widespread

---

336 https://www.vice.com/en/article/epxxkn/musicians-are-dragging-spotifys-ceo-for-funding-a-military-ai-company
337 https://www.theguardian.com/technology/2017/jun/02/airbnb-faces-crackdown-on-illegal-apartment-rentals-in-barcelona
338 https://www.businessinsider.com/cities-fighting-airbnbs-with-regulations-for-short-term-rentals-2022-5

movement to regulate the impact of short-term rentals on local communities

Uber has faced numerous challenges, including regulatory issues where governments and regulators in various cities and countries have contested its business model, leading to operational bans and restrictions[339]. Legal challenges have also been significant, with lawsuits from drivers seeking employee classification and claims related to safety concerns, such as insufficient measures to prevent sexual harassment and assault by drivers. The competitive landscape is another area of concern, with rivals like Lyft and Didi Chuxing competing for market share, some benefiting from strong relationships with local governments and transportation entities.

# All that glitters is not gold

William Shakespeare

The startup ecosystem increasingly prioritizes achieving "unicorn" status, driven by a societal fascination with identifying the next billion-dollar company, often at the expense of genuine value creation. This phenomenon can lead to a cycle where early investments are made not on the basis of a startup's fundamental

---

339 https://thebrandhopper.com/2023/05/01/the-rise-and-challenges-of-uber-a-story-of-disruption-and-innovation/

value or sustainable business model, but on the potential for inflated valuations, enticing subsequent investors. Such practices risk turning the startup landscape into a speculative bubble, where valuations are more reflective of hype and investor expectations than actual economic performance and value. This shift towards valuation over value underscores the need for a recalibration in the startup world, emphasizing the importance of building companies with solid foundations, ethical business practices, and long-term contributions to society and the economy. We are in an urgent need for a more permaculture infused startup-culture. But be aware that it usually works the other way round.

The intersection of startup culture and permaculture lifestyle presents a nuanced dynamic, particularly when considering the financial disparities between individuals in high-earning positions within startups and those dedicated to permaculture as a way of life. It's not uncommon for successful individuals from the startup world to channel their earnings into establishing permaculture homesteads, equipping them with resources and tools – like acquiring expensive animal or high-end equipment or buying 20 different varieties of hazelnuts for their newly build off-grid Eco-lodge – that might be beyond the reach of those who practice permaculture not as a hobby but as a core life philosophy.

This influx of capital can create a stark contrast in the permaculture community, where the principles of sustainability, self-sufficiency, and ethical living are often pursued within the constraints of modest means. For those deeply embedded in permaculture, the journey involves a gradual building and nurturing of their environment, often relying on ingenuity, time, and community rather than substantial financial investment.

The disparity raises important conversations about accessibility and authenticity in the permaculture movement. While financial resources can accelerate the establishment of permaculture projects and potentially amplify their impact, there's a risk of overshadowing the grassroots, inclusive ethos that underpins permaculture. It challenges the community to find balance, ensuring that permaculture remains accessible and relevant to those from all economic backgrounds, not just those with the means to expedite their transition to a permaculture lifestyle.

This situation also invites reflection on the values of permaculture, encouraging all practitioners, regardless of their financial background, to consider how they can contribute to the sustainability, resilience, and ethical integrity of the movement, ensuring it remains grounded in its core principles and inclusive to all who wish to participate.

In the long run, we can aspire for startups to evolve beyond mere valuation metrics, embracing value-driven models with permaculture principles at their core. The question we must ask ourselves is, what worth does a billion-dollar valuation hold in a world deprived of natural beauty and resources? The future we should strive for is one where businesses thrive not just economically but sustainably, contribution to the 8 forms of capital[340], nurturing the planet and its inhabitants in a fair for everyone way.

# Subscription culture

It is 2007. DSL (digital subscriber line[341]) was introduced around 7 years ago and the speed of the consumer internet was finally fast enough to send and receive videos. I'm sitting in this cozy Irish pub called Messr Maguire, pint in hand, good music in the background. Me and my friends had just visited the local micro brewery and we were having a conversation about TV series. The conversation with my friend then took an intriguing turn. He was animated about this new service called Netflix his friend hat told him about. It was a revelation – the idea that you could watch what you wanted, when you wanted, without the intrusion of ads or the constraints of a broadcast schedule. Finally be free of all those limitations. It sounded intriguing.

Fast forward to today, in the meantime I moved from Ireland to Germany and then to Finland, and now the numbers speak volumes about the transformative wave Netflix has ridden and propelled. From a modest base of subscribers in its early days, it swelled to a staggering 209 million by 2021[342], reshaping not just TV but our entire consumption landscape. This was no mere shift; it was a

---

340 https://www.researchgate.net/figure/Eight-Forms-of-Capital-Permaculture-Finance-Appleseed-Permaculture_fig5_321110833
341 https://en.wikipedia.org/wiki/Digital_subscriber_line

cultural upheaval, setting the stage for a plethora of subscription-based services like Spotify, Disney+, Adobe and others, each carving out their niche in this new digital dominion.

This subscription economy, however, extends beyond entertainment. It's morphing into a broader societal ethos where ownership seems passé. Software, music, even essentials like groceries, are all ensnared in this subscription model. It's as if life itself is parcelled out on a monthly plan, with giant corporations holding the reins. This paradigm promises convenience and an ever-refreshing smorgasbord of choices, but at what cost?

Beneath this veneer of endless access lies a stark reality: the dilution of ownership and personal autonomy. We're nudged from owning to merely accessing, from being proprietors to perpetual subscribers. This shift is seismic, challenging the very fabric of how we define possession and value in our lives.

Moreover, as everything morphs into a service, the power dynamics tilt overwhelmingly towards a handful of tech behemoths. They dictate the terms, curate our options, and in many ways, shape our desires and consumption patterns. This isn't just about entertainment or software; it's a fundamental reorientation of our societal structures towards a future where we might own nothing and live perpetually tethered to subscription services.

---

342 https://www.statista.com/statistics/250934/quarterly-number-of-netflix-streaming-subscribers-worldwide/

The subscription economy, for all its allure, beckons us to scrutinize its implications. It's a call to reflect on the sustainability of this model, not just in environmental terms but as a blueprint for our lives and communities. In a world veering towards digital omnipresence, finding a balance that respects our planet's limits and our need for genuine choice and ownership is imperative. This isn't merely about resisting the tide but about charting a course that harmonizes with the principles of sustainability, equity, and community that lie at the heart of a conscientious society.

Should I say thank you internet? I for myself hold only one subscription and even that has to be re-evaluated every year. What subscription services are you using? What do they cost you? Are they worth the money? Are they necessary?

# The digital divide – a social problem

The digital divide is a growing concern in today's increasingly technology-driven world. It represents the disparities in access to and use of information and communication technology (ICT) between different groups of people, regions, or socio-economic backgrounds. As the digital landscape continues to expand, understanding the factors that contribute to the digital divide is crucial to ensuring equal opportunities for everyone.

# Access to technology

One of the primary factors contributing to the digital divide is the uneven distribution of technology and internet infrastructure. Access to devices, such as computers and smartphones, as well as the availability of broadband or mobile networks, can vary significantly between urban and rural areas, and between developed and developing countries. Closing the gap in access to technology is essential for ensuring equal opportunities for individuals, households, and businesses across different regions.

Before we relocated to Finland, Pekka from the local artisan cheesemaker[343], reached out to the residents of the village and proposed the idea of creating our own fiber optic network. This plan was promptly set into motion, and ever since, we have been enjoying the convenience of broadband internet at home, which also enables home office working in our rural area.

---

343 https://juustola.fi

# Affordability

The cost of devices and internet services can pose a significant barrier for some individuals or households, particularly in low-income communities. When people cannot afford to purchase or maintain the necessary technology, they are unable to participate in the digital world, leading to disparities in access to information, education, and economic opportunities. Addressing the issue of affordability is critical to bridging the digital divide and fostering social and economic inclusion.

While I would call myself an early adapter when it comes to the internet, I couldn't afford a mobile plan for mobile internet and therefore experienced digital divide first hand. Not that I was intrinsically lacking something – it was the advantage people with a mobile plan had over me, like access to public transportation plans, maps and information in general. It made me feel like a 2nd class citizen even back then. I think our culture has long way to go to understand what the digital divide can truly cause.

# Digital literacy

Digital literacy[344], or the ability to use digital technology effectively, is another essential aspect of the digital divide. Individuals with limited digital skills may struggle to navigate the digital landscape, hindering their ability to access and benefit from online resources and services. Disparities in digital literacy can exist between different age groups, education levels, or socio-economic backgrounds. Developing and promoting digital literacy programs can help bridge this gap and empower people to fully participate in the digital world.

At the Permaculture Design Courses[345] (PDC) at Beyond Buckthorns I have integrated a lecture about Digital Permaculture. I think it is a must have for every PDC. Too many people who attend those courses are digital illiterates and can't make any sound decisions regarding digital tools.

When I suggested a digital learning platform to the Nordic Permaculture Academy, they explained to me that a PDF document and email were the furthest they could go with digital technology for their students.

---

344 https://en.wikipedia.org/wiki/Digital_literacy
345 https://www.beyondbuckthorns.com/courses

# Quality of access

Even when people have access to technology and the internet, the quality of their connection or devices can significantly impact their experience[346]. Slow or unreliable internet connections, outdated devices, or limited access to high-quality content and services can create barriers to fully utilizing digital resources – it could also be the content itself. Ensuring that people have access to reliable, high-speed internet connections and up-to-date devices is essential for reducing the digital divide. It also requires web developers to make sure that website don't use up a lot of bandwidth or transfer huge amounts of data.

On the other hand we have the mentality of "I need the internet everywhere" in over-developed countries. Why is it necessary to ensure that enough bandwidth is available so that everyone on the train is able to watch their Netflix show in 4K on a 6.5" smartphone screen?

Our bandwidth is already good enough to pass through all the information necessary to learn whatever can be learned. There is enough bandwidth[347] (in Europe) to transfer millions of emails per second. What is eating into bandwidth is our hunger for entertainment. We amuse ourselves to death[348].

---

346 https://www.imf.org/en/Blogs/Articles/2020/06/29/low-internet-access-driving-inequality
347 https://ec.europa.eu/eurostat/web/products-eurostat-news/-/ddn-20220822-1
348 https://en.wikipedia.org/wiki/Amusing_Ourselves_to_Death

# Content and language barriers

The internet is dominated by content in a few languages (one of which is English)[349], which can create barriers for individuals who do not speak these languages. Furthermore, locally relevant content may not be readily available or accessible, amplifying the digital divide. Encouraging the development of diverse and locally relevant content, as well as promoting multilingualism online, can help ensure that the internet is more inclusive and accessible to a broader range of users.

# Data sovereignty

Data Sovereignty[350] is the concept of data being under the jurisdiction and control of a specific nation, community or individual. In a digital permaculture context data sovereignty can be used to ensure that personal data is protected by the laws and regulations of the user's country, rather than being controlled by global companies.

Data sovereignty encompasses several key principles and ideas:

---

349 https://www.statista.com/statistics/262946/most-common-languages-on-the-internet
350 https://en.wikipedia.org/wiki/Data_sovereignty

# Data privacy

Data privacy is from a users point of view simple: don't f*ck with my data. But as we have seen over the years some companies don't care – and even sell data[351] or the stolen data gets sold [352].

Registering with services like Facebook, Google, etc. means we are giving away data freely. The more we click, the more we like, the more precise the profile of us gets. After that we are ripe for microtargeting[353].

In a permaculture world our data would belong to us – and no one else.

It's crucial to contemplate the methods through which personal data is gathered, retained, and employed, while also safeguarding our authority over our own data. This necessitates the establishment of robust privacy policies, employing encryption and other protective measures, and granting individuals the option to abstain from data collection. Alternatively, a paradigm shift in data collection could be pursued—where the standard assumes no data collection, and users must actively choose to participate.

---

351 https://www.theguardian.com/news/2018/mar/17/cambridge-analytica-
    facebook-influence-us-election
352 https://cybernews.com/news/stolen-data-of-500-million-linkedin-users-being-
    sold-online-2-million-leaked-as-proof-2/
353 https://en.wikipedia.org/wiki/Microtargeting

When the Finnish Permaculture Association transitioned to WordPress in 2023, they also made a significant change in their analytics platform by switching from Matomo to Google Analytics. However, this switch raised concerns regarding privacy and compliance with data protection regulations. The association did not provide clear information about cookie consent or update their privacy policies to address the use of Google Analytics.

## Data security / cybersecurity

Ensuring the security of personal data is crucial to protect individuals from identity theft and other malicious activities. This can include implementing strong security measures, such as firewalls, encryption, and multi-factor authentication, and regularly monitoring for and responding to security breaches.

And while the data is securely stored on a server the human factor is always there. Dumpster diving[354] for data

---

354 https://powerdmarc.com/dumpster-diving-in-cybersecurity/

or social engineering[355] are some of the tactics to target humans in order to obtain data.

And while I was writing this book I read about for how long USB cables have been used to hack in smartphones. The technical term is "Juice Jacking"[356]. Be aware of the cables and chargers you are using!

## Technological independence

Digital sovereignty encourages the development and use of technology solutions that are not reliant on foreign or external technologies. It promotes the idea of creating and maintaining indigenous digital technologies and infrastructure.

It is nice to have an off-grid house, but when you look closer you realized that the batteries come from the US, the panels from China, the cables from Vietnam. Off-grid is just as good as the technological independence is. Basically off-grid as in energy autonomy is useless in the wider consideration of technological independence.

355 https://en.wikipedia.org/wiki/Social_engineering_(security)
356 https://en.wikipedia.org/wiki/Juice_jacking

# Transparency

Digital permaculture should be always transparent about how data is collected, used, and shared, and provide individuals with the ability to understand and control their own data.

In 2018 the EU published the GDPR, the General Data Protection Regulation and with it came the cookie consent. Suddenly everything was transparent and the cookie lists of some website were longer than the websites itself.

Of course we also then got dark patterns[357]. Dark patterns use design to make the consent to all instead of some cookies more likely. Don't click the red button without looking!

# Cultural and linguistic sovereignty

Digital sovereignty also extends to protecting cultural and linguistic diversity in the digital space. It emphasizes the importance of using and preserving native languages and cultural content online.

------------------------

357 https://en.wikipedia.org/wiki/Dark_pattern

It's easy to understand why the Finnish permaculture community wants to translate all permaculture terms into Finnish, given that Finnish is a minority language compared to English or German. They've done a great job so far!

## Digital inclusion

Ensuring that all citizens have equal access to digital resources and technologies is another aspect of digital sovereignty. It seeks to bridge the digital divide and promote digital inclusivity.

## Ethical AI

In 2018 so called Large Language Models[358] (LLM) emerged. It took some 4 years until version 3 of GPT[359] (Generative Pre-trained Transformer) became available as ChatGPT for the public.

---

358 https://en.wikipedia.org/wiki/Large_language_model
359 https://en.wikipedia.org/wiki/GPT-3

Those new LLMs treat everything as language – text, voice, image, video. But language, especially storytelling, is the basis of our culture. According to philospher Yuval Noah Harari[360] culture, and with that also permaculture, is threatened by AI. What if the AI is the better story teller, more believable than our fellow human beings? According to Tristan Harris and Aza Raskin AI will be about intimacy[361]. Who will we believe? What is real, what is fake?

The images generated with Midjourney[362] are stunning and sometimes very hard to distinguish from photos. Is it fake or true? Can and should I still believe what I see?

AI needs regulation and as Yuval Harari expressed it: it needs regulation yesterday.

Ethical AI, also known as responsible AI or trustworthy AI, involves developing and deploying artificial intelligence (AI) systems that promote social good and uphold ethical principles. These principles include fairness, transparency, accountability, privacy, and social responsibility.

**Fairness** in AI systems means avoiding bias and discrimination against individuals or groups based on factors such as race, gender, or ethnicity.

360 https://www.economist.com/by-invitation/2023/04/28/yuval-noah-harari-
    argues-that-ai-has-hacked-the-operating-system-of-human-civilisation
361 https://www.youtube.com/watch?v=xoVJKj8lcNQ
362 https://en.wikipedia.org/wiki/Midjourney

**Transparency** involves making the decision-making processes of AI systems clear and understandable. Transparency is also needed when it comes to the training data.

**Accountability** requires AI systems to take responsibility for their actions and have mechanisms in place to identify and address any issues or errors that arise.

**Privacy** is essential to protecting individuals' personal information from unauthorized access or use.

Lastly, **social responsibility** means that AI developers and users have a responsibility to ensure that AI systems promote social good and contribute to the betterment of society.

## Other things to consider

There is of course always more. Things that I haven't thought of. But that's not the point. While researching and surveying Digital Permaculture I came across a lot of new topics. I didn't have a chapter about Startup Culture in the first iteration. The point is, the topic itself is as endless the every expanding digital landscape. It can not be tamed. I would have liked to have integrated design justice but that's for a book about design itself. I'd also like to go deeper into the startup culture – but that's also another book. Let's continue – let's analyze some of our findings!

# 5. Analysis

Having surveyed our current state – the tools, techniques, and alternatives available for sustainable digital living and how we are using them right now – we now transition to the analysis stage of our permaculture design. This stage is crucial in evaluating our findings, determining their alignment with the permaculture principles, and identifying areas for improvement. Our goal is to achieve digital sustainability, a harmonious integration of technology within the permaculture ethics.

In this phase, we apply various analytical tools to assess our digital practices. This process allows us to discern whether we are on the right track towards our goal and where adjustments are necessary. Remember, the essence of permaculture lies in starting with ourselves and gradually extending our influence outward. This aligns with the prime directive of permaculture, where we take responsibility for our actions and their impact on our immediate environment and community. Thus, we begin our analysis at Zone 0 – our personal digital space – hard & software layer – and work our way outward, concentrating on our most-used digital products and services.

As we go deeper into analysis, keep in mind that while the use cases we explore may vary, the underlying principles and tools remain universally applicable. We start with some numbers, then focus on personal communication, particularly examining the use of messengers and emails, and gradually broaden our scope to encompass wider community interactions. This structured approach ensures that we cover the spectrum of digital engagement, providing insights and strategies that are adaptable to your unique digital landscape.

# Hardware

| Layer | Year | What | OS | Conscious |
|---|---|---|---|---|
| 0 | 2015 | Self build PC | Windows, Linux | Yes |
|  | 2012 | E-Book reader | Linux | Yes |
|  | 2019 | Smartphone | Google Android | Yes |
| 1 | 2015 | Laptop | Linux | Yes |
| 2 | 2020 | Camera | Proprietary | Yes |
|  | inherited | Tablet | Lineage Android | - |
|  | inherited | Tablet | Lineage Android | - |
| 3 | 2013 | Raspberry Pi | Linux | Yes |
| 4 | 2018 | Raspberry Pi | Linux | Yes |
|  | 2021 | Drone | Proprietary | Yes |
| 5 | 2019 | Gimbal | Proprietary | Yes |

Hardware Layers 1 to 5

The survey of my hardware inventory has yielded insights into the technological ecosystem I navigate. Among the 11 devices that constitute my digital toolkit, a majority – 7 devices, accounting for approximately 64% – are powered by open-source operating systems. This preference underscores my inclination towards the flexibility, transparency, and community-driven innovation that open-source software embodies.

However, not all devices in my arsenal align with this open-source paradigm. Specialized equipment such as my camera, drone, and a gimbal are tethered to proprietary software, reflecting a common trend in niche, high-specification hardware where customized solutions often prevail. Additionally, my computer represents a deviation from my open-source preference, as it operates on Windows, a proprietary system. This choice is influenced by specific requirements or software compatibilities that necessitate a balance between open-source ideals and practical functionality.

This hardware survey not only catalogs the tools of my digital engagement but also reflects the broader dynamics of technological adoption, where open-source and proprietary systems coexist, each catering to specific needs and preferences. The predominance of open-source software in my collection underscores its value and versatility, yet the presence of proprietary systems underscores the complexities and compromises inherent in our technological choices.

I also then compiled a table to show the energy consumption, lifespan and repairability of the devices from  Hardware Layer 0 to 2

| What | Energy | Lifespan | Repairability |
|---|---|---|---|
| Self build PC | - 115 Watt | open | High |
| E-Book reader | - 3.9 Watt | open | Fair |
| Smartphone | 1.5 – 16 Watt | EOL | Difficult |
| Laptop | - 55 Watt | open | Fair |
| Camera | - | EOL | Difficult |
| Tablet | - 7 Watt | EOL | Fair |
| Tablet | - 6 Watt | EOL | Fair |

In evaluating my hardware setup, a pressing concern has emerged with my smartphone. It has nearly reached its End-of-Life (EOL) stage, meaning it will soon no longer receives official updates, including crucial security patches. While there is unofficial support through LineageOS, the security patch level remains outdated. This lack of current support compromises the device's security and functionality, necessitating its replacement sooner rather than later. The camera's focus issue further exacerbates the need for a new phone, marking a definitive end to this device's serviceable life. I also have to think what to do with it.

Aside from the smartphone, my hardware inventory appears robust, with no other devices requiring imminent replacement. This stability allows me to concentrate on maximizing the efficiency and utility of my current setup, avoiding unnecessary consumption and waste.

The personal computer's energy consumption presents a different challenge. Despite selecting energy-efficient monitors, the PC's overall power usage remains relatively fixed, highlighting the limitations of post-purchase energy reduction. This experience reinforces the critical importance of initial hardware selection, emphasizing energy efficiency and long-term sustainability as key factors in purchase decisions.

# PMI

PMI stands for "Plus, Minus, Interesting," and it's a decision-making tool designed to help analyze options or situations from different perspectives. It was developed by Dr. Edward de Bono[363], a renowned psychologist, author, and expert in creative thinking and lateral problem-solving. He introduced this method to encourage balanced thinking and comprehensive evaluation.

In the context of permaculture design, PMI is often used to assess various elements, strategies, or choices during the design process. Here's how it works:

**Plus:** This step involves listing the positive aspects or benefits of a particular option. These could be advantages, strengths, or favorable outcomes associated with the choice.

**Minus:** Here, we consider the negative aspects or drawbacks of the option. These could be challenges, limitations, or potential disadvantages.

**Interesting:** In this step, we explore the interesting or novel aspects of the option that might not fall under strictly positive or negative categories. These could be potential learning experiences, new opportunities, or unique features.

Permaculture designers use PMI as a way to systematically evaluate various elements of a design, ensuring that they consider

---

363 https://en.wikipedia.org/wiki/Edward_de_Bono

both the advantages and disadvantages of each option. It helps in making more informed decisions that align with permaculture principles, such as "Observe and interact", "Use and value diversity", and "Apply self-regulation and accept feedback".

Let's apply a PMI onto the different soft- and hardware licensing models available:

## PMI on licensing models

| Aspect | Plus | Minus | Interesting |
| --- | --- | --- | --- |
| **Proprietary Software** | High-quality, polished products | Expensive licensing fees | Driven by market demand |
| | Professional customer support | Vendor lock-in | Protected by intellectual property rights |
| | Regular updates and improvements | Limited customization options | |
| | | Source code not accessible | |
| **Open-Source Software** | Access to source code | Limited support options | Encourages collaboration |
| | Can be modified and customized | May have less polished interfaces | Can foster innovation |
| | Community-driven development | Development may be slower | Development can be unpredictable |
| | Often more cost-effective | | |
| **Free and Open-Source Software (FOSS)** | Access to source code | Limited support options | Aligned with open knowledge sharing |

| | Can be modified and customized | May have less polished interfaces | May challenge traditional models |
| --- | --- | --- | --- |
| | Community-driven development | Development may be slower | (e.g., support, services) |
| | Free to use, distribute, and modify | | |
| | Encourages collaboration | | |

PMI comparing Proprietary Software, Open source and FOSS

# Permaculture ethics for licensing models

In a second step we could evaluate the licensing models against the Permaculture Ethics:

| Permaculture Ethic | Proprietary Software | Open-Source Software | Free and Open-Source Software (FOSS) |
| --- | --- | --- | --- |
| **Earth Care** | Low alignment | Limited alignment | **Better alignment** |
| | Higher resource usage | Encourages collaboration | Promotes sharing and reuse |
| | Limited sustainability | May reduce resource consumption | Supports sustainable practices |
| **People Care** | Low alignment | **Better alignment** | **Best alignment** |
| | Less accessible | Encourages collaboration | Accessible and collaborative |
| | Limited customization | Supports knowledge sharing | Empowers individuals and communities |
| **Fair Share** | Low alignment | Moderate alignment | **Best alignment** |
| | Concentrated power | Equitable distribution | Promotes equitable |

|  |  | of knowledge / resources | distribution |
|---|---|---|---|
|  | Limited access to source code | Some financial barriers | Removes financial barriers |
|  |  |  | Encourages sharing and cooperation |

Comparison of alignment of permaculture ethics with software licensing models.

The Open source and the permaculture communities overlap nicely in their ideals and as we know: **a community, like a forest, grows on the edges.**

# Sectors of influence in software choices

**Data analysis and visualization**

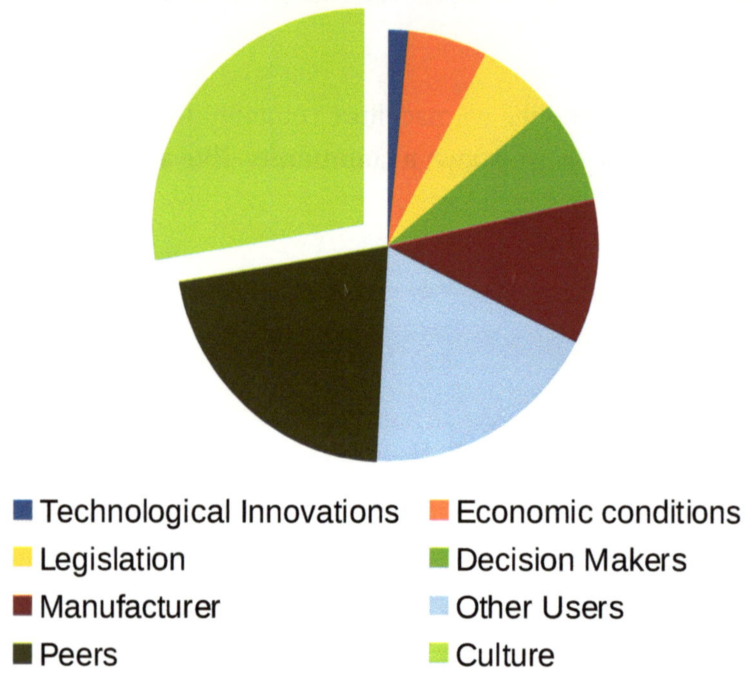


The survey I conducted on the software I use revealed some surprising sectors that influence my decisions.

Culture turned out to be the biggest influence, which makes sense since I've been involved with the open-source community for a long time. The values and shared practices of this community evidently shape my software choices more than I realized.

It was also surprising to see that peers and the opinions of other users affect my choices quite a lot. It shows that the software tools used by friends and people among my social circles play a significant role in what I end up using.

On the other hand, I thought that as someone who likes new technology, the latest tech innovations would be a major deciding factor. But the survey showed that new technologies don't influence my decisions as much. This tells me that it's not just about the newest features or tech; it's about what fits well with the culture I'm part of and what my peers are using.

How do your results look? What sectors do have influence over your software decisions? Do you use a lot of software because someone else decided it for you? Do you use it because it is innovative?

**Be aware of your sectors!**

# Communication Zones

During our survey we came across the *Zone 0* dilemma – the problem that while we are connected with the internet all *Zones* are collapsed on *Zone 0*. I brought the netiquette back and also spent some time going over quantity and quality of communication.

For the quantity part it is mainly the same as with the *Sectors*. Get your numbers and find the time thieves. When it comes to quality we have to go a different path.

I'd like invite you to use the "Roses, Buds, Thorns"' tool. It is a popular feedback and reflection technique used in various settings, including education, design thinking, and team meetings. It's a metaphorical framework that helps us to reflect on and share our experiences, thoughts, and feelings about a particular topic, project, or period of time.

# Roses, buds, thorns

Permaculture teacher Katie Shepherd[364] introduced me to "Roses, Buds, Thorns". Over the years I've found it to be very helpful.

Here's what each element represents:

---

364 https://www.ktshepherdpermaculture.com

**The "Roses"** represents something <u>positive</u>, a success, highlight, or something that went well. It's akin to stopping and smelling the roses – taking a moment to appreciate what's flourishing or bringing joy.

- What was the highlight of this experience for you?
- What achievements or successes stood out?
- What aspects brought you the most joy or satisfaction?
- Can you share a moment that you felt was particularly rewarding?


**The "Buds"** symbolizes <u>potential</u> or something that's emerging. It could be a new idea, an opportunity for growth, a developing skill, or an area that's showing promise but hasn't fully blossomed yet.

- What new ideas or opportunities are emerging?
- What are you looking forward to exploring or developing further?
- Is there a particular area where you see great potential for growth?
- What skills or knowledge do you wish to cultivate based on this experience?


**The "Thorns"** stands for <u>challenges</u>, obstacles, or areas of difficulty. It's something that might be causing discomfort or needs attention and problem-solving.

- What obstacles did you encounter, and how did they affect you?

> - Were there any aspects of the experience that caused frustration or
> difficulty?
> - What would you change or improve for next time?
> - Can you identify a specific moment or aspect that didn't go as
> planned?

We now have to adapt the questions to our *Zone 0* dilemma.

**Roses (Positives):** What benefits have arisen from the accessibility
and immediacy of information and connectivity provided by the
internet in your personal space (*Zone 0*)? How has this digital
integration enhanced your learning, productivity, or well-being
within your immediate environment? Can you identify any specific
instances where this collapse of zones has led to positive outcomes,
such as community building or access to resources?

**Answer:** For me the *Zone 0* dilemma is actually a great opportunity
as I've been working from home since 2007. Over the years I've
taken part in many online courses, workshops, etc – because they
finally became available online.

**Buds (Potential):** What potential opportunities do you see in this
new, digitally landscape for personal growth, learning, or community
engagement? How can the principles of permaculture be applied to
navigate and optimize this digital convergence for future
sustainability and resilience? Are there emerging technologies or

digital practices that could help restore or redefine the boundaries between zones, aligning more closely with permaculture ethics?

**Answer:** The shift towards digital communication, particularly the ease of teleconferencing, holds significant potential for sustainability. The convenience of connecting with others across the globe at the touch of a button offers a clear reduction in the carbon footprint compared to traditional in-person meetings, which often involve travel. However, this convenience also presents a paradox known as the rebound effect, where the energy savings from individual teleconferences could be offset by the sheer increase in their frequency.

Just because digital tools make it possible to host countless meetings doesn't mean we should. The ease of initiating a teleconference, devoid of the logistical considerations tied to physical meetings, can lead to an increase in unnecessary virtual gatherings. Over time, the cumulative energy consumption and carbon footprint of these additional digital interactions could rival, if not exceed, those of fewer in-person engagements.

Embracing the principles of permaculture, such as "Produce no waste" and "Apply self-regulation and accept feedback", can guide us in making sustainable choices in our digital habits. By critically assessing the necessity and frequency of virtual meetings, we can harness the potential of teleconferencing for sustainability, ensuring that our shift towards digital communication truly benefits the planet.

**Thorns (Challenges):** What challenges have emerged from the blurring of boundaries between traditional permaculture *Zones* due to the Internet's omnipresence in *Zone 0*? How has the digital overload or constant connectivity affected your personal well-being, privacy, or connection with the natural environment? What steps could be taken to mitigate the negative impacts of this *Zone* collapse, ensuring a balance between digital integration and the preservation of distinct *Zones* for diverse functions and interactions?

**Answer:** Addressing the challenges posed by the digital realm, particularly in terms of communication via smartphones and the broader implications of social media usage, necessitates a personal and introspective approach. In my own experience, maintaining a disciplined and focused approach to digital communication has been crucial. By consciously limiting interactions and engagements, especially those mediated through smartphones, I've managed to avoid the pitfalls of digital overload, which can often lead to a sense of overwhelm and distraction.

The impact of social media on mental well-being is a significant concern, one that I've confronted firsthand. The realization that the pursuit of "likes" and validation on these platforms can lead to a detrimental comparison with others was a turning point for me. Recognizing this addictive mechanism[365] – engineered to captivate attention and drive engagement for the platforms' benefit[366] – prompted a decisive shift in my digital habits. The decision to step back from social media was driven by an understanding of its

---

365 https://www.theguardian.com/global/2021/aug/22/how-digital-media-turned-
   us-all-into-dopamine-addicts-and-what-we-can-do-to-break-the-cycle
366 https://www.arte.tv/en/videos/RC-017841/dopamine/

potential to foster discontent and unease, counteracting the principles of mindfulness and contentment that I strive to uphold.

This journey underscores the importance of mindful engagement with digital technologies and platforms. It serves as a reminder of the need to critically assess how our digital interactions align with our values and well-being. In navigating the digital landscape, drawing upon permaculture principles such as "Apply self-regulation and accept feedback" can offer guidance, encouraging us to adapt our habits in response to the feedback we receive from our own experiences and well-being.

## Conclusion

The notion of "quality" in communication is inherently elusive, varying significantly from one individual to another. It's a term frequently invoked, especially within permaculture circles, where the pursuit of "high quality" is often lauded yet seldom defined with clarity. This ambiguity prompts a critical question: what exactly constitutes "high quality" in the context of communication?

The answer, it seems, is deeply personal and subject to the collective values of a group. To genuinely grasp the essence of quality in our interactions, it's imperative that we first establish clear criteria that resonate with our personal or shared objectives. Without such definitions, the term "high quality" remains an abstract ideal, rather than a tangible goal to strive towards.

Ultimately, the quest to define and achieve high-quality communication is a dynamic process, one that demands ongoing introspection, dialogue, and adaptation. By embracing tools like "Roses, Buds, Thorns" for reflection, we equip ourselves with the means to navigate this process, continuously shaping and elevating the quality of our interactions in alignment with our permaculture principles and personal values.

## Communication tools

As we refine our approach to communication, grounding our efforts in thoughtful reflection and the permaculture principles, we turn our attention to the tangible implements of our digital interactions: our communication tools. These tools, from emails to messengers and video conferencing, are the conduits of our digital discourse, directly under our fingertips and integral to our daily lives. In the following exploration, we'll apply the PMI (Plus, Minus, Interesting) method to dissect and understand these tools' roles and impacts, ensuring our digital toolkit not only serves our needs but also aligns with our commitment to sustainable and mindful digital permaculture practices.

# PMI primary communication tools

Let's see an example of PMI for communication tools and messengers.

| Aspect | Plus | Minus | Interesting |
|---|---|---|---|
| **Face-to-Face Meeting** | Builds stronger relationships | Travel contributes to carbon emissions | Adapts to non-verbal cues and body language |
| | Enhances communication clarity | Can be time-consuming and costly | Can foster collaboration and creativity |
| | Immediate feedback and problem-solving | Limited by geographical constraints | Encourages active participation |
| | Supports local communities and businesses | Scheduling can be challenging | |
| **Email** | Reduces travel and associated emissions | Can lead to miscommunication | Enables asynchronous communication |
| | Saves time and resources | Lacks personal touch and non-verbal cues | Can be more efficient for certain tasks |
| | Overcomes geographical limitations | May contribute to digital waste and energy consumption | Easily searchable and organized |
| | | Can create a sense of isolation | |
| **Telephone** | Allows for real-time, voice-based interaction | Lacks visual cues and body language | Can quickly address questions and concerns |
| | Reduces travel and associated emissions | May contribute to miscommunication | More personal than email |
| | Saves time and resources | Dependent on network connectivity | Can support collaboration and |

| Aspect | Plus | Minus | Interesting |
| --- | --- | --- | --- |
| | | | problem-solving |
| | Overcomes geographical limitations | | |
| **Messenger** | Instant text based messaging | Privacy and security concerns | Integration with other apps/tools |
| | Multimedia sharing | Distractions from notifications | Evolution of emojis and stickers |
| | Group chat and collaboration | Platform specific limitations | Innovative features and trends |
| | Quick response time | Storage limitations | Impact on informal communication |
| | Read receipts and status | Potential for addictions | |
| | Wide variety of platform options | | |

PMI comparing Face-to-Face meetings, E-Mail, Telephone and Messenger

In a questionnaire I conducted via the Nordicpermaculture.org website 87.5% gave e-mail as their primary, 75% telephone as secondary and 62,5% use face-to-face as their tertiary communication tool.

# Email

With the PMI about communication tools we got a broad overview of the subject. Because of personal preference I pick e-mail to demonstrate how I would analyses any give subject further.

Let's imagine you're trying to choose a new email system for yourself and go through some steps of analyzing them, thus making an informed choice. While we're at it, you'll also get to know a few more great analysis tools you can use in all your permaculture design work.

The first tool we are using is a functions, systems, elements analysis.

## Functions, systems, elements (FSE)

The FSE analysis is a versatile tool used in various fields, including engineering, business management, and problem-solving. It is especially valuable when dealing with complex systems that may not be easily understood at first glance. Breaking down a system into its functions, the underlying processes, and its constituent elements provides a clearer perspective and facilitates decision-making and problem-solving.

As for its origin, the FSE analysis is derived from systems thinking and engineering principles. Systems thinking involves examining the interactions and interdependencies of various components within a system to understand its behavior and optimize its performance. Engineers and system analysts often use FSE analysis to design and improve systems, ensuring they meet their intended objectives efficiently and effectively. Over time, this analytical approach has been adapted for use in various contexts beyond engineering, making it a valuable tool in diverse fields.

**Function (What does it do?):**

The "Function" part of the analysis focuses on the purpose or role of the system, process, or concept. It answers the question: What is its primary function or intended outcome?

**System (How does it work?):**

The "System" part is about the mechanisms and processes that enable the system or concept to function. It answers the question: How does it operate, and what are the key components of this operation?

**Elements (What are the parts?):**

The "Elements" aspect identifies and describes the specific components or parts that constitute the system, process, or concept. It answers the question: What are the individual pieces that contribute to the overall function and system?

# FSE for email

**Function (What does it do?):**

- Communication: Email is a digital communication tool that allows individuals to send and receive messages, including text, images, and documents, to and from others over the internet.
- Documentation: It provides a means of documenting conversations and exchanges, creating a digital paper trail.
- Notification: Email can serve as a notification system for various events, such as receiving messages, updates, newsletters, or alerts.

**System (How does it work?):**

- User Interface: Email systems typically have user-friendly interfaces that display received messages, allow composition, and manage contacts.
- Server Infrastructure: Email relies on servers (computers) that store, send, and receive messages. These servers are maintained by email service providers (or by yourself).
- Protocols: The system operates using standardized protocols like SMTP (Simple Mail Transfer Protocol) for sending emails and POP/IMAP for retrieving them.
- Security Measures: To protect against unauthorized access and data breaches, email systems employ security measures like password authentication, encryption, and spam filters.

**Elements (What are the parts?):**

- Email Address: Users have a unique email address, typically in the format "username@domain.com."
- Folders: for Inbox, Draft, Sent, SPAM, etc. It helps oragnize our mails
- Contacts: An address book or contact list for storing email addresses.
- Attachments: The ability to attach files (documents, images) to emails.
- Search function: Allows users to search for specific emails or content within emails.
- Settings: Users can customize email settings, such as signatures, notification preferences, and security options.
- Compose: The feature for creating and sending new emails.


## Level of commitment

We should now have a better understanding what email entails but we still need more information. We have three options for obtaining an email address that we need to evaluate:

**Email providers.** An email provider, also known as an email service provider (ESP), is a company or organization that offers email services to individuals, businesses, or other entities.
- Knowledge needed: low to moderate
- Using email services provided by established email providers like Gmail, Outlook, or ProtonMail requires minimal

technical knowledge. Users need to understand how to create an email account, send and receive emails, organize their inbox, and configure basic settings. These providers offer user-friendly interfaces and handle most technical aspects, making it accessible to the average user.

**Domain-Based Email Services** (e.g., business email with your custom domain): An e-mail would then be yourname@yourdomain.com
- Knowledge needed: moderate
- Domain-based email services allow individuals and businesses to use their custom domain name (e.g., yourname@yourdomain.com) for email communication. Setting up and managing domain-based email typically requires a moderate level of technical knowledge. Users need to understand domain management, DNS (Domain Name System) configuration, and email account setup.

**Own e-mail server.** In this option we then host the sever that delivers e-mail on our own.
- Knowledge Needed: High to Expert
- Running our own email server is the most complex option and requires a high level of technical expertise. Users need in-depth knowledge of email protocols (e.g., SMTP, IMAP), server administration, security measures, DNS configuration, spam filtering, and ongoing server maintenance. Managing an email server involves regular updates, troubleshooting, and security monitoring. It's a task typically undertaken by IT professionals or experienced system administrators.

Here we already have a decision to to make: **The level of commitment to setting up an email**. For most permaculturists running their own email server is out of the question. That's why we are going to compare email providers and domain services in the next chapter.

I received an email from one of my friends telling me that another person couldn't reach me because his emails got rejected by my mail server. I took a closer look into the log-files. It turned out that his mail server was not correctly configured, and hence emails from him were being rejected.

## Comparing providers / domain services

If we continue to think that you are looking for a new email system for yourself, you would have compiled a list of email alternatives in the *Survey* phase of our design. Let's assume that has resulted in a list of email providers and some domain services. We could name them here and run a PMI to get an overview, but as this is a book, the information would become outdated sooner or later. Services come and go, but the fundamentals are universal. Let's focus on what we should be looking for within that PMI.

What we want to see in **plus:** Strong privacy and security, End-to-end encryption, Zero-access encryption, Web-mailer available.

What we don't want to see in **minus:** Proprietary, Privacy and security concerns and collection of user data, No web-mailer.

What we are looking for in **interesting**: Security focused, commitment to reducing carbon, sustainability focus.

At the end we might have 2 to 3 candidates we can choose from.

Our next logical step is to determine how we are actually going to access our mails. There are two options: web-mailer or local email client.

| aspect | web-mail | email client |
| --- | --- | --- |
| **plus** | Accessibility: Accessible from any device with internet access. | Offline Access: Emails can be read and composed offline, |
| | No Installation: No software installation required; access via a web browser. | Enhanced Features: Typically offers advanced features like filtering, sorting, and email organization. |
| | Cross-Platform: Works on various operating systems without compatibility issues. | Privacy Control: Users have more control over data privacy and security settings. |
| | No Storage Limit: Typically, webmail services offer ample cloud storage for emails. | Integrated Services: May integrate with calendar, contacts, and productivity apps |
| **minus** | Internet Dependency: Requires a reliable internet connection for access. | Installation Required: Software must be installed and set up on each device. |

| | | |
|---|---|---|
| | Limited Offline Access: Often provides limited offline functionality, if any. | Learning Curve: New users may need time to learn and configure the software. |
| | Data Privacy: Some concerns about data privacy and security with data stored on remote servers. | Storage Space: Emails may consume local storage space on devices over time |
| | Limited Features: May lack advanced features compared to email clients. | Device-Specific: Settings and configurations may need to be duplicated on each device. |
| **interesting** | Synchronization: Real-time syncing of emails and data across devices. | Customization: Users can customize the email client with extensions and add-ons. |
| | Accessibility on Public Computers: Can be accessed from public computers and shared devices. | Backup Options: Users can create local backups of emails for added security. |
| | Integration with Other Services: May integrate with cloud storage and collaboration tools. | Offline Search: Some email clients offer powerful offline search capabilities. |

Ultimately, the choice between using a web-mailer and a locally installed email client, like Thunderbird, comes down to personal preference. Each option has its own set of advantages, disadvantages, and notable features (PMI). What's important is understanding these aspects to make an informed decision that best suits your needs.

# Messenger

After exploring email options, we turn our attention to messengers. These tools provide a quicker way to communicate, different from email. We'll look at their advantages, disadvantages, and what makes them stand out, helping us decide which messenger fits our needs and values in digital communication.

## PMI of messengers

In the same questionnaire I mentioned earlier 62.5% gave Facebook as their primary messenger app, followed by WhatsApp as secondary with 37.5 %, and then Signal and Telegram as tertiary with 25% each. A few use more than 3 messengers.

| Messenger | Positive | Minus | Interesting |
|---|---|---|---|
| **WhatsApp** | Wide user base, easy to connect with others | Owned by Facebook (Meta), a company with questionable privacy practices | Supports group chats, voice, and video calls |
| | Provides end-to-end encryption | Possible data sharing with Facebook | Frequent updates and new features |
| | Supports group chats, voice, and video calls | | Encourages global communication |
| | End-to-end encryption | | |
| **Signal** | Strong focus on privacy and security | Smaller user base, may not find all contacts using Signal | Offers end-to-end encryption |
| | End-to-end encryption | Lacks some features found in other messaging apps | Supports group chats, voice, and video calls |
| | Open source, | | Developed by a |

| Messenger | Positive | Minus | Interesting |
| --- | --- | --- | --- |
|  | promoting transparency |  | non-profit organization |
|  | Non-profit organization, no ads or tracking |  | Encourages secure communication |
| **Facebook Messenger** | Wide user base, easy to connect with others | Owned by Facebook (Meta), a company with questionable privacy practices | Supports group chats, voice, and video calls |
|  | Integrated with Facebook, easy to find friends and contacts | Questionable privacy practices | Frequent updates and new features |
|  | Supports group chats, voice, and video calls |  | Encourages global communication |
| **Telegram** | Wide user base, easy to connect with others | End-to-end encryption only in secret chats, not by default |  |
|  | Open source, promoting transparency | Ownership unclear |  |
|  | Supports group chats, voice, and video calls |  |  |
|  | Cloud-based, allowing for easy syncing across devices |  |  |

PMI of different messengers used by permaculture practitioners.

# Permaculture ethics for messengers

Another evaluation tool we can use is to evaluate against the permaculture ethics "Earth Care", "People Care" and "Fair Share" and see if and how the software in question aligns with the ethics.

| | Facebook Messenger | WhatsApp | Telegram | Signal |
|---|---|---|---|---|
| **Earth Care** | Reduces physical travel, lowering emissions | Reduces physical travel, lowering emissions | Reduces physical travel, lowering emissions | Reduces physical travel, lowering emissions |
| | | | Cloud-based, reducing device storage needs | |
| **People Care** | Connects people globally | Connects people globally | Connects people globally | Connects people globally |
| | Supports group chats, voice, and video calls | Supports group chats, voice, and video calls | Supports group chats, voice, and video calls | Supports group chats, voice, and video calls |
| | Integrated with Facebook for convenience | Provides end-to-end encryption | Offers channels and bots for extra features | Strong focus on privacy and security |
| | | | | End-to-end encryption and file encryption |
| **Fair Share** | Owned by Facebook (Meta), raising concerns about data privacy and sharing | Owned by Facebook (Meta), raising concerns about data privacy and sharing | Offers Open source, transparency | Developed by a non-profit organization |
| | | | End-to-end encryption only in secret chats | Open source, promoting transparency |
| | | | | No ads or tracking |

Value the messengers against their alignment with permaculture ethics.

All four messaging apps help reduce physical travel and associated emissions, aligning with Earth Care. People Care is met by providing global connections and support for group chats, voice, and video calls. However, Fair Share is where the apps differ in alignment with permaculture ethics. Signal aligns the best with Fair Share due to its non-profit nature, open-source transparency, and focus on privacy and security.

## SWOC

To analyze and evaluate the software used in permaculture, a SWOC analysis tailored to your specific context can be highly beneficial.

The SWOC analysis is a variation of the more well-known SWOT[367] analysis. SWOT stands for Strengths, Weaknesses, Opportunities, and Threats, and it's widely used in strategic planning and decision-making processes. The SWOC analysis, with "Challenges" instead of "Threats," is an adaptation that some individuals and organizations use, especially when they want to focus on potential challenges or difficulties rather than external threats.

The SWOT analysis, in its traditional form, is attributed to Albert S. Humphrey[368], a management consultant who developed the

---

367 https://en.wikipedia.org/wiki/SWOT_analysis
368 https://en.wikipedia.org/wiki/Albert_S._Humphrey

framework in the 1960s and 1970s while working at the Stanford Research Institute (SRI) in California, USA. It was initially designed as a tool for assessing the internal and external factors affecting a business or organization.

In the following SWOC we are evaluating digital tools for permaculture design:

## Strengths:

**Alignment with permaculture ethics:** Identify software that aligns with permaculture principles, such as open-source options that promote resource-sharing and collaboration.

**Functionality:** Recognize software that effectively meets the needs of permaculture design, such as GIS tools for mapping and design software for planning.

**Community Support:** Highlight software with active user communities and development teams that provide ongoing support and updates.

**User-Friendliness:** Consider software that is user-friendly and accessible to individuals with varying levels of technical expertise.

## Weaknesses (W):

**Limited Features:** Identify software that may lack specific features or capabilities required for comprehensive permaculture design.

**Compatibility:** Recognize software that may not integrate well with other tools or may not be available on all platforms.

**Cost:** Acknowledge any software that comes with high licensing or subscription fees, which might not be budget-friendly for permaculture practitioners.

**<u>Opportunities (O):</u>**

**Open-Source Alternatives:** Explore opportunities to replace proprietary software with open-source alternatives, reducing costs and promoting resource-sharing.

**Training and Education:** Leverage opportunities to provide training and education on the use of selected software within the permaculture community.

**Collaboration:** Encourage collaboration between permaculture practitioners to collectively identify and adopt software that best serves their needs.

**Customization:** Explore options for customizing or extending existing software to better align with permaculture design principles.

<u>**Challenges (C):**</u>

**Resistance to Change:** Recognize that some individuals or organizations may be resistant to switching from familiar software tools to new ones.

**Technical Barriers:** Acknowledge the potential technical barriers for users who may not have extensive experience with certain software applications.

**Data Migration:** Anticipate challenges related to migrating data and projects from one software to another, ensuring a smooth transition.

**Resource Constraints:** Address potential resource constraints, such as the availability of hardware or internet connectivity for using specific software.

## SWOC for Signal messenger

Due to the PMI and permaculture ethics analysis before we already narrowed down our list of candidates. In order to narrow it down further let's run a SWOC on the messenger Signal.

| Strengths | Weaknesses |
| --- | --- |
| • Strong end-to-end encryption<br>• Core Messaging features<br>• Available on multiple devices<br>• Focus on privacy advocacy<br>• Open-source transparency | • Smaller user base<br>• Limited third-party integration<br>• Smaller developer team |
| **Opportunities** | **Challenges** |
| • Growing concerns about privacy & data security<br>• Expanding feature set<br>• Cross-Platform compatibility<br>• Engaging in an active community supporting privacy | • Encouraging users to switch from less secure platform<br>• addressing potential platform-specific issues<br>• scaling development to match user-growth |

Using a SWOC always helps me to see where the design is heading. It offers opportunities and comes with challenges. We can leverage its strengths and acknowledge its weaknesses.

## Social media platforms

Let's imagine we are running a homestead and we want to become more visible in and engage with the community. In the survey phase we would have compiled a list of social media platforms that are available to us.

What we should know from them is:

**Audience and Reach**  →  Understand the demographics and interests of the audience on each platform. Consider whether your target audience is active and engaged on a particular platform. Look at the platform's user base, including age, gender, location, and interests. Choose platforms where you can reach and connect with your intended audience effectively.

**Content and Engagement:** Assess the types of content that perform well on each platform and the level of engagement they generate. Some platforms are better suited for visual content like images and videos, while others are more text-centric. Consider the nature of your content and whether it aligns with the platform's format. Additionally, evaluate the level of interaction and engagement your content can achieve on each platform, as this varies widely.

**Privacy and Data Security:** Examine the platform's privacy policies and data security practices. Pay attention to how the platform collects, stores, and shares user data. Ensure that the platform complies with privacy regulations and provides users with adequate control over their data. Prioritize platforms that prioritize user privacy and data security, especially if you're handling sensitive information.

# DAFOR for audience and reach

## DAFOR

DAFOR[369] is an acronym used to remember different stages of vegetation found in a field or landscape. Each letter in DAFOR represents a specific stage or category of plant growth, and this system is often used by ecologists and botanists to assess and describe vegetation in an area. Here's what each letter in DAFOR stands for:

**Dominant (D):** This category includes the most abundant plant species in a given area. Dominant species are usually the largest or most numerous and play a significant role in shaping the landscape.

**Abundant (A):** Abundant species are not as prevalent as dominant ones but are still well-represented within the vegetation. They may be numerous but not as influential as dominant species.

**Frequent (F):** Frequent species are moderately common in the area but are not as abundant as the dominant or abundant species. They may occur throughout the landscape but not in large numbers.

**Occasional (O):** Occasional species are present but not common. They might be found sporadically or in small patches within the landscape.

---

369 https://www.researchgate.net/figure/The-DAFOR-scale-used-to-determine-species-abundance-cover_tbl4_47929583

288

**Rare (R):** Rare species are infrequently encountered and are not a prominent part of the vegetation. They may be scarce or limited to specific microhabitats.

A more general definition of DAFOR is a qualitative scale that categorizes the frequency or prevalence of elements within a given system, thus demonstrating its multipurpose.

There are several possibilities for adapting DAFOR to the digital realm. For example **DAFOR can also be applied to categorize Social Media platforms according their user base numbers.**

Let's run a DAFOR about active monthly users on social media platforms.

| Dominant | Abundant | Frequent | Occasional | Rare |
|---|---|---|---|---|
| Facebook | YouTube | WeChat | LinkedIn | Snapchat |
| | TikTok | Instagram | Vimeo | X (Twitter) |
| | | Reddit | | Pinterest |
| | | | | Mastodon |

DAFOR for active users on social media platforms, October 2023[370]

## Limits and helps for content and engagement

From Looby Macnamara's book "People and Permaculture"[371] and especially her "Design Web" we'll use the Limits and Helps anchor

370 https://www.statista.com/statistics/272014/global-social-networks-ranked-by-number-of-users/

371 https://loobymacnamara.com/people-and-permaculture/

points to evaluate the platforms further. Both anchors help us navigate the design process by considering both the constraints we need to work within (limits) and the assets and opportunities we can use to your advantage (helps). This balanced approach encourages more realistic, sustainable, and effective designs in permaculture and other fields.

## Limits:

**Content suitability:** Determine the type of content that is most suitable for your message or brand. For example, if your content is highly technical and requires in-depth explanations, platforms with character limits may present limitations.

**Time constraints:** Assess the time and resources available for content creation and engagement. Some platforms demand more frequent updates and interactions, which may be challenging if you have limited resources.

**Algorithm changes:** Recognize that social media algorithms can change, affecting how your content is displayed and who sees it. Stay informed about algorithm updates and be prepared to adapt your content strategy accordingly.

## Helps:

**Audience alignment:** Choose platforms where your target audience is active and engaged. When your content aligns with the interests of the platform's users, it's more likely to resonate and generate engagement.

**Visual content tools:** Leverage platforms with built-in tools for creating and sharing visual content if your message benefits from images or videos. Tools like Instagram Stories or TikTok's editing features can enhance your content.

**Engagement features:** Utilize platforms with engagement-boosting features, such as polls, Q&A sessions, or live streaming. These features can help you interact with your audience more effectively.

**Analytics tools:** Take advantage of platforms that offer robust analytics and insights into your content's performance. These tools can provide valuable data to refine your content strategy and increase engagement.

After stepping through the Helps and Limits check the remaining platforms in the table below.

| Dominant | Abundant | Frequent | Occasional | Rare |
|---|---|---|---|---|
| Facebook | YouTube | ~~WeChat~~ | LinkedIn | ~~Snapchat~~ |
| | TikTok | Instagram | ~~Vimeo~~ | ~~X (Twitter)~~ |
| | | ~~Reddit~~ | | ~~Pinterest~~ |
| | | | | Mastodon |

Remaining social media platforms

# Permaculture ethics on privacy and data security

## Earth Care:

**Minimal Data Collection:** Practicing Earth Care in privacy and data security means minimizing the collection of personal data to reduce the environmental impact associated with data storage and processing. By only collecting necessary data, we can lower energy consumption and resource use in data centers.

## People Care:

**User Consent and Transparency:** People Care in data security involves obtaining informed consent from individuals before collecting their data. It means being transparent about data collection practices, respecting user preferences, and providing control over personal information. Prioritizing user privacy and well-being is essential.

**Data Protection:** Safeguarding personal data from unauthorized access, cyberattacks, and data breaches demonstrates care for people's privacy and security. Implementing robust security measures and promptly addressing vulnerabilities is crucial for people's peace of mind.

## Fair Share:

**Data Ownership:** Fair Share in the context of privacy means acknowledging that individuals should have ownership and control over their personal data. They should have the right to decide how their data is used, shared, or monetized. Fair compensation for the use of personal data is also a consideration.

**Data Responsiveness:** Fair Share extends to ensuring that organizations respond to data breaches responsibly and fairly. This includes timely notification to affected individuals, taking accountability for security lapses, and providing remedies in case of harm.

| Platform | Earth Care | People Care | Fair Share |
| --- | --- | --- | --- |
| Facebook | - | - | - |
| YouTube | - | - | - |
| TikTok | - | - | - |
| Instagram | - | - | - |
| LinkedIn | - | - | - |
| Mastodon | + | + | + |

Which Social Media platform aligns with permaculture ethics?

Mastodon aligns most closely with permaculture ethics. It respects Earth Care by offering a decentralized, energy-efficient platform. It prioritizes People Care by giving users control over their data and interactions. It follows Fair Share principles by ensuring user ownership and control over their content.

# Cloud storage

Our next example is cloud storage, which usually involves multiple people. It's commonly utilized for transferring files or storing data for groups, teams, entire organizations, and companies. To understand who will be impacted by our decisions, let's conduct a stakeholder analysis.

## Stakeholder analysis

1. **Identification of stakeholders:** The first step is to identify all potential stakeholders. This includes internal stakeholders like employees and managers in companies or volunteer in associations, as well as external stakeholders like customers, suppliers, competitors, government agencies, and community groups.

2. **Stakeholder mapping:** Once stakeholders are identified, they can be categorized based on their level of influence or interest in the project. Common categories include "high influence, high interest," "high influence, low interest," "low influence, high interest," and "low influence, low interest."

3. **Understanding interests and needs:** For each stakeholder, it's essential to understand their interests, needs, and objectives concerning the project. This information helps in tailoring communication and strategies to address their concerns.

4. **Mapping relationships:** Stakeholders don't exist in isolation. They often have relationships and alliances with other stakeholders. Mapping these relationships can provide insights into how information or influence may flow.

# Identification of stakeholders

- General users (individuals / teams)
- Administrators / IT
- Data security and compliance officers
- Procurement /  Purchasing
- External consultants / experts

## Stakeholder mapping

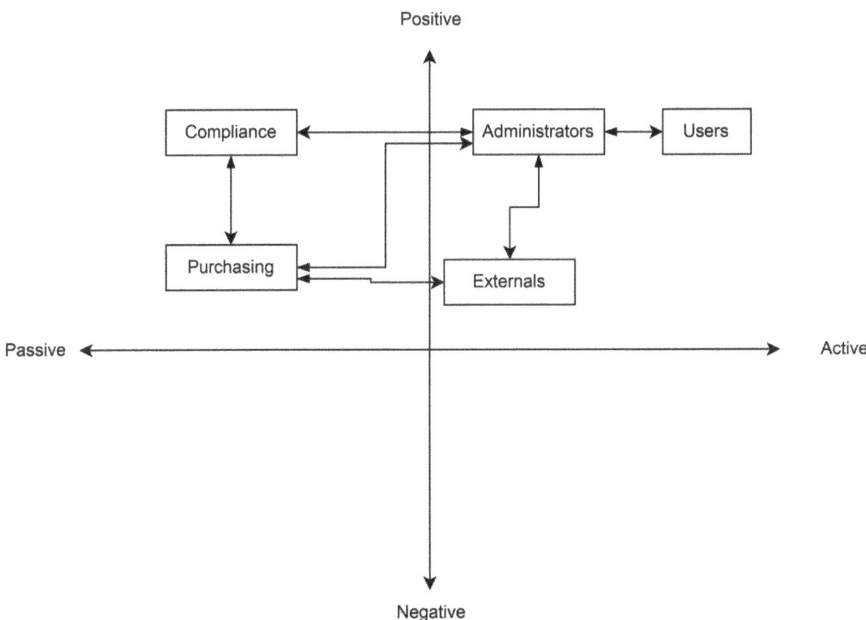


Stakeholder analysis of people involved in a cloud storage project

**X-Axis (Horizontal Axis):** This axis represents the **level of stakeholder involvement or activity**.

**Y-Axis (Vertical Axis):** This axis represents the stakeholders' **attitude or sentiment** toward the project.

**Active and positive:** Engage them as key allies. Keep them informed, involve them in discussions, and leverage their support to drive the decision forward.

**Active and negative:** Address their concerns proactively. Listen to their feedback, provide clarifications, and work collaboratively to mitigate any issues.

**Passive and positive:** Encourage their participation and seek their input, even if they tend to be less vocal. Recognize their positive attitude as a valuable asset.

**Passive and negative:** While they may not actively engage, monitor their concerns and attempt to convert them into more supportive stakeholders through targeted communication and addressing their reservations.

## Understanding interests and needs

- General users
  - Providing input on their storage needs and preferences

- o Testing and evaluating the usability and functionality of the service
  - o Expressing concerns about data security and privacy
- IT
  - o Assessing the service's compatibility with existing IT infrastructure
  - o Evaluating the service's security features and compliance with data protection regulations
  - o Managing user accounts and access permissions
- Compliance
  - o Conducting a risk assessment to evaluate the service's security measures.
  - o Ensuring that the service aligns with data protection requirements (e.g., GDPR, HIPAA).
  - o Recommending security enhancements or alternatives if needed.
- Purchasing
  - o Evaluating the financial aspects of the service, including costs and licensing models.
  - o Negotiating terms and conditions with the service provider.
  - o Ensuring that the chosen service aligns with the organization's budget.
- Consultants
  - o Providing independent assessments and recommendations.
  - o Assisting in the selection process based on industry best practices.

- o Ensuring that the chosen service aligns with industry standards.

## Mapping relationships

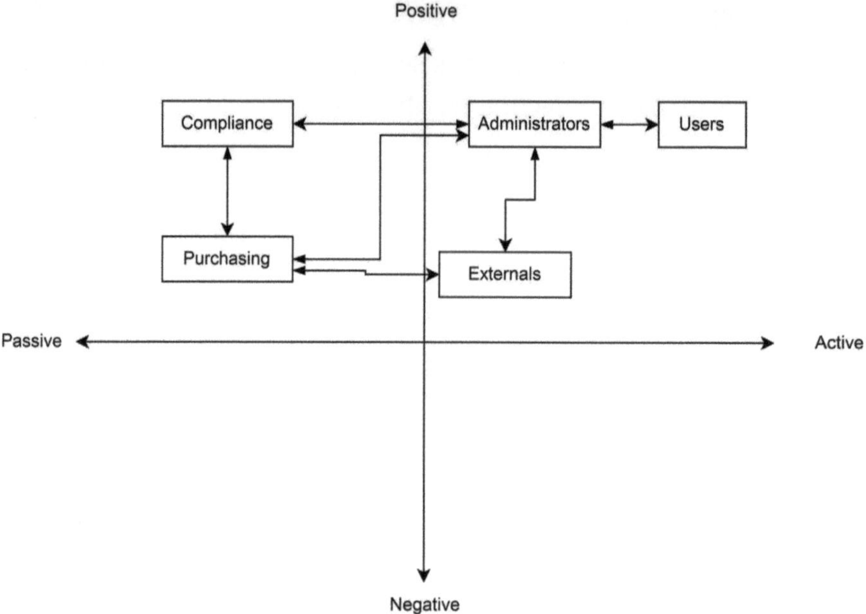


Mapping of relationships of stakeholders

Especially in small associations one person might be responsible for all the duties from administration to purchasing. That's why the involvement of people with extensive IT knowledge in associations is important. They have the duty to change the course of action and lead us towards digital sustainability.

In bigger companies there might be more stakeholders, hence the stakeholder analysis gets more difficult. Nevertheless: it needs to be done if multiple people are involved.

> Over the years I have seen multiple sustainability projects fail because their chair or CEO neglected the administrator(s) or treated them very badly – as replaceable. We have to remember that as permaculture designers we have to value the marginal.

Since administration, compliance and purchasing can be a one-man-show in a small associations / companies, we can simplify the analysis process further. Let's assume our "IT department" has already surveyed several cloud storage services and compiled a list.

## Permaculture ethics on cloud storage

We could then evaluate that list against the permaculture ethics:

- **<u>Earth Care:</u>**
  - Minimize environmental impact through energy-efficient data centers or renewable energy sources.
  - Implement sustainable data center practices to reduce energy consumption.

- **<u>People Care:</u>**
  - Prioritize user data ownership and privacy.
  - Offer user-friendly collaboration features and tools.
  - Enhance data security to protect user information.
- **<u>Fair Share:</u>**
  - Provide equitable access with free storage options and affordable premium plans.
  - Offer open-source, self-hosted solutions for users who want more control and autonomy over their data.

Here is an example:

| Criteria | Google Drive | Dropbox | Nextcloud |
|---|---|---|---|
| **Earth Care** | Data centers have significant energy consumption concerns. | Data centers have environmental impacts due to energy consumption. | Can be hosted on energy-efficient servers or renewable energy sources. |
| | | | Poorly managed instances may have environmental consequences. |
| **People Care** | User-friendly collaboration features. | User-friendly collaboration tools and enhanced security features. | Emphasizes user data ownership and privacy. |
| | Concerns about data privacy and security. | Concerns about data security breaches. | Self-hosting requires technical expertise. |
| **Fair share** | Offers free storage and affordable premium plans. | Offers free and paid plans. | Offers open-source, self-hosted solutions promoting equitable |

| Criteria | Google Drive | Dropbox | Nextcloud |
|---|---|---|---|
|  |  |  | access. |
|  | Concerns about data collection and advertising practices. | Pricing and storage limitations on free plans. | May not be as user-friendly for non-technical users. |

Example of using permaculture ethics to evaluate cloud storage services / software based on services available in the time of writing, early 2024

# Conclusion

The analysis phase heavily relies on the data collected during the survey stage. However, the process of analysis often uncovers the need for further surveying. Don't hesitate to return to the survey stage, continue your observations, and integrate new findings into your existing data. The 'Survey' and 'Analysis' stages are interdependent and frequently circular, allowing for deeper insights before moving on to the 'Design' stage.

Remember, there are numerous tools available for analyzing your findings. Choose the tools that best suit your specific situation.

Now, let's proceed to the 'Design / Decisions' stage!

# 6. Design / Decisions

The design stage is also often called the decision stage. Over the past couple of chapters we have gathered a lot of information, evaluated it and already came up with a lot of solutions for choosing and using different kinds of products and services for ourselves and our organisations to use. Now is the time to make decisions and craft the actual solutions based on our work so far.

## Patterns

When we analyze things in depth, patterns begin to appear.

Wikipedia states a pattern as: "A pattern is a regularity in the world, in human-made design, or in abstract ideas."[372]

A pattern generally refers to a repeated arrangement, design, or sequence of elements that can be found in a variety of contexts such as nature, art, behavior, or systems. Patterns can range from simple, like a recurring sequence of colors or shapes, to complex, such as the organization of leaves on a plant or the structure of a social network.

---

372 https://en.wikipedia.org/wiki/Pattern

Identifying and comprehending patterns enables us to better understand intricate systems, anticipate results, and establish successful approaches for tackling problems and making decisions.

## Patterns of abundance

During our survey and analysis we came across several patterns:

- Open-source software aligns best with permaculture ethics.
- In terms of internet tools, self-hosted software aligns best with permaculture ethics.
- Within each software category there is an open-source pendant which has been available for as nearly as long as its proprietary counterparts, or even longer.
- In each category there is usually an abundance of Open-source software to choose from.
- There is often a driver, main developer or company, backing the Open-source software.
- There are often entire communities of developers / contributors around a specific software.

In general Open-source software offers more transparency, collaboration, and sharing of resources, adhering to the Fair Share principle. Additionally, when talking about internet tools, self-hosted solutions provide users with greater control over our data and privacy – data sovereignty, which is important for People Care. Most of the communication software I considered as Earth Care because the amount of energy used for an online meeting is usually far less than for a face-to-face meeting.

> As permaculture designers we know that only if all 3 ethics are in play it can be called permaculture. As designers we need to make sure our solutions align with them.

## Patterns of erosion

Patterns of erosion are those which we have to break in order to generate a more sustainable or regenerative outcome.

I explicitly listed the annual revenue of some of the larger IT companies during my survey. What we could clearly see is that **proprietary software is primarily focused on growing capital wealth**, often leaving sustainability, regeneration, and social impact out of the equation. We have no influence over these companies' decisions; to them, we are merely consumers. It is mostly a one-way street from the producer to the consumer.

One pattern of erosion is a behavioral one: **we tend to often use easy and fast solutions in the digital realm**, instead of evaluating their tools according to permaculture principles and ethics. Convenience! Or "use small and slow solutions!"

While permaculturists consider permaculture to be knowledge and imagination-intensive, permaculture ethics and principles are not applied if the subject is not perceived as related to permaculture. For example, a food forest is seen as a subject of permaculture, whereas the use of software to create a food forest is not. Consequently, the ethics and principles are not applied to software.

When we look at the dominating software within a category and how many people are using a specific software one pattern emerges: **the digital monoculture.** A few companies dominating an entire category.

Another pattern of erosion, which more or less goes hand in hand with the previous one is to **default to the leader in the sector**. We don't teleconference, we zoom. We don't search, we google. Using brand names as verbs instead of the actual verb plays to the benefit of the leader. I never google – I search. I never zoom – I teleconference – it takes the free advertisement away.

In concluding the discussion on digital permaculture, it's clear that adopting open-source and self-hosted solutions aligns with permaculture ethics, fostering transparency and community. However, we must also tackle patterns of erosion by moving away from convenience-driven choices and the dominance of a few tech giants. By applying permaculture principles to our digital choices, we can transform our engagement with technology to be more sustainable and ethical. This shift is essential as we extend the values of permaculture beyond the natural environment to our digital interactions, striving for a balanced and thoughtful approach in the digital realm.

# The digital permaculture principles

Transitioning from our exploration of patterns in digital permaculture, we now turn our focus towards defining "The Digital Permaculture Principles". These principles are derived from our survey and analysis, aiming to guide our interactions and decisions in the digital landscape. They serve as a framework for making choices that are in harmony with permaculture ethics, promoting sustainability, transparency, and community engagement.

Though most of the given examples pertain mostly to digital tool development and maintenance, they can be applied by digital tool users too – especially the last one.

## 1. Design for privacy and transparency

*"Honesty is the best policy"*

Promote the ethical design of digital tools that prioritize transparency, privacy, and user empowerment. By placing honesty and transparency at the forefront, we ensure that digital solutions respect user privacy, provide clear information about data practices, and empower individuals to make informed choices about their personal information.

Here are some considerations:

**Data collection and storage:** Limit the collection of user data to the minimum necessary for site functionality. Be transparent about what data is being collected and how it will be used. Avoid unnecessary tracking mechanisms.

**User consent:** Implement clear and easily accessible consent mechanisms for data collection, cookies, and any analytics tools used on the website. Users should have the option to opt in or out of data collection.

**Data sharing:** while I find data sharing with $3^{rd}$ parties a difficult topic and avoid it as much as possible I suggest strongly to be as transparent as possible about data sharing.

**Encryption:** Use HTTPS to ensure secure communication between users and the website. Encrypt user data when storing it on servers to prevent unauthorized access.

**Privacy policy:** Have a well-drafted and easily accessible privacy policy that outlines the types of data collected, the purposes of collection, and how users can exercise their rights to their data.

**User control:** Provide users with the ability to access, correct, or delete their personal data. Allow them to manage their preferences for data collection and communications.

**Third-party services:** I find the usage of 3$^{rd}$ party services in general problematic and I avoid it as much as possible. If necessary then clearly disclose the use of any third-party services that might collect user data, such as analytics or advertising platforms.

**Open-source software:** Use open-source software components whenever feasible, as they tend to have better transparency and community-driven security.

**Transparency in content:** While I usually don't allow any sponsored content on my websites I suggest to clearly label sponsored content, advertisements, and any content that might have a commercial interest. Provide information about the sources of the news and articles presented.

**Updates and communication:** Inform users about any changes to the website's data collection practices, privacy policy, or terms of use. Maintain clear channels of communication for users to ask questions or voice concerns.

**User Education:** Provide educational content about online privacy, data protection, and responsible online behavior. Empower users to make informed decisions about their online activities.

# 2. Consider the connected whole

## *"A chain is only as strong as its weakest link"*

Acknowledge the interconnections and interdependencies within the digital realm and broader systems. By understanding the bigger picture, we can make more informed and ethical decisions that consider the implications and consequences of our choices.

Here are some examples:

**Interconnected content:** Ensure that the content presented on a website is interconnected, providing readers with a comprehensive understanding of topics. Include cross-referencing, related articles, and tags for easy navigation. Link external resources.

**Collaborative content creation:** Allow guest authors, experts, and community members to contribute content, encouraging a diverse range of perspectives and collaborative knowledge sharing.

**Community engagement:** Incorporate features that facilitate discussions and interactions among users. Include comments, forums, or discussion threads to create a sense of community around the content.

**Multi-media integration:** Utilize various media formats such as text, images, videos, and infographics to convey information in multiple ways, catering to different learning styles and preferences.

**Cross-platform compatibility (Responsiveness):** Ensure that the website is accessible and functional across various devices and screen sizes, promoting a seamless user experience.

**Networked partnerships:** Collaborate with other permaculture organizations, websites, and content creators to amplify the reach of valuable information and create a more extensive digital permaculture network.

**Information flow:** Design the website layout to guide users through a logical flow of information, ensuring that related content is easily discoverable.

**User feedback:** Encourage user feedback, suggestions, and contributions to continuously improve the website's content and functionality, making it a platform that evolves based on community input.

**Localization:** Consider providing content in multiple languages or catering to specific regional interests, thereby connecting with a broader and more diverse audience.

**Data integration:** Utilize APIs and data integration to pull in relevant data from external sources, providing users with up-to-date and relevant information.

**Ecosystem integration:** Develop tools that integrate seamlessly with existing ecosystems, avoiding disruption to established natural and social systems while providing innovative solutions.

# 3. Innovation only with regeneration

*"Necessity is the mother of invention"*

Foster the development of diverse and regenerative digital solutions that contribute to a more sustainable future. Encouraging innovation that reduces resource consumption and promotes regeneration aligns with ethical decision-making in the digital space.

**Renewable energy usage:** Embrace innovative technologies powered by renewable energy sources, minimizing the carbon footprint associated with digital infrastructure.

**Circular economy:** Design digital products with the principles of a circular economy in mind. Consider the entire lifecycle, including sourcing sustainable materials, reducing waste, and enabling easy recycling.

**Minimal environmental footprint:** Innovate technologies that have a minimal impact on the environment, including low-energy consumption, reduced electronic waste, and sustainable production processes.

**Bioinspired design:** Draw inspiration from nature's patterns and processes when designing digital tools, mimicking the efficiency and resilience found in natural ecosystems.

**Adaptive solutions:** Create digital technologies that can adapt and evolve to changing conditions, mirroring the adaptive nature of regenerative systems.

**Data regeneration:** Develop data-driven solutions that contribute to the regeneration of ecosystems or communities, such as using data to optimize resource allocation, reduce waste, or enhance environmental monitoring.

**Open innovation:** Foster an open-source and collaborative approach to innovation, allowing for collective input and diverse perspectives to drive regenerative technological advancements.

**Ethical tech:** Innovate technologies that prioritize social and environmental ethics, ensuring that they contribute positively to people and the planet. Foster Digital Permaculture.

**Regenerative design thinking:** Apply regenerative design principles to the entire innovation process, from ideation to implementation, to ensure that the end result enhances overall sustainability.

# 4. Involve the users

*"Unity is strength"*

Emphasize the value of community involvement and collaboration in digital decision-making processes. By including diverse perspectives, experiences, and knowledge, we can create more inclusive and impactful digital solutions that address the needs and aspirations of the community.

Here are some ideas:

**Participatory design:** Engage users and stakeholders in the design process from the outset, ensuring that their needs, preferences, and feedback shape the development of the technology.

**User-centered approach:** Prioritize the user experience and create intuitive interfaces that are easy to navigate, understand, and use, enhancing accessibility for a wide range of users.

**Co-creation:** Collaborate with users to co-create digital solutions, fostering a sense of ownership and investment in the technology's development.

**Feedback loops:** Establish mechanisms for users to provide ongoing feedback, allowing for iterative improvements and adjustments based on real-world usage.

**User testing:** Conduct user testing to identify pain points, areas for improvement, and potential enhancements, refining the technology based on user insights.

**Customization:** Provide users with options for customization and personalization, allowing them to tailor the technology to their specific needs and preferences.

**Empowerment:** Design tools that empower users to actively engage with and contribute to the technology's functionality, fostering a sense of agency and control.

**Inclusive design:** Ensure that the technology is accessible to a diverse range of users, including those with disabilities or different levels of digital literacy.

**Community engagement:** Create opportunities for users to connect with one another, fostering a sense of community and enabling knowledge sharing and mutual support.

**Continuous learning:** Develop resources and support mechanisms that enable users to continuously learn and adapt to new features and capabilities.

**Transparency:** Provide clear information about the technology's functionalities, data collection practices, and privacy measures, enabling users to make informed decisions.

**Open collaboration:** Embrace open-source and collaborative approaches that invite users to contribute code, ideas, or suggestions, fostering a sense of shared ownership.

**User-driven innovation:** Encourage users to propose innovative ideas and solutions, recognizing that their insights can lead to breakthroughs and novel approaches.

# 5. Use and value FOSS

*"Many hands make light work"*

Prioritize the use of Free and Open-Source Software (FOSS) over proprietary software whenever possible. Recognize that FOSS fosters transparency, collaboration, and user empowerment, aligning with ethical considerations and promoting a more ethical and sustainable digital landscape.

**Community collaboration:** Engage with open-source communities to contribute code, report bugs, suggest improvements, and actively participate in the development and enhancement of the software.

**Avoid vendor lock-in:** Opt for open-source alternatives to avoid being locked into proprietary systems, which can limit flexibility and increase costs in the long run.

**Security and transparency:** Leverage the transparency of open-source software to assess its security, identify vulnerabilities, and address them promptly.

**Customization and flexibility:** Utilize open-source tools that can be customized to fit specific needs, enabling a tailored experience and efficient workflows.

**Compatibility and interoperability:** Embrace open standards and protocols to ensure compatibility and interoperability between different software applications and platforms.

**Knowledge sharing:** Benefit from the collaborative nature of open-source communities to learn from others, share insights, and collectively enhance your skills and expertise.

**Ethical considerations:** Support the ethical values of sharing knowledge and resources for the common good by using and contributing to open-source projects.

**Cost-effectiveness:** Utilize open-source software to reduce licensing fees and associated costs, making efficient use of resources.

**Longevity:** Choose open-source tools that are backed by active communities and have a history of continuous development, ensuring the longevity of the software.

**Global perspective:** Engage with open-source projects that have a global reach, enabling contributions from diverse perspectives and enriching the software's functionality.

**Contribute back:** Whenever possible, contribute to open-source projects by reporting issues, submitting code, or supporting the community financially, ensuring a cycle of mutual benefit.

# Specific decisions

We have surveyed and analyzed several different real-world digital applications, most of the time from a permaculture designer's perspective. We looked for patterns and even developed new principles – the Digital Permaculture Principles. We can now turn this into real-world decisions. Let's use the example from the analysis to decide what we are going to do:

## Smartphone

The end-of-life status of my phone, identified during the analysis of my hardware, necessitates the search for a replacement. Ideally, a Fairphone[373] would align with my values, but its 700,- € price tag is

---

373 https://en.wikipedia.org/wiki/Fairphone_5

beyond my budget. (Perhaps, if enough people have bought this book I'm able to buy a Fairphone – but let's for the moment go with the assumption I can't spend that amount of money.) I'm looking to spend around 200,- €. To maximize longevity, I need a recent model with the latest OS, potentially extending its usability to about five years. I usually wait for the World Mobile Congress[374] in Barcelona, a significant event where new models are announced, to make my decision. After the event, I use resources like gsmarena.com[375] to shortlist phones that meet my criteria: the latest Android version, Dual-SIM capability, and a decent camera. I then consult the XDA-Developer Forum[376] to see if these models are supported and if there's active custom ROM development. This step is crucial for gauging the potential to extend the device's life beyond the manufacturer's support through alternative operating systems.

Let's see through the lens of the principles:

- I have observed the topic and then acted on the findings → I need a phone. My initial idea to buy a new one might not be the right idea. I could go for a used one. The workflow will be the same → gsmarena.com → XDA → but then buy a used one
- I use & value diversity → different websites to obtain the information in order to make an informed decision
- I uses edges & value the marginal → developers who work on free and open-source software like custom ROMS

---

374 https://en.wikipedia.org/wiki/Mobile_World_Congress
375 https://www.gsmarena.com
376 https://xdaforums.com

- I can see if I can spent some time helping out the XDA forum. I can try to integrate myself into the XDA community – giving back → Fair Share, or support the developers with money

# Messenger

The only messenger that complies with permaculture ethics is Signal. The SWOC showed that one of the challenges is to get people to use it. Hence more education regarding data sovereignty and security is needed. Also form my perspective it simply needs tenacity.

**My setup would be:**

*Communication Zone 0 / 1* → Signal. Means I require family and close friends to use Signal. Installed on my phone. Front screen. HL0 / SL0

*Communication Zone 2 / 3 / 4* → WhatsApp. Due to its huge user base and often acquaintances and colleagues use it. Installed on my phone. Not necessarily front-screen. If someone requires me to use another messenger then I have to check. HL0 / SL1

*Communication Zone 5* → Matrix / Facebook. You never know who contacts you. Not installed on my phone. HL0 / SL5

Let's see through the lens of the principles:

- I observed the topic, identified the problems and acted upon them.
- In the beginning I asked everyone to switch to Signal. The feedback wasn't that good. I changed the design to incorporate other Zones.
- With using different messengers I can reach different groups / people. I can integrate them into my life.
- Changing the messenger is a small and slow solution for me.
- With using multiple messengers while focusing on the one that closer aligns with permaculture ethics I use and value diversity.
- Using Signal as my *Zone 0 & 1* messenger will bring new people to Signal. I use and value diversity.
- The edge is at the new systems, in my example Matrix.

# Email

This choice heavily depends on the depth of commitment. For the sake of argument we are homesteaders with no prior knowledge in administrating servers or web-hosting.

Our choice would be one of the more privacy driven email providers like Posteo or Protonmail.

We could either use their web-mailer or we could install Thunderbird on our computer.

Let's look at our design pathway through the lens of the principles:

- We had a long a deep look into email. We observed and interacted
- Email is communication between people. It is people's time. We properly and securely catch and store it.
- Some of Protonmail's data-centers are run with green energy → Here it might make sense to look a little bit further into the email providers. Perhaps there is one that offers all what we are asking + green energy hosting. Survey needs to be more extensive.
- Switching email provider is a slow and small solution. But it is very effective in creating diversity when suddenly more people have different email domains like @permaculture-network.eu or @beyondbuckthorns.com instead of just @gmail.com
- There is a diversity of solutions out there. I use them → you could too!
- I've been using Thunderbird for a long time. Good software that is around for years and open-source is highly appreciated.

## Social media platforms

Our choice falls on an open platform like Mastodon, since they are more in alignment with the permaculture ethics.

During the analysis we found some limits. Let's flip the limits from the analysis and see if they can become helps:

- **Time Constraints:** Limit the time in social media, maybe to specific hour on the day and then to a specific duration – See "Embrace the offline mode" page 334.
- Additionally we remove all existing social media apps from our *Zone 0* – Hardware *Layer 0* – Software <u>Layer 0</u> and put them into Hardware *Layer 1 or 2* and Software *Layer 1 or 2* – banning them from disrupting our life. → we then evaluate after some time. If it is not enough then we ban the device to *Zone 1 or 2.*
- **Algorithm Changes / Privacy:** Use Social media platforms that have no history with violating privacy (data sovereignty).
- **Remember:** Social media should be only one of many elements in our dissemination strategy (multiple elements for important functions).

We will slowly phase out the already used social media systems by notifying family, friends and followers of the change. Time horizon is 1 year.

Let's see through the lens of the principles:

- We observed the usage of social media and the problems it is causing. We analyzed our findings and can now act upon it.

- We make sure that our caught energy (time and energy to produce social media posts) and stored energy (the post itself) is in a system that aligns with the permaculture ethics.
- We value the marginal by not following the leader in the space and choosing a platform that is marginal. → we will meet new people outside of our bubble.
- Marginal is time itself. Spending two hours on the smartphone per day to scroll to social media is too much. We make sure we free time for us.

## Cloud storage

The cloud storage example (page 293, 123)  is a little bit different since we have to take the stakeholders into account. It also highly depends on the availability of people with IT knowledge. That's why it is imperative to have IT knowledge within teams / associations. If not we should build capacity, means we have to train existing members and those costs need to be accounted for. Associations and companies into sustainability shouldn't pay for training in proprietary products: we only support open-source.

The decision is to use a self-hosted cloud storage software. We then have the chance to educate the users, creating a workshop for them, contributing to their life-long learning efforts. In that workshop we can then emphasize the importance of digital permaculture and digital sustainability. It also offers the possibility for the teacher to sell the newly acquired knowledge – make the workshop available for the wider public.

Let's see through the lens of the principles:

- We observed the situation, analyzed it and we now act upon our findings.
- People's work, especially in groups needs a place to be. A selfhosted cloud is a good place to catch and store people's energy (work).
- If we open the service up to others we might be able to obtain a yield.
- I have seen small teams to use selfhosted cloud platforms and the feedback so far is very good.
- My selfhosted cloud platform will run on a server with green energy.
- This is still on a pattern level. This design will need more time and effort to decide how the details will play out.
- It will take some time until other individuals, groups and teams will follow. It is slow and small.
- There are multiple selfhosted cloud software available.

# Use case: EuPN

On different occasions I mentioned the European Permaculture Network (EuPN)[377]. In 2023 we switched from WordPress to Drupal after years of problems with WordPress. Once we had Drupal running we integrated a Single-Sign-On server for all other services offered. Members can log in to the internal forum, which of course is open-source software. Members who volunteer their time can also log in to the self-hosted cloud, including calendar software and document collaboration and Kanban. The same login allows access to other EuPN-related websites.

Following the Digital Permaculture Principles:

- The design keeps privacy and transparency in mind. We have a clear privacy policy. All data collected stays with the EuPN.
- We consider the connected whole. We run interviews with members and publish them in the different communication Zones. We have a robust assurance program going. There are no social media accounts, but there is a Matrix channel.
- We only introduce innovations based on permaculture design, following its ethics and principles.
- All software used, including team communication software, is FOSS (Free and Open Source Software).

---

377 https://permaculture-network.eu

The website is hosted at a green energy hoster and the whole site is optimized for a low data usage. The site was rated with A+ at the Website Carbon Calculator [378]

> My examples are just for you to get an idea on how a design process in the digital realm can be. The amount of soft- and hardware we are using determines the amount of survey, analysis and decisions we need to go through. Let's align them with permaculture ethics & principles!

# General decisions

A holistic system change also requires the digital tools and habits to change accordingly. If we apply permaculture ethics and principles onto the digital realm, there would be no way we would end up with those big players we constantly support now.

## Switch software

In the survey and analysis stage we have made our homework and listed all the software we are using, and we also categorized them according to *Zones* and *Sectors*. We checked whether it is open-source or not. We checked the revenue of the company behind it. We checked if its usage was conscious decision. And last but not least: checked if there are alternatives around.

---

378 https://www.websitecarbon.com/website/permaculture-network-eu/

We now have a comprehensive list and it is time to **prepare the switch!**

Switching software to an FOSS or Open source alternative and to a self-hosted variant is small and slow solution in general. But we will value diversity and we will value the marginal. Train yourself in using Open-source software. AND always check if there is a (F)OSS alternative available.

The next step is to create an implementation list. Below is an example, though yours can also look different to it:

|    | Software | Switched away to (✓) | When? |
|----|----------|----------------------|-------|
| 1  | Web search | | |
| 2  | Website software | | |
| 3  | Mail provider | | |
| 4  | Project management | | |
| 5  | Newsletter | | |
| 6  | Messenger | | |
| 7  | Mailing list | | |
| 8  | Collaboration Platform | | |
| 9  | Document collaboration | | |
| 10 | Cloud storage | | |
| 11 | Teleconference | | |
| 13 | Social media | | |
| 15 | Login Provider | | |
| 16 | Calendar | | |

Example for an implementation list – which software are you going to switched when?

# Switching behavior

Switching the software is just one part of the story. Switching behavior is another one. Soft- and hardware gets produced by people and those people are often in need of support. Using Open-source software of course drives the whole system into the right direction but wouldn't it be great that when we observe it from the developers side the Fair-Share part would be really fair? Wouldn't it be great if we wouldn't just use the FOSS but also contribute to it, by either helping in the their issue queue, or committing code, or paying the developer(s)?

There are several options (helps) we can apply:

**Educate yourself:** First you need to research and learn about ethical software choices, Open source alternatives, and the impact of different software options on the environment and society. The more informed you are, the better decisions you can make. I hope this book helps you with it.

**Evaluate your current software usage:** Assess the tools and services you currently use, and identify areas where you could switch to more ethical or sustainable alternatives. Use the PMI!

**Prioritize changes:** Determine which software transitions are most important to you and create a plan to gradually replace those tools with more ethical options. Start with the easiest changes first to build momentum. The list to switch is just a prioritized example. Make your own switch list!

**Seek out resources and support:** Look for guides, tutorials, and communities that can help you learn about and adopt new software. Connect with others who share your values and can provide advice or assistance.

**Be patient and persistent:** Changing habits and learning new tools can take time. Be patient with yourself and recognize that it's okay to encounter challenges or setbacks along the way. Keep working towards your goals, and celebrate your progress. Create your own permaculture design about it!

**Share your experiences:** Talk to friends, family, and colleagues about the changes you've made in your software choices and why they matter to you. Your story can inspire others to reconsider their own software usage and make more ethical decisions. Again: publish your design!

**Advocate for change:** Support organizations and initiatives that promote ethical software development and Open source projects. Sign petitions, participate in campaigns, or donate to causes that align with your values. And of course: help the developers in a way that is in accordance with your Fair Share!

**Stay informed:** Keep up to date with the latest developments in ethical software and technology. This will help you stay aware of new tools and opportunities to improve your software choices further.

Behavioral change is necessary. If you are not yet on the track please start! We need a sustainable, even regenerative approach on our digital technologies. Your commitment counts!

## Community: turn the switch

**Education and awareness:** Raise awareness within the community about the importance of aligning software choices with permaculture ethics. Share information about Open source and ethical alternatives to popular mainstream tools. → **Please inform your colleagues about this book!**

**Skill development:** Encourage the development of technical skills within the community, so that members can better understand, adopt, and support Open source and ethical software solutions. Be a digital permaculture advocate!

**Community support:** Create a support network within the community to help members transition to more ethical software choices. This could include workshops, online forums, or mentorship programs to assist with the adoption of new tools. → The International Permaculture Colab[379] is good starting point.

**Collaboration:** Work together with other like-minded communities and organizations to develop, improve, and promote Open source and ethical software solutions that align with permaculture principles.

---

379 https://www.perma.earth/colab/

**Holistic approach:** Consider the entire life-cycle of digital tools, from production to disposal, when making choices. This means taking into account energy consumption, waste generation, and the overall environmental impact of a tool. → **Use 5R!** See chapter – page 332

**Lead by example:** Demonstrate the effectiveness of ethical software choices within the permaculture community by documenting successes, challenges, and lessons learned. Share these experiences with the broader community to inspire others to adopt similar practices. → **Simply use ethical software!**

By taking these actions, permaculture practitioners can help to create a shift in their community's digital habits, moving towards software and services that better align with permaculture ethics and principles.

# Counteract (e)-waste

We need to counteract e-waste, and we need a strategy to do so.

I call it the 5R strategy (derived from the 4R – for which I couldn't find the originator):

- Refuse: You don't need everything that is advertised
- Rethink: There might be other options
- Reduce: Here less is really more
- Reuse / Re-purpose: Things can be used differently, extend life
- Recycle: Make sure when it goes to waste it goes into the right channels

 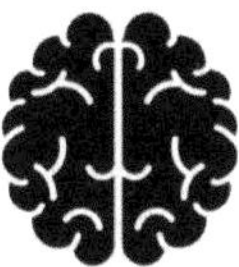   

The 5r: Refuse, Rethink, Reduce, Reuse, Recycle

I have already given some example of how to extend the lifespan of electronic gadgets like smartphones, tablets, computers, etc. I'd like to emphasis that the refuse part is the hardest one.

I have encountered individuals who identify as permaculturists but have not embraced the principles of resourcefulness and reuse. It is disheartening to witness their reluctance to purchase second-hand items or repurpose materials for different purposes. Instead of retrofitting their existing homes to improve sustainability, some choose to construct entirely new houses, often relying on imported resources like timber and glass.

In permaculture, there is a strong emphasis on reducing waste, conserving resources, and minimizing our ecological footprint. This includes finding creative ways to reuse and repurpose existing materials, opting for second-hand items whenever possible, and embracing the concept of "refuse, rethink, reduce, reuse, recycle." By doing so, we can contribute to a more sustainable and regenerative lifestyle.

It is important to continue promoting awareness and education within the permaculture community about the value of resourcefulness, reusing materials, and making conscious choices when it comes to building, renovating, and consuming. By inspiring others to adopt these practices, we can work together towards a more sustainable future and truly embody the principles of permaculture.

## Embracing the "offline" mode

Encouraging people to disconnect from the digital world, and embrace the "offline" mode, can reduce the dependence on digital systems and increase the resilience of communities in the face of digital disruptions.

Here are some tips for going "offline":

**Digital detox periods:** Set specific timeframes each day or week where you disconnect from digital devices entirely. Use this time to engage in analog activities, connect with nature, or spend quality time with loved ones.

**Prioritize offline activities:** Allocate time for hobbies, reading physical books, gardening, or practicing other offline skills that bring you joy and fulfillment.

**Offline knowledge:** Invest in offline resources such as printed manuals, guides, and books related to your interests or professional field. These resources can be valuable during periods of limited or no internet access.

**Local networking:** Foster in-person relationships by attending community events, workshops, or meetups. Building strong local connections enhances your resilience and offers offline resources.

**Offline note-taking:** Carry a notebook for jotting down ideas, reflections, and important information. This habit reduces reliance on digital note-taking apps and keeps your thoughts accessible without technology.

**Offline entertainment:** Explore activities that don't require a screen, such as board games, puzzles, playing musical instruments, or crafting.

**Emergency preparedness:** Have essential information, contacts, and resources printed or stored offline for unexpected events where digital access might be limited.

**Learn practical skills:** Acquire skills like cooking, woodworking, or basic repair that empower you to address daily needs without relying on digital solutions.

**Unplugged workspaces:** Designate spaces where digital devices are not allowed, such as a tech-free bedroom or an area for meditation and relaxation.

**Mindful digital usage:** When online, adopt mindful practices like focusing on specific tasks, disabling non-essential notifications, and using website blockers to prevent mindless browsing. Use *Zone* and *Layers* to organize your virtual workspace

**Offline creativity:** Engage in creative activities like drawing, painting, or writing by hand to tap into your imagination without digital tools.

**Nature connection:** Spend time outdoors, appreciating natural surroundings and connecting with the environment. Nature offers a powerful way to recharge and recalibrate.


## Fostering a culture of repair and reuse

Encouraging people to repair and reuse their digital devices, rather than constantly buying new ones, can reduce electronic waste and increase the lifespan of digital devices, making them more sustainable. → The Repair Café is a wonderful solution! See the chapter about the design principle "Produce no waste" at page 48.

# Creating digital commons

Digital commons refer to shared digital resources that are collectively owned or managed by a community, rather than by private individuals or companies. These resources can include software, data, research, educational materials, and other digital content that is freely accessible and reusable. The concept promotes collaboration, openness, and inclusivity, allowing people to contribute to and benefit from these resources. This approach fosters innovation, democratizes access to information and technology, and helps to ensure that knowledge and tools are available to everyone, not just those with the ability to pay.

Creating digital commons, such as Open-source software and open data, can increase the resilience and sustainability of digital systems by making them accessible to everyone, and fostering a culture of collaboration and sharing. Technology that is available for everyone helps to close the digital divide. By making digital content and tools freely available and accessible to all, regardless of economic status, digital commons can help level the playing field. This can empower individuals and communities with knowledge, skills, and opportunities that were previously out of reach due to financial constraints or lack of access. However, closing the digital divide also requires addressing other factors such as internet access, digital literacy, and the availability of appropriate hardware. See the chapter about the Digital Divide.

# Support device neutrality

Device Neutrality[380] is a concept aimed at ensuring users have the freedom to choose and control the software that runs on their devices, promoting competition and innovation in the digital market. It's about making sure that devices do not limit or dictate the use of applications, services, or functions, allowing users to fully personalize their digital experience. This principle is becoming increasingly relevant as our reliance on digital devices grows, highlighting the need for regulations that support an open and user-centric digital ecosystem.

In 2024 the fsfe[381] (Free Software Foundation Europe) published an article on their website "Let's make Device Neutrality a reality in Europe!"[382]. In that article the fsfe discusses the implementation of the Digital Markets Act (DMA) in the EU, marking a step towards Device Neutrality, aimed at giving users control over their devices and promoting software freedom. The DMA addresses big tech companies, imposing rules to foster competition in digital markets. However, FSFE notes that the DMA alone isn't enough to ensure Device Neutrality fully and highlights the need for continuous monitoring and broader application beyond large platforms to include all device manufacturers, promoting a more inclusive and open digital environment.

**Let's support Device Neutrality!**

---

380 https://en.wikipedia.org/wiki/Device_neutrality
381 https://fsfe.org/
382 https://fsfe.org/news/2024/news-20240307-01.en.html

# Developing digital literacy

Digital literacy is important. Even for permaculture folks there is no way around it.

Here are some steps to help you enhance your digital literacy

**Start with basics:** Begin by understanding fundamental concepts such as hardware, software, operating systems, and internet connectivity.

**Explore operating systems:** Familiarize yourself with different operating systems (e.g., Windows, macOS, **Linux**) to understand their features and functionalities.

**Learn about devices:** Gain knowledge about various digital devices, including computers, smartphones, tablets, and wearables.

**Navigate the internet:** Develop effective internet search skills, understand website navigation, and learn how to evaluate online information for credibility.

**Master productivity tools:** Learn to use common office productivity tools like word processors, spreadsheets, and presentation software.

**Improve communication:** Understand various communication tools such as email, instant messaging, and video conferencing. Practice effective online communication etiquette.

**Stay safe online:** Educate yourself about online security, privacy settings, and safe browsing habits to protect your personal information.

**Use digital resources:** Discover online learning platforms, tutorials, and educational websites to expand your knowledge on specific topics.

**Digital creativity:** Experiment with creative tools such as graphic design software, video editors, and music production applications.

**Coding and programming:** If interested, explore basic coding concepts and programming languages to understand how software works.

**Online collaboration:** Learn to collaborate effectively using tools discussed earlier

**Adapt to new technologies:** Stay open to learning about emerging technologies like artificial intelligence, augmented reality, and blockchain.

**Stay Curious:** Embrace a curious mindset and don't hesitate to explore new apps, tools, and platforms as they emerge.

**Continuous Learning:** Digital literacy is an ongoing journey. Regularly seek out new resources, courses, and updates to stay current.

**Seek assistance:** Don't hesitate to ask for help from friends, colleagues, or online communities when you encounter challenges or have questions.

**Practice patience:** Learning new technologies may take time and practice. Be patient with yourself and celebrate your progress.

**Apply learning:** Use your digital skills in real-life scenarios. For instance, create documents, manage your digital files, or explore hobbies online.

**Reflect and review:** Periodically reflect on your digital literacy goals, assess your progress, and identify areas for further improvement.

**Teach others:** Share your knowledge with friends, family members, or colleagues who might benefit from improving their digital literacy.

# Sustainable websites

On my websites I apply some simple rules, which I call Nick's "Fast and compressed". They can be found at my companies website[383]. They are based on the spectrum of of data. Here they are:

- Don't use videos, especially not on the front-page and don't use auto-play. Auto-play sucks anyway and every website that comes along with it gets banned for lifetime
- Compress images as far as possible and use modern codecs that are supported by the browsers
- Use lazy loading for images which are not in the First Contentful Paint.[384]
- Responsive images. Different image sizes according the browsers resolution
- Compress js + css
- Minify js, css, HTML
- Optimize js
- Optimize frontend used, lean css
- Use webfont formats like woff2[385]
- Enable Gzip compression on your webserver[386]
- Usew http/2 for SSL[387]
- Long caching period for static content
- Deliver static HTML where possible
- If you want to go further

---

383 https://www.chaseandsnow.com/sustainable-websites
384 https://web.dev/fcp/
385 https://css-tricks.com/understanding-web-fonts-getting/
386 https://en.wikipedia.org/wiki/HTTP_compression
387 https://web.dev/performance-http2/

- ○ no loading of 3<sup>rd</sup> party plugins from remote
- ○ only static sites, no database in between
- ○ reduction of objects in the Document Object Model[388] (DOM)
- ○ images dithering[389]

Over the years I guess more and other techniques will be added or deleted on my "Fast and compressed" list. Just see what has changed online:

After implementation I suggest to check your website at https://www.websitecarbon.com – mine usually score an A or even an A+.

---

388 https://developer.mozilla.org/en-US/docs/Web/API/
    Document_Object_Model/Introduction
389 https://en.wikipedia.org/wiki/Dither

# *7. Implementation – the way away*

All the unconscious, forced and unsustainable decisions create an unsustainable reality.

But we have made some conscious decisions and we need to implement them to lead us to a sustainable or even regenerative world!

## Implementation list

From all your survey, analysis and design you have got an implementation list

Schedule the time and **execute, execute, execute!** Use whatever productivity tool serves you best to execute – of course it should be according to permaculture ethics.

| | |
|---|---|
| Create list of all the software in use | |
| List all the hardware in use | |
| **Survey** software<br>• *Zones, Layers* and *Sectors*<br>• What is the license model? Proprietary or Open-source?<br>• Why are we using that software?<br>• Was it a conscious decision to use that software?<br>• Who is developing that software?<br>    ○ If a company → What is their revenue?<br>• What alternatives are there? Are there any?<br>• Are we in a locked-in system or can we install software freely from different sources? | |
| **Survey** hardware<br>• *Zones, Layers* and *Sectors*<br>• When have I bought that hardware?<br>• Was it a conscious decision to start / continue using it?<br>• Which operating software is it running?<br>    ○ Licensing model?<br>• Am I locked in?<br>• Am I using leased hardware or hardware given to me by e.g. the company I work for?<br>• Check the energy consumption | |
| **Analysis** using different tools<br>• PMI, SWOC, DAFOR, permaculture ethics, etc. | |
| **Decisions**<br>• Check with what you have come up so far against permaculture principles & Digital Permaculture Principles<br>• Make your decisions | |
| Create an **Implementation** list for the changes you will implement and then start executing it | |
| Create a **Maintenance strategy and list** | |
| **Evaluate** your choices after 1 year | |
| **Tweak** where necessary | |

Permaculture design process list for Digital Permaculture as an example. This could also function as your pattern view implementation list – to keep the general process on track.

# 8. Maintenance

Applying permaculture ethics and principle in a design process should result in a low maintenance system that serves the planet and its inhabitants. Digital Permaculture should be no exception.

## Updates

Updates are important. Believe me. A long time ago, in a galaxy not so far away, I ran an outdated FTP client. The security vulnerability was exploited, and I had a lot of work to do for several days as a result. The attacker gained access to my server, compromising sensitive data and disrupting services. It was a valuable lesson in the importance of keeping software up-to-date.

If you are using software, there will be release cycles, security patches, and other updates. It's important to get familiar with these processes. How do updates work? What do you need to know? Some self-hosted software comes with auto-update mechanisms, while others require manual updates (or can be set to auto-update by writing a script, plugin, module, etc.).

For locally installed software, the update process depends on your operating system. For example, Linux typically comes with a package manager that simplifies the management of software packages and updates. Other operating systems, like Windows and macOS, have their own update management systems.

**You have your list of devices** – make sure to include them in a yearly review. Do they need to be updated? When will their EOL (end of life) be? What will you do with the devices afterward? Practice digital mindfulness by staying aware of the software and hardware lifecycle and making informed decisions about updates and replacements.

| Layer | What | OS | Updates | When |
|---|---|---|---|---|
| 0 | Self build PC | Windows, Linux | Semi-automatic | |
| | E-Book reader | Linux | Manual | ¼ year |
| | Smartphone | Google Android | Semi-automatic | |
| 1 | Laptop | Linux | Semi-automatic | |
| 2 | Camera | Proprietary | Manual | ½ year |
| | Tablet | Lineage Android | Automatic | |
| | Tablet | Lineage Android | Automatic | |
| 3 | Raspberry Pi | Linux | Automatic | |
| 4 | Raspberry Pi | Linux | Automatic | |
| | Drone | Proprietary | Semi-automatic | Every flight |
| 5 | Gimbal | Proprietary | Manual | ½ year |

Updates for my hardware. Semi-automatic means that I get notified about the update but I have to start it on my own.

There are some considerations for updates. Updates are often important for security, as unpatched software can be a significant vulnerability. For crucial systems, consider **testing the update** in a staging environment. A staging environment is a copy of your live (production) environment used for testing and validation before making changes available to all users. Think of it as a "dress rehearsal" where you can ensure everything works correctly before going live. **Automate updates** where possible, and make sure the automation works as intended. **Stay up to date** – subscribe to security newsletters / bulletins for the software you use.

One last thing: always create a **backup before** performing an update!

# Backups

Backups are important. Believe me. I once lost an entire hard drive of dear data – private files, digital artwork from my teenage years, digital photos, and so on. It hurt.

## Backup strategy

Make sure you have a backup strategy in place. The 3-2-1 strategy might be a good choice:

- 3 copies of data
- On 2 different media (drive, tape)
- With 1 copy being off-site

The benefits of the 3-2-1 backup strategy:
- **Redundancy:** Multiple copies ensure that even if one or two backups fail, there is still another copy available.

- **Risk Mitigation:** Different storage media and off-site storage reduce the risk of total data loss due to hardware failure, software issues, or physical disasters.
- **Data Integrity:** Regularly updating backups and storing them in different locations helps maintain the integrity and accessibility of your data.

**Security:** Off-site backups can be encrypted to ensure data security, protecting it from unauthorized access.

Here is how I run backups:
- **Primary backup:** I have my computer and smartphone **automatically** backed up and synced to my local cloud. This happens **continuously**.
- **Secondary backup:** A flash drive copy is created **every month**.
- **Off-site backup:** I take one flash drive to an off-site location and bring the one that was stored there back to be used again.
- **Cloud backup:** I don't use any cloud storage systems that would store my file somewhere on the internet
- **Integrity check:** Every quarter I check the integrate of the backups to see if I can restore files from it.

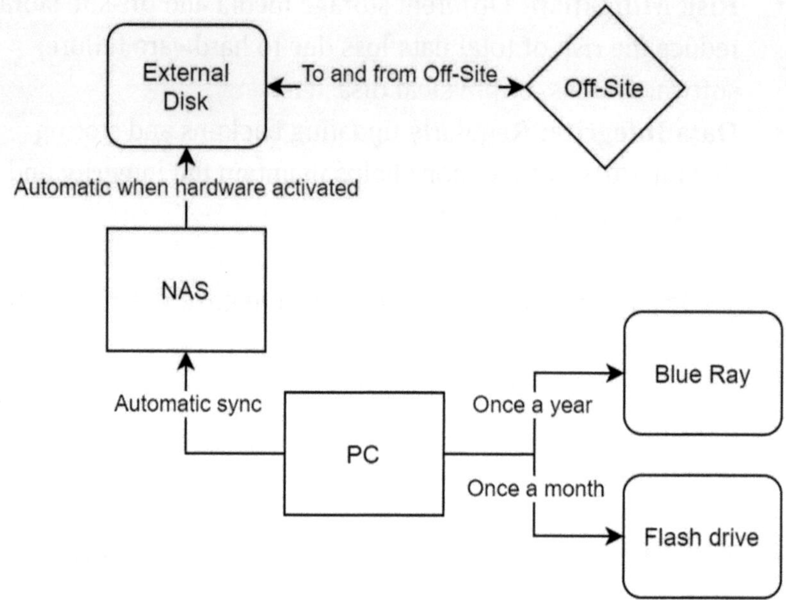


Backup Strategy

# 9. Let's end on high note

We have stepped through the SADIM parts of the SADIMET design process. The next two steps are to evaluate our design and then tweak it according to our findings. You have to do that, too!

We conducted extensive surveys in the digital realm and thoroughly analyzed our findings. You have gathered and been provided with numerous resources to make ethical decisions, and I will do my best to further raise awareness about the topic of digital permaculture.

It is now up to you to find the way away – away from the monopoly, oligopoly and locked-in systems, from the excess production of e-waste, etc. – into a permaculture world. Use the design skills and information you've learned in this book to start your journey.

Learn more about permaculture by reading books or taking part in a Permaculture Design Course (PDC) somewhere close to you. Or even get a Diploma in Applied Permaculture Design.

The path is personal for everyone. I can't design it for you as I don't know your starting point, your level of commitment, your level of understanding, your knowledge, etc. Every path is different but if we apply Digital Permaculture it will lead to a better world. A world where permaculture will extend beyond the garden gate.

You are always welcome to send me feedback. I have a contact form on my website https://dominikjais.com/contact